ROUTLEDGE LIBRARY EDITIONS:
HUMAN RESOURCE MANAGEMENT

Volume 28

PROFESSIONAL INTERVIEWING

T0384439

PROFESSIONAL INTERVIEWING

ROB MILLAR, VALERIE CRUTE AND
OWEN HARGIE

Routledge
Taylor & Francis Group

LONDON AND NEW YORK

First published in 1992 by Routledge

This edition first published in 2017
by Routledge
2 Park Square, Milton Park, Abingdon, Oxon OX14 4RN

and by Routledge
711 Third Avenue, New York, NY 10017

Routledge is an imprint of the Taylor & Francis Group, an informa business

British Library Cataloguing in Publication Data
A catalogue record for this book is available from the British Library

ISBN: 978-1-138-80870-6 (Set)
ISBN: 978-1-315-18006-9 (Set) (ebk)
ISBN: 978-0-415-38616-6 (Volume 28) (hbk)
ISBN: 978-0-415-39189-4 (Volume 28) (pbk)
ISBN: 978-1-315-23095-5 (Volume 28) (ebk)

Publisher's Note
The publisher has gone to great lengths to ensure the quality of this reprint but
points out that some imperfections in the original copies may be apparent.

Disclaimer
The publisher has made every effort to trace copyright holders and would welcome
correspondence from those they have been unable to trace.

Professional interviewing

Rob Millar, Valerie Crute
and Owen Hargie

London and New York

First published in 1992
by Routledge
11 New Fetter Lane, London EC4P 4EE

Simultaneously published in the USA and Canada
by Routledge
a division of Routledge, Chapman and Hall Inc.
29 West 35th Street, New York, NY 10001

Typeset in Times by LaserScript, Mitcham, Surrey
Printed in Great Britain by Mackays of Chatham PLC, Chatham, Kent

British Library Cataloguing in Publication Data
Millar, Rob *1951*–
   Professional interviewing.
   1. Interviewing
   I. Title II. Crute, Valerie *1959*– III. Hargie, Owen IV. Series
   658.31124

Library of Congress Cataloging in Publication Data
Millar, Rob, 1951–
   Professional interviewing/Rob Millar, Valerie Crute, Owen Hargie.
   p. cm. – (International series on communication skills)
   Includes bibliographical references and index.
   1. Interviewing. 2. Interpersonal communication. I. Crute, Valerie, 1959– .
   II. Hargie, Owen. III. Title. IV. Series.
   BF637.I5M55 1992
   158′.3 – dc20   91-9631
                                                                         CIP

ISBN 0–415–04084–1
     0–415–04085–X (pbk)

To Dot and the boys, Stephen, Aaron and Jonathan, Patricia and Ethel

Contents

Figures and tables

FIGURES

TABLES

Chapter 1

Introduction

This book is concerned with the professional practice of interviewing as a strategy for achieving specific objectives. A very large number of professional groups regularly utilise some form of interview in their face-to-face encounters with clients (Downs *et al.*, 1980). In some cases this will be the main interpersonal strategy employed (e.g. by counsellors), while in other instances this will be one among a number of interpersonal approaches within the armoury of the professional (e.g. a nurse will make particular use of the interview to take a medical history from a patient). Regardless of the extent to which interviewing is the central job function of the professional, however, it is now generally accepted that there is a need for all those who use this method to have a deeper understanding of the core elements involved (Stewart and Cash, 1985). The approach which we will adopt in this book to the analysis of interviewing is based upon the tenet that this is a skilled activity, and as such is amenable to description, analysis and evaluation in the same way as is any other type of skilled performance.

The book itself is structured into ten chapters. This introductory chapter 'sets the scene' by addressing a number of basic introductory issues; it examines definitions and purposes of interviewing and outlines the main settings within which this activity occurs. Chapter two then presents a social interactional model of interviewing, which encompasses the main processes inherent in dyadic interaction. This model examines interviewing in terms of the goals, mediating factors, responses, feedback and perceptions of the participants, as well as taking into account both personal and situational influences which affect their behaviour. This model, in turn, forms the basis for the remainder of the book, in that the central components of the model are explored in detail in succeeding chapters. Chapter three develops this model to complete the theoretical foundation for the book by linking the study of interviewing directly to the discipline base of social psychology. Chapter four is concerned with aspects of person perception, chapter five examines the role of goals and goal-setting, chapters six and seven explore a range of communication skills and strategies available to interviewers, and in chapter eight attention is given to the interviewee's perspective on the interview process. Chapter nine focuses upon a number of wider and crucially important ethical and professional issues pertaining to the practice of interviewing, while the final chapter provides an overview drawing together the significant issues raised throughout the book.

THE NATURE OF INTERVIEWING

As a starting point, any analysis of the nature of interviewing should begin with an examination of the question 'What is an interview?' While this question has been answered in a number of different ways, there tends to be general agreement regarding the core defining features with regard to what constitutes an interview. In order to illustrate this degree of consensus, it is useful to examine a sample of the definitions which have been proffered.

A fairly basic, although not atypical, definition is that given by Hodgson (1987, p.2) who, in recognising the goal-directed nature of this activity, characterises the interview simply as 'A conversation with a purpose'. Gorden (1975, p.50) provides a more extended version of this theme when he notes that:

> Any two-way conversation involves many of the same skills and insights for 'successful interviewing'. The main difference is in the *central* purpose of interviewing as opposed to other forms of conversation.

This definition is elaborated upon by Beveridge (1975, p.73) who also includes the notions of context and interviewer control when he refers to the interview as:

> a conversation within a specific context and having a specific purpose, the pattern of which is directed by the interviewer.

Dickson (1986, p.146) builds upon this to add the concept of self-disclosure within a dyadic context when he describes the interview as:

> a generic term encompassing a range of largely dyadic interpersonal encounters. It should be interpreted broadly to refer to a conversation engaged in for a particular purpose. The interviewer is the participant who has the major responsibility for conducting the transaction and...the interviewee is much more likely to reveal information to the interviewer, and especially personal information, than *vice versa*.

Lopez (1975, p.8) highlights two further facets of interviews, namely that they are usually associated with specific environments and do not just occur in isolation from preceding or forthcoming events, when he states that:

> An interview is initiated to achieve one or several objectives, takes place in a particular physical and social setting, and occurs as part of a procedural sequence of events. Further, it focuses on the present, past or future behavior, beliefs, opinions, attitudes or convictions of the interviewee.

In relation to the latter dimensions of this definition, Gorden (1975, p.39), in discussing the most appropriate content focus for the interview, emphasises the covert domain when he asserts that:

Interviewing is most valuable when we are interested in knowing people's beliefs, attitudes, values, knowledge, or any other subjective orientations or mental content.

From these definitions a number of themes emerge. Beveridge (1975) argues that the defining features of the interview are that it: is not a casual conversation; is limited to a particular set of topics; is organised; is directed by the interviewer; is purposeful; and takes place within a set context. In like vein, Skopec (1986) identifies the central facets of the interview as normally being: dyadic; purposeful; concerned with restricted subject matter; and characterised by questions and answers which occur in face-to-face oral communication. Rae (1988) additionally notes that interviews are: usually structured affairs; are pre-planned, preferably by both sides; are formal or at least semi-formal situations; both participants are aware that an interview is taking place and know who is to play the role of interviewer and interviewee, and they are normally seated during the encounter.

Bearing all of this in mind, the definition which we would propose for the interview is: *A face-to-face dyadic interaction in which one individual plays the role of interviewer and the other takes on the role of interviewee, and both of these roles carry clear expectations concerning behavioural and attitudinal approach. The interview is requested by one of the participants for a specific purpose and both participants are willing contributors*. This definition emphasises the following features:

(i) The interview is a *face-to-face* encounter. Although recent and rapid developments in video technology have increased the availability of mediated 'down the line' interviews where the participants are in different physical locations but can see one another on TV screens, such encounters are as yet by no means commonplace. They also necessitate specialised analysis given the impinging variables which remove this type of interaction from the norm and which may influence the responses of the participants. Indeed, an interesting field of study has, in fact, developed in relation to what is now known as the 'news interview' which can be defined as:

> a functionally specialised form of social interaction produced for an over-hearing audience and restricted by institutionalised conventions.
>
> (Heritage, 1985, p.112)

In other words, these media news interviews are conducted for the benefit of a third party – the audience. However, the study of this type of format is beyond the scope of the present book, and we will restrict our analysis to face-to-face interviews carried out for the direct benefit of at least one of the participants. (The interested reader may wish to refer to Cohen, 1987 for a useful analysis of the news interview.)

(ii) The interview is *dyadic* in nature. It is, of course, possible to have interviews involving more than two people. For example, many selection interviews are comprised of panels of two or more interviewers. However, for the most part interviews are dyadic affairs, and often the presence of a third person would adversely affect the interaction, especially where the subject matter being disclosed by the interviewee involves highly personal information.

(iii) Both the interviewer and interviewee are expected to behave in a manner consistent with their respective, and complementary, *roles*. Thus, a candidate at a selection interview will be expected to answer questions posed by the interviewer and demonstrate an interest in the vacant position, while a counsellor will be expected to listen carefully to, and show sensitivity towards, the concerns expressed by the client during a helping interview. More general expectations of many interviews are that interviewers will ask most of the questions while interviewees will make almost all of the self-disclosures (Hargie *et al.*, 1987).

(iv) The interview will be *requested* by one of the participants, and this may be either the interviewer or interviewee. For instance, a research interview will normally be requested by the interviewer whereas a counselling interview is usually requested by the client.

(v) There is a clear *purpose* to the interview. The actual purpose will, of course, vary from one context to another. Indeed, Shouksmith (1978, p.1) argues that 'there is no such thing as the interview but that there are many interviews'. In other words, the exact nature of an interview is dependent upon the purpose for which it has been initiated. This is emphasised by Hunt and Eadie (1987, p.5) who assert that:

> All interviews can be characterised by the existence of purpose on the part of at least one of the participants.

A large number of different types of interview are carried out in different contexts and to achieve different objectives. The range of categories would include appraisal, counselling, discipline, journalistic, medical (history-taking and diagnostic), news (mediated), psychiatric, research, sales and selection.

(vi) Both parties are *voluntarily* involved in the interview. In this sense an interrogation would not meet our criteria for inclusion within the analysis of interviewing, since in this instance the interviewee would usually be a less than willing participant.

These six features contain the essence of 'the interview', and they therefore set the parameters for the content of the remainder of this book. It is also recognised, of course, that all interviews take place within a set context, and that this context includes the specialised and well-defined nature of certain types of interview.

TYPES OF INTERVIEW

Although many different types of interview have been described in the literature, those which have been the central focus for research and evaluation would seem to fall into five main categories, namely counselling (or helping), selection (or employment), research, medical and appraisal. While this book is concerned with interviewing in general, we will use examples from these five categories to illustrate particular issues and highlight their relevance to practice. It is therefore useful at the outset to examine each type of interview briefly, in order to provide an outline of a range of situational contexts which can then serve as a precursor for examples employed in the remainder of the book.

The counselling interview

The term 'counselling' is in some senses much abused, in that it is used by many different people to refer to many different activities. There are financial counsellors, employment counsellors and beauty counsellors, to name but a few. In most of these cases, counselling is seen as being synonymous with advice-giving. A similar usage can be found in the medical sphere where patient counselling and education are frequently viewed as the same activity (Morrow and Hargie, 1989).

However, there is another perspective to the concept of counselling, as detailed by the British Association for Counselling (1979, p.1) whereby:

> The task of counselling is to give the client an opportunity to explore, discover and clarify ways of living more resourcefully and toward greater well-being.

This meaning of the term is underlined by Hopson (1981, p.267) who defines counselling as:

> helping someone to explore a problem, clarify conflicting issues and discover alternative ways of dealing with it, so that they can decide what to do about it; that is, helping people to help themselves.

Counselling in this therapeutic sense is a field of study and practice which has witnessed an enormous growth of interest in the past decade. This is evidenced by the vast proliferation of publications pertaining to research, theory and practice, by the increasing number of courses aimed specifically at counsellor training and by the growth in full-time employment opportunities for counsellors in the private and public sectors. All of this has led to an increasingly professional approach to counselling. At the same time, as with any field of academic endeavour, it has also led to a diversification of theoretical and practical perspectives. Thus, there are now a number of theories relating to the nature of counselling, each with its own conceptual base and accompanying practical implications for implementation (Ivey *et al.*, 1987).

There is, however, a core thread running through all of these approaches. Thus, Hopson (1981) has identified the main general objectives of counselling as being to help clients to:

- develop a relationship where they will feel understood and will be prepared to openly and honestly discuss personal matters;
- acquire a deeper insight and understanding of their situation;
- fully discuss alternative courses of action and decide which one to pursue;
- devise, and implement, a specific action plan;
- produce a change of feeling, or an adjustment to a situation that is unlikely to change.

One approach to the conceptualisation of counselling is to consider it as a strategy composed of a number of well-defined component parts. For example, the counselling model proposed by Egan (1982) adopts such a standpoint. In effect, this model portrays counselling as a process involving four main stages, namely attending, exploring, understanding and action. The operational use of this approach can be explained by briefly examining each of these stages separately.

1. Attending. At the outset, it is necessary for counsellors to demonstrate to clients that they are willing to become involved with them and are prepared to devote time to the interaction. Thus an attentive listening style should be portrayed by counsellors from the time of initial meeting with clients. In addition, care and consideration should be given to methods whereby the client can be made to feel 'settled' (see chapter seven for a discussion of interviewing skills).
2. Exploring. Once a relationship has been established, the next step is for the counsellor to attempt to gain a full and accurate understanding of the client's situation. This necessitates allowing the client as much freedom as possible to present her situation. The central skills at this stage are those of questioning, reflecting and summarising (see chapter seven).
3. Understanding. Here the counsellor is concerned with ensuring an optimal awareness of all the issues, thoughts and feelings raised during the exploration stage. The counsellor should also convey this understanding to the client. A central dimension at this stage is therefore that of empathy, whereby the counsellor demonstrates that he can see the world through the eyes of the client.
4. Action. The final phase of counselling is the action stage. At this juncture, the client should have been allowed to explore fully, and have achieved as deep an understanding as possible of, the underlying problem and should then be ready to take the appropriate steps to overcome it. The client is always regarded as the decision-maker with the counsellor acting as a facilitator to action. In this way, the client is encouraged to decide upon a course of action and work out a series of objectives which need to be attained in order to be successful. The role of the counsellor at this point is to provide support and encouragement. The final part of the action stage involves terminating the counselling relationship.

Although a considerable volume of research has been conducted in the field of counselling, there is no clear picture of the qualities of the effective counsellor (Gallagher, 1987). One reason for this is that counselling occurs in such a wide range of settings, involving variations in the type of client, the role of the counsellor and the nature of the problem, that any comparison of studies is inevitably fraught with difficulties. In general terms, however, it would seem that effective counselling tends to occur where the counsellor: is able to participate fully in the client's communication; clearly understands how the client feels and is able to demonstrate this understanding; closely follows the client's line of thought; and treats the client as an equal co-worker on a common problem (Authier, 1986).

The selection interview

A simple and direct definition of this type of interview is given by Skopec (1986, p.49), who states that:

> Selection interviews are usually defined as interviews conducted by employers for the purpose of matching candidates to available jobs.

The selection, or employment, interview is pervasive within our society. It is the pivot method whereby individuals are evaluated, assessed and recruited for employment (Einhorn *et al.*, 1982). Within the process of selection, there seems to exist an:

> unquestioning faith in interviewing as a tradition...despite a volume of evidence over many years that interview judgements are often inadequate, biased and always highly subjective.
>
> (Goodworth, 1979, p.1)

Thus, regardless of the often voiced and widely recognised limitations of this method, it clearly has a very strong face validity among those responsible for recruitment. McHenry (1981) in fact argues that perhaps too much attention has been devoted to the interview *per se* since:

> Good selection interviewing depends mostly on the efficient use of a system for selection in which the interview itself plays only a small part. (p.1)

However, although there is now a wide range of objective-type tests which can be employed to aid the selection process, it is still the case that most people faced with the task of selecting individuals for particular jobs will make use of an interview. This allows the interviewer the opportunity to interact with the interviewee, and assess her social skills, general attitudes to others and to work, dress and appearance, and overall personality. As Goodworth (1979) puts it, at the very least:

> A face-to-face interview is necessary and well justified in terms of the human relations value involved. (p.2)

On the other hand, interviews can be dysfunctional when they result in mistaken decisions being made, often through subjective interviewer evaluations. McHenry (1981) identifies several main sources of error in selection interviews.

- The primacy effect. Here, interviewers are unduly influenced by the early part of the interview and ignore the later performance of the interviewee. In fact there is evidence to illustrate that selection decisions are often made within the first few minutes of an interview (Arvey and Campion, 1984).
- The cosmetic effect. In this case, the appearance of the interviewee (dress, height, attractiveness, etc.) results in an unjustified evaluation about the true ability of the individual.
- The contrast effect. Interviewees are often judged in the light of the preceding candidates. This may cause distortion if, for example, an average candidate is seen immediately following two mediocre ones.
- The similarity effect. Interviewers may over-rate candidates who are similar to themselves in attitudes, educational background, race, religion, social class and so on. We tend to like people who are similar to ourselves, and such liking can blur the issue of actual suitability for the job (Greenwald, 1981). Conversely, of course, we can hold negative views of those who are dissimilar to us and this may result in the failure to appoint suitable candidates.
- The halo effect. Once an interviewer has identified a few positive attributes in an interviewee, this may lead to an overall positive evaluation regardless of true potential (Schuler and Funke, 1989).
- The negative effect. Interviewers often search for, and overemphasise, negative information about candidates without a counterbalance with regard to seeking out positive attributes.

During interviews, these sources of distortion need to be borne in mind. The actual process of selection interviewing can be categorised as comprising four main stages, namely: establishing rapport, getting information, giving information and closing (Lopez, 1975).

1. Establishing rapport. This usually involves an attempt by the interviewer to put the interviewee at ease by offering a welcome, confirming the post for which the interview is taking place, making any necessary introductions, explaining the purpose of the interview and the procedure to be followed, and saying how long the interview will last. By the end of this stage, the interviewee should feel settled and ready to answer the questions to follow.
2. Getting information. Here the interviewer will ask a range of questions, and this stage will, in fact, comprise the major part of the interview. The interviewee will accept that the questions may be awkward and personal, providing they are directly relevant to the appointment process. Questions asked will include the areas of education and training, previous experience, disposition, hobbies and interests, health, reasons for applying for the present position and aspirations for the future. In interviews for senior managerial positions, more

difficult, higher-order questions will be asked (Hargie *et al.*, 1987). However, most interviews begin with factual biographical questions which are easy to answer, and then progress to more difficult questions.

3. Giving information. Approaching the end of the interview, there is the convention that the interviewee is invited to ask questions of the interviewer. The norms here suggest that only one or two questions should be asked by interviewees, since interviewers do not expect to be 'grilled' at this point!

4. Closing. The final part of the selection interview involves a closure by the interviewer which includes thanking the interviewee for attending and answering the questions, indicating when a decision will be taken and letting the candidate know how and when she will be informed of this decision. The interviewee reciprocates the thanks and final parting behaviours are carried out.

As with counselling, although there is a large body of research in the field of selection interviewing it is difficult to reach any definite conclusions about what constitutes effective interviewing in this field. Indeed in their comprehensive text on research in the employment interview, Eder and Ferris (1989, p.11) point out that:

> much of the research on the interview is fragmented and disjointed....In reality the gap between interview research and the practice of interviewing remains considerable.

McHenry (1981), however, suggests that decisions taken about candidates can be improved by the adoption of a system where: there is a structured system upon which to evaluate the interviewees; a team of interviewers work independently using the same guidelines to interview candidates and then pool their information; and interviewers concentrate on the performance of interviewees in situations similar to those prevalent in the position to be filled.

The research interview

This is a field which has attracted an enormous volume of literature, and indeed 'There are more books in this field than articles in most other fields' (Dillon, 1990, p.109). The research interview has been defined as:

> a two-person conversation initiated by the interviewer for the specific purpose of obtaining research-relevant information and focused by him on content specified by research objectives.
>
> (Cannell and Kahn, 1968, p.530)

In this setting, the interview is therefore part of an overall research strategy. As such, interviewing may be a major part of a research investigation or just one among many methods being employed. The actual function of the interview must be fully worked out by the researcher. In discussing this issue, Cohen and Mannion (1980, p.243) point out that:

As a distinctive research technique, the interview may serve three purposes. First, it may be used as the principal means of gathering information.... Second, it may be used to test hypotheses or to suggest new ones....[third] it may be used to follow up unexpected results...to go deeper into the motivations of respondents and their reasons for responding as they do.

There is therefore no one set research interview since the purpose of the specific research investigation will determine the style of the interviewer. Sommer and Sommer (1980) identify two main types of interview, which in essence represent a continuum, namely the structured and the unstructured. Carlson (1984) further delineates interviews into four types within this continuum:

– Highly structured standardised. Here the sequence and exact wording of questions to be asked are specified in advance and the respondents' response options are also predetermined with the answers being recorded on a standardised schedule. It is akin to an oral questionnaire, since no leeway is given to respondents to modify the nature of questions or responses. French (1983) identifies three reasons why this type of interview rather than a self-completed questionnaire may be necessary. First, it allows for some degree of probing at certain points. Second, it allows the interviewer to code answers (e.g. for later computer analysis). Finally, the interviewer can clarify any uncertainties regarding particular questions, and can also provide motivation for the respondent to complete the task.
– Highly structured. This is similar to the above category with the exception that the interviewee response options are not predetermined. Thus, although questions to be asked are decided in advance, a degree of flexibility is allowed in relation to the respondent's answers.
– Moderately structured. In this case, while the major questions to be asked are decided upon before the interview is conducted, these do not have to be posed in a set, pre-ordained sequential order. Rather, they can be asked in the context of a more natural conversational style of interaction.
– Nonstructured. Here the interviewer has decided, in only general terms, some of the main themes and topics to be covered. No exact questions are prepared in advance and there is no pre-designed order in which the interview is expected to progress. The interviewer takes a more subordinate role and encourages the interviewee to express himself fully and spontaneously.

Each of these types of interview will have advantages and disadvantages when compared to the others, and they are all therefore equally valid within different contexts. There are three main stages in the research interview, regardless of type.

1. Opening. The first task is often to motivate interviewees to participate fully in the interview. This can be facilitated by a careful explanation of the purpose of the interview and its relevance, what the functions of the respondent and interviewer will be, how the interview will be conducted and what length of time it will require.

2. Conducting the interview. During the main body of the interview it is important for the interviewer to encourage the interviewee to maintain a high level
of participation. As such, skills of listening and reinforcing are very important,
while the skill of questioning will, of course, be crucial (see chapter seven). It
is also vital that the respondent answers all the questions without being
subjected to interviewer bias. Steps need to be taken to safeguard the accuracy
of information provided, by attempting to reduce those factors which may bias
responses. There is clear evidence to indicate that respondents will often try to
please interviewers by offering the responses they feel are expected or are
socially desirable (Sudman and Bradburn, 1982). The verbal and nonverbal
reactions of the interviewer to interviewee responses must therefore always be
neutral and non-judgemental. Bias can be very difficult to eliminate, however,
since it would seem that factors such as the age, gender, social class and race
of the interviewer can all have marked effects upon the responses of interviewees (Brenner, 1981). Furthermore (and without any encouragement),
respondents consistently over-report behaviours such as voting, reading
books, going to the theatre and giving to charity, and under-report aspects such
as illnesses, illegal behaviour, disabilities and financial status (Bradburn and
Sudman, 1980). These findings need to be borne in mind when designing a
research project, since steps need to be taken (e.g. in the design and wording
of questions) to overcome such pre-occurring response bias.
3. Closing. At the end of the interview, the interviewer will thank the respondent
for his participation and may explain how and when the results of the research
will be made available.

The medical interview

The medical interview is a core feature of the work of many health professionals.
For example, Elliot (1980, p.xxiii) argues that: 'Among the skills needed...in
nursing is a highly developed competence in interviewing.' Likewise, Hunt and
Eadie (1987, p.119) point out that 'a doctor's best "bedside manner" is the ability
to interview skillfully'. Within the health professions, there is no one set medical
interview, but rather there are a range of different types of interview which take
place within a medical setting, and the nature and conduct of each type of
interview will vary depending upon the actual context. In discussing this issue,
Sheppe and Stevenson (1963) concluded that all medical interviews have three
main goals:

  (i) to establish a conducive working relationship with the patient;
 (ii) to elicit specific information from the patient;
(iii) to observe the patient's behaviour.

More specifically, Bernstein and Bernstein (1980) delineated four central
characteristics of the medical interview, namely that:

(i) it is held primarily for the benefit of the patient rather than that of the practitioner;

(ii) it has a clear purpose;

(iii) it involves a formal interaction;

(iv) the focus of the interaction is directly related to the problems, needs or concerns of the patient.

As Dickson *et al.* (1989) have illustrated, all health professionals are involved in some form of interviewing. For example, nurses carry out medical history interviews, general practitioners employ diagnostic interviews and hospital pharmacists conduct interviews to obtain drug histories. Within each of these contexts it is possible to further identify specific types of interview. Thus, Gill (1973) has identified three main types of interview conducted by doctors:

(i) the short diagnostic medical interview which is solely concerned with physical symptoms;

(ii) the personal interview which is longer and in which the doctor also deals with psychosocial dimensions of the patient's situation;

(iii) what Gill refers to as the 'flash' type of interview during which there is a free-flowing interaction. This facilitates the occurrence of a sudden flash of insight involving a mutual understanding by patient and doctor about what has caused some of the former's problems.

The medical interview can be characterised as comprising three main stages.

1. The opening stage. Here, it is important for the practitioner to establish rapport with the patient at the outset (see chapter seven). The actual objectives of the interview and the main areas to be explored should be highlighted, the likely duration should be stated, and the role of the patient explained. Thus, in his analysis of nurse–patient interaction, French (1983) proposes that the practitioner should complete some or all of the following tasks at the beginning of interviews.

a. Inform the patient what the practitioner is going to do and what the procedures will be.

b. Provide reasons as to why certain information will be sought.

c. Allow the patient to express any reservations, and answer any questions by giving a full explanation.

d. Explain what the patient's role will be, and what is expected of him.

e. Check the accuracy of any information already collected (e.g. on the patient's file).

f. Obtain the full attention and cooperation of the patient before proceeding to the next stage of the interview.

   If the patient expresses resistance, disagreement or concern at this juncture, Klinzing and Klinzing (1985) recommend the following course of action:

    (i) The purpose of the interview can be restated.

    (ii) The benefits to the patient of cooperation can be re-emphasised.

    (iii) The importance of obtaining the required information can be stressed.

    (iv) The patient's fears should be fully identified, recognised and openly discussed.

Where none of these tactics works the interview may have to be postponed or another practitioner asked to conduct it, since for the interview to be successful it is vital that the confidence of the patient be obtained at the outset. However, in highlighting the results of research into this phase of medical interviews, Dickson *et al.* (1989) conclude that there is evidence to support the view that 'more attention [should] be devoted to the importance of opening skills during medical training' (p.113).

2. The information collection and evaluation stage. This is the main body of the interview during which the substantive business is carried out. Here the practitioner needs to employ effectively skills such as questioning, listening, reflecting, reinforcing and explaining (see chapter seven), in order to gather full and accurate information from the patient, and if appropriate make a diagnosis and prescribe treatment. This latter aspect is of core importance in many medical interviews, since patients clearly value careful, lucid explanations from practitioners regarding their medications or the actions they are expected to carry out and the reasons for them (Ley, 1988). In many interviews the practitioner will have to take notes. Where this occurs, the reasons for note-taking should be explained as should the content of the notes. Furthermore, there is evidence to suggest that note-taking interchanged, rather than concurrent, with conversation is more effective in terms of remembering what has been said (Watson and Barker, 1984), while also being more conducive to the encouragement of a natural dialogue. (For a further discussion on note-taking see chapter nine.)

3. The closing stage. It is important for practitioners to lead in gradually to the closure of the interview. In discussing doctor–patient interaction, Heath (1986, p.150) points out that:

> Bringing the consultation to an end is a progressive, step-by-step process in and through which doctor and patient co-operate and co-ordinate their actions.

At this stage the practitioner should summarise the main decisions which have been made as a result of the interview, check for patient comprehension, indicate what will happen next and reward the patient for his participation (see chapter seven). One phenomenon which is quite common in doctor–patient interviews is the 'By the way...' syndrome, whereby the patient introduces new and often crucial information at the end of the consultation (Byrne and Long, 1976). This causes problems for doctors in terms of deciding whether to extend the interaction or arrange a new appointment. Livesey (1986), however, argues that doctors often terminate consultations prematurely, and suggests that the 'By the way...' syndrome can be circumvented by encouraging patients to participate fully and freely from the outset of the interview.

The appraisal interview

Systems of appraisal are part of the managerial operation of many private and public corporations (Fletcher and Williams, 1985). Appraisal has been defined as:

the process by which an organization measures and evaluates an individual employee's behavior and accomplishments for a finite time period.

(Devries *et al.*, 1981, p.2)

Pratt (1985, p.1) also takes into account developmental aspects by referring to appraisal as 'a formal or systematic method of staff assessment and development'.

The increasing popularity of appraisal structures can be understood by examining the benefits of the appraisal interview. Hodgson (1987) identifies the following eight benefits:

(i) It offers a formal opportunity to review the performance of individual members of staff.
(ii) It provides a means of discovering ways in which staff performance can be improved.
(iii) It can help to rectify poor staff performance.
(iv) It results in the agreement of a set of performance objectives for the individual over a specified period.
(v) The potential for individual development and promotion can be evaluated.
(vi) The 'worth' of the individual can be ascertained (e.g. for a bonus payment).
(vii) Problems faced by the individual can be discovered.
(viii) It is a useful method for gathering information to aid manpower planning so that staff performance overall can be improved.

These benefits are recognised by Beveridge (1975, p.11) who asserts that the purpose of appraisal is to answer the questions:

What does this man do and if he were given further resources, training or experience, what else could he also do? How can we develop him so that he is not only enabled to do his present job even more effectively but will be encouraged and prepared to do an even more demanding job in the future, and one that will be required to be done?

Hunt and Eadie (1987) concur with this view when they identify four main functions for the appraisal interview. First, to ascertain the current performance of the employee, as compared to the time of the last appraisal. Second, to compare this performance with that of other employees doing the same job. Third, to allow the manager to obtain an overall assessment of how the employee is currently performing. Finally, to identify what opportunities for development are available to the employee both immediately and in the longer term.

Most appraisal interviews are based upon and guided by some type of proforma or appraisal form, which is completed by the interviewee and submitted to the interviewer prior to the interview (Williams, 1972). This proforma will typically include sections in which the interviewee lists the actual job functions performed during a specified period, offers an evaluation of how well these have been carried out, highlights perceived difficulties or obstacles to the performance of these duties and suggests areas where further training and development would be useful. These sections then provide a chronological sequence for the interview with each area being discussed in turn, and this culminates in the final interview stage in which new objectives should be agreed for a future period leading up to the next appraisal, where necessary a programme of training and development is formulated and a commitment made by the interviewer to rectify any organisational impediments which are obstructing the achievement of the objectives. These decisions are then usually ratified in writing on the proforma.

The actual progress of the interview will, however, depend upon the extent to which the employee is performing at a satisfactory level. As Lopez (1975) notes, where this performance has been at a high level the interview will largely take the form of an opportunity for the interviewer to reinforce the interviewee and encourage her to continue to maintain the present standard of work. However, where performance has been unsatisfactory the interview will become more difficult. The interviewee will need to accept that his performance has not been at a high level and be committed to effecting an improvement, reasons for the poor performance will have to be identified and a programme of remedial action agreed upon.

While appraisal interviews have advantages for organisations, there can also be disadvantages. There can be a degree of embarrassment inherent in the process, particularly where appraiser and appraisee are working closely together on a day-to-day basis; for example one of the authors of this book was required to appraise the other two as part of the appraisal system of the university. Where there is a need for a cooperative working relationship between appraiser and appraisee, this could militate against an open, honest appraisal. When staff are working as part of a closely-knit team many of the functions of appraisal are carried out on a regular basis, although the formal nature of the actual appraisal interview can still be useful since it allows appraisees to raise issues they may not wish to voice on a more informal basis. Where there is a dearth of opportunities for staff training, development or promotion within an organisation, however, the appraisal system may be seen as a waste of time. Indeed, appraisal systems usually involve considerable time and effort, especially for the interviewer who may have to conduct a number of appraisal interviews each involving fairly lengthy paperwork. As a result appraisal can be an expensive procedure. Finally, where the interviewer is incompetent the appraisal can be dysfunctional. The effective appraisal interviewer is well organised and is familiar with all the necessary documentation, demonstrates that the interview is of importance, encourages self-evaluation by the appraisee, listens to and accepts suggestions (even if this involves accepting responsibility for previous unsatisfactory arrangements), acknowledges successful performance, emphasises the positive cooperative nature of the exercise, ensures that the encounter is not transformed into a discipline interview and at the end of the appraisal agrees a set of objectives for future action (Gill, 1977; Williams, 1972).

SUMMARY

This chapter has been concerned with the definition and delineation of the nature of interviewing. Given the wide range of different types of interview which are carried out it is hardly surprising that there is a diversity of definitions regarding the nature of the interview. However, there does seem to be general agreement regarding the main characteristics of the interview, in that it usually comprises a face-to-face, dyadic interaction requested by either the interviewer or the interviewee for a specific purpose.

Having identified the core features of the interview, five main types of interview were examined, namely counselling, selection, research, medical and appraisal, since these have been the primary focus for research and evaluation. Throughout the remainder of the book we will use examples from each of these interview contexts to illustrate specific aspects pertaining to the practice of interviewing. Overall, therefore, this chapter has set the scene for the in-depth study of interviewing which is the focus of this book.

Chapter 2

A social interactional model of the interview

INTRODUCTION

In the previous chapter we set the scene for the study of interviewing by defining the activity and outlining five main types of interview. The present chapter builds upon this necessary foundation by conceptualising interviewing primarily as a process of interpersonal interaction, which can be interpreted by utilising methods developed for the study of the latter. The interview can be a complex system to analyse, given that it is affected by a myriad variables such as the nature of the participants and their previous experience, the physical location, the time of day, the objectives of both parties, the actual function of the interview and so on. In order to facilitate our understanding of this phenomenon, it is useful to have an overall framework with which to evaluate any particular interview.

In this chapter we present a model of interpersonal communication which can be applied directly to the analysis of interviewing. This model, as outlined in Figure 2.1, was developed by Hargie and Marshall (1986) to account for the main processes inherent in dyadic interaction, and is therefore of direct relevance to the study of interviewing. The model contains five core processes pertaining to the performance of both interviewer and interviewee, namely: goal/motivation, mediating factors, responses, feedback and perception. These processes are all operative in any interviewing context.

Thus, an interviewer who is *motivated* to help a client may have the *goal* of encouraging maximum participation early in the interview. In order to achieve this goal, the individual will employ a range of *mediating factors* to allow various plans of action to be worked out (e.g. ask an open question; stay silent but look receptive; invite the interviewee to take the lead). One of these plans will be decided upon and enacted in terms of a *response* (e.g. asking a question). The *feedback* to the interviewer will then be the *perception* of the effects of the question upon the interviewee, and this will, in turn, determine the extent to which the interviewer's goal has been achieved. At the same time, the interviewee will be pursuing her own goals, and will likewise devise and implement responses and monitor the reactions of the interviewer to these in order to evaluate personal goal attainment.

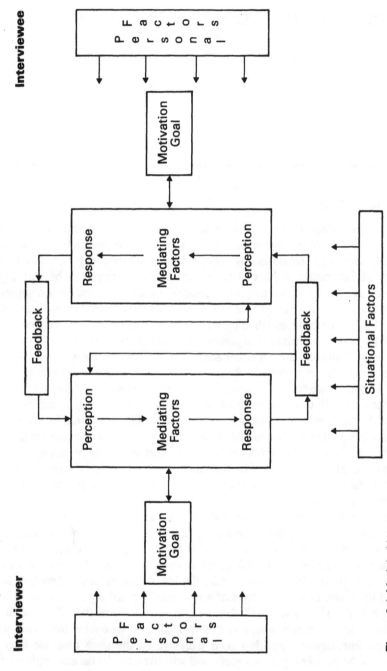

Figure 2.1 Model of interpersonal interaction

The two remaining elements of the model concern *personal* and *situational* factors, and both are crucially important during social interaction. The age, gender and physical appearance of the participants will influence how they are perceived, and responded to, by others. Similarly, situational factors, such as the roles of the interactors, the physical environment and the expected sequences of behaviour, all affect the responses of those involved in any interview situation.

All of these elements need to be taken into consideration in any analysis of interviewing. Thus, the model of interpersonal interaction, as illustrated in Figure 2.1, highlights the central dimensions of dyadic interaction, and as such can serve as a template for the study of interviewing. The application of this model to the interviewing situation can best be explained by examining each of the components separately.

GOALS AND MOTIVATION

As discussed in chapter one, a central defining feature of the interview is the function or purpose which it is intended to achieve. In this sense, the goals of both interviewer and interviewee are of vital import, since, for the interview to be effective, the goals of both parties must be compatible. For example, effective counselling will only occur when the counsellor wants to help the client, and the client genuinely wants to engage meaningfully with the counsellor. For this reason, it would be very difficult to *make* a client accept counselling.

Goals are therefore a useful starting point in any analysis of interviewing. The goals which people pursue are directly influenced by their motivation to achieve these goals. Generally, people pursue goals that are valued and tend to engage in behaviour that is likely to maximise goal achievement. In discussing the relationship between goals and motives in the context of interviewing, Lopez (1975, p.19) points out that: 'Underneath every human action lies a complex series of motives. A *motive* is simply a connection between a felt *need* and a perceived *goal*.' There are a large number of human needs, some of which will be central depending upon the context. Various analyses of needs have been posited, one of the best known being the hierarchy of human needs put forward by Maslow (1954).

At the bottom of this hierarchy (see Figure 2.2), and therefore the most important, are physiological needs, which are concerned with the physical survival of the individual. If we are very hungry, thirsty or cold, we will be highly motivated to rectify this deprivation, and our goal will be to seek food, water or heat. Interviewers need to take account of these needs in the interview by ensuring adequate temperature and ventilation in the room, offering tea or coffee and checking that the interviewee is generally 'comfortable'. The fact that the interviewer has recognised these basic needs will be appreciated by the interviewee.

The second most important needs as recognised by Maslow are those associated with the safety of the individual, including security and freedom from fear. In

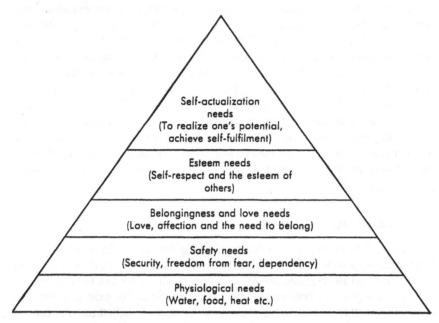

Figure 2.2 Maslow's hierarchy of human needs

appraisal interviews, for example, the interviewee may well be concerned about the satisfaction of these needs, and about whether a negative appraisal will affect promotion, or even employment, opportunities. Where appropriate, it is therefore useful for the interviewer to begin such interviews with a positive statement concerning the performance of the interviewee, thereby giving reassurance that the interview is not intended to be in any way threatening. At the next level are belongingness and love needs, which are concerned with the need for acceptance and affection. People seeking counselling are often in a situation where these needs are not being met (e.g. following bereavement or separation). In such circumstances the counsellor may be in the position of playing the part of a 'good friend'. This befriending function can be very important in certain helping interviews.

The next set of needs are to do with esteem, which includes the need for both self-esteem and the respect of others. In interviews where the client may be suffering a loss of self-respect, it is important for the interviewer to be especially sensitive. Such a context may be where the client is unemployed, since for many people esteem needs are met through occupational status. Likewise, attention may need to be devoted to esteem needs when dealing with sensitive issues such as marital breakdown. The importance of self-esteem, in the form of 'recognition', is highlighted by Gorden (1987) as one of the core needs of interviewees. He asserts that:

by attention from people outside the individual's intimate circle....The skilful and insightful interviewer takes advantage of every opportunity to give the respondent sincere recognition. (Gorden, 1987, p.142)

Locke and Latham (1984) also regard recognition as an important dimension, in terms of contributing to employee motivation within the work setting. The final level of need relates to the desire for individuals to realise their true potential. Again, during appraisal interviews this type of need should be recognised, as it should in careers guidance and other types of helping interview.

Maslow argues that the importance of this hierarchy is that it illustrates how the satisfaction of basic needs takes priority over the achievement of higher-order goals. In other words, individuals who are starving with hunger will be pre-occupied with obtaining food and will not be so concerned with personal esteem (thus they may be prepared to compromise their dignity by begging). The ramifications of this for interviewing are that interviewers should ensure that basic creature comforts (heat, comfortable seating, food, drinks, security in the form of privacy, etc.) are provided at the outset of the interview, thereby allowing the interviewer to concentrate on the achievement of more specific goals directly relating to the interview.

It should be realised that Maslow's hierarchy does not hold in all cases. An extreme exception to the hierarchy is the case of hunger strikers who starve themselves to death, thereby forgoing basic needs, in order to attempt to achieve what they regard as higher-order political goals. In most cases, however, the hierarchy will give a true representation of the relative importance of human needs, and this is useful for interpreting the behaviour of individuals, which can in turn be related to their levels of need.

Goals and behaviour

There is a clear link between goals and behaviour. Indeed, Miller and Steinberg (1975, p.62) argue that:

the basic function of communication is to control the environment so as to realize certain physical, economic and social rewards from it.

The importance of goals is further underlined by Argyle et al. (1981, p.6) who iterate that:

Most social behaviour is goal-directed, and cannot be understood until the goal or goals are known.

During social encounters, therefore, we carry out certain behaviours in order to achieve particular goals. This pursuit of goals is not always a conscious process, since our behaviour is guided for the most part by subconscious goals. Indeed this is a feature of skilled performance, in that the experienced interviewer does not think consciously 'I want to obtain specific information so I will ask a factual closed question', but rather will do so almost 'without thinking'. This is similar to the experienced car driver who will put the gear in neutral, switch on the ignition, depress the clutch, etc., without having to think consciously about these actions. Thus, skilled behaviour is usually executed without conscious reference to guiding goals. In fact a conscious focus upon underlying goals can result in impaired performance. This was illustrated by the goalkeeper for the English first division soccer team West Ham United, Allen McKnight, who explained his recent poor performances as follows:

> I've started to think about things rather than rely on instinct. When you do that you tend to make silly decisions....You are considering two options and sometimes you choose the wrong one. When you rely on instinct, it just tells you what is right.

> (*Independent*, 18 February 1989)

However, Ellis and Whittington (1981) point out that what they refer to as 'super-normal interactors' are able to carry out skilled behaviours while being consciously aware of the goals they are trying to achieve. In this way, a skilled physician will have carefully formulated goals concerning a diagnosis of a patient's illness, will be aware of these at each stage of the medical interview and will employ appropriate behaviours to achieve these goals. Nevertheless, even with highly skilled individuals not all goals will be conscious during interaction, in that, for example, smiles, head nods and other such rewarding behaviours usually will be carried out without direct awareness of each individual behaviour as it is being employed. Generally, in interviewing, the more aware we are of our behaviour and of the goals we are seeking the better able we should be to adjust to the demands of any given interview.

Likewise, as illustrated in Figure 2.1, we need to take cognizance of the goals of the interviewee. It is therefore important for the interviewer to ascertain the objectives of the interviewee at the outset, and either to proceed to attempt to meet these objectives or to explain why they cannot be facilitated. (See chapter seven for further discussion of this issue.) The goals of the interviewee will, of course, vary depending upon the type of interview being conducted and these goals may be seen by the interviewer as being of more or less importance. For example, in counselling the goals of the client are usually regarded as being of paramount importance, whereas in selection the interviewer's goals normally take precedence over those of the candidate.

Another distinction which can be made is between long-term and short-term goals. In order to attain long-term goals it is necessary to formulate a series of related short-term goals. The latter then act as a route for the achievement of the former. Our moment to moment behaviour is therefore guided by short-term goals. For instance, a personnel officer may have a long-term goal of selecting the best candidate for a vacant post. To achieve this goal he will have to devise and execute a large number of short-term goals including: writing a suitable job description; advertising the vacancy in appropriate locations; drawing up a short-list of candidates for interviewing; and arranging the interviews. At the actual interview stage the main goal will be to assess each candidate, and again this involves shorter-term goals such as welcoming the candidate, asking a range of pertinent questions and evaluating the responses, allowing the candidate to ask questions, and so on. The failure to achieve each of these short-term goals will usually mean that the long-term goal will not be attained.

At times, there may be conflict between the long-term and short-term goals, and this can pose particular difficulties for interviewers. One example of such goal conflict can be found in counselling when the counsellor has to confront or challenge the client with inconsistencies in his presentation, while at the same time ensuring that this confrontation does not damage the overall relationship. As Nelson-Jones (1983, p.111) points out:

> though a good challenge may accelerate the counselling process, premature or clumsy challenges, especially with vulnerable clients, may retard the coun-selling process or cause clients to terminate counselling.

Goal conflicts of this type clearly require careful and skilled handling by interviewers.

Goals, therefore, represent an essential base line in the communication model, since they play a pivotal role in interpersonal communication, influencing how information is received, processed and acted upon. Interviewers should ensure that they have carefully formulated plans of action to guide their behaviour in interviews and should also pay attention to the goals of the interviewees. Success-ful interviewing occurs when there is concurrence between the goals of inter-viewer and interviewee.

MEDIATING FACTORS

Mediating factors can be defined as those internal states, activities or processes within the individual which mediate between the goals that are being followed, the feedback which is being perceived and the action that will be taken. As Glassman (1979, p.144) puts it:

> events within the person are referred to as mediational processes or *mediators*, because they come between external stimulus and the response.

The process of mediation is important since it allows the person to evaluate to what extent goals can be achieved, and whether different actions need to be taken, or different goals adopted. In other words, this is the decision-making stage of the interactive process. In terms of such decision-making the two main mediating factors are cognitions and emotions.

Cognition

The importance of the role of cognition in interpersonal communication has long been recognised. Pillsbury and Meader (1928, p.92) noted that 'man thinks first and then expresses his thoughts in words by some sort of translation'. The actual nature of cognition has been explained by Neisser (1967, p.4), who asserts that this involves:

All the processes by which the sensory input is transformed, reduced, elaborated, stored, recovered and used.

This definition encapsulates the central facets of cognition. This involves *transforming*, or decoding and making sense of the sensory information that is perceived. To be effective in doing so, it is necessary to *reduce* the amount of information attended to, in order to avoid overloading the system. Paradoxically, it is also sometimes necessary to *elaborate* on minimal information received from others by making interpretations, judgements or evaluations (for example, if an interviewee refuses to speak to us we will attempt to work out why this is happening). Some of the incoming information will be *stored* in either the short-term or the long-term memory store. This storage is vital since 'a critical requirement for successfully completing any interaction is a functioning memory' (Stafford and Daly, 1984, p.379). Short-term memory involves the retention of information for a few minutes, whereas long-term memory refers to retention for days, weeks or years. In medical interviews problems can be encountered with patients who are suffering from impairments to short-term memory. For example, a geriatric patient may have forgotten the interviewer's name seconds after being introduced, but be able to recall vividly instances from their childhood. Information which has been stored in memory can then be *recovered and used.*

In terms of interviewing, we are concerned with social cognition which can be defined as 'organised thoughts people have about human interaction' (Roloff and Berger, 1982, p.21). This is an important field of study since:

human communication, whether interpersonal or mass, involves more than overt behavior. The communication behaviors we observe directly reflect a great deal that is purely cognitive. We communicate based upon what we know about the world and what we know about communicating. Even more, it seems as though most, if not all, of our communication behaviors are generated through cognition. We must think to communicate.

(Hawkins and Daly, 1988, p.191)

Furthermore, there is an 'accumulation of evidence that individuals use schemas to process information' (Hawkins and Daly, 1988, p.201). Experienced professionals develop a range of cognitive 'schemas' which can be utilised to facilitate the process of decision-making during interpersonal encounters (Carroll, 1980; Ellis and Whittington, 1983). Thus, the experienced counsellor will have a number of schemas, such as 'she is getting embarrassed' and 'he needs time to think this through', each with accompanying action plans – 'use a reassuring self-disclosure', 'keep silent and provide nonverbal signs of attending'. These schemas are used both to evaluate situations and to enable appropriate responses to be implemented without delay. The capacity to respond quickly and competently is a central feature of skilled performance. In discussing this issue, McCroskey (1984, p.264) notes:

> Communication competence requires not only the ability to perform certain communication behaviors, it also requires an understanding of those behaviors and the cognitive capacity to make choices among behaviors.

The skilled interviewer will have acquired a wide range of cognitive schemas and strategies to facilitate problem-solving and decision-making during interviews. This includes the ability to formulate a number of contingency plans which can readily be implemented should the initial response be unsuccessful. As discussed in the previous section, these plans of action are for the most part subconscious. The skilled interviewer will also pay attention to the thoughts of the interviewee, which, as Wessler (1984, p.112) puts it, involves 'the capacity to form cognitive conceptions of the other's cognitive conceptions'. This process of meta-cognition therefore involves an ability to be aware of how the interviewee is thinking.

Emotions

Emotions also have an important role to play in social interaction (Frijda, 1986). There are three main components of emotion. First, the direct conscious experience or 'feeling' of emotion; second, a series of physiological processes which accompany the feeling of emotion; and third, the actual verbal and non-verbal behaviours which are used to express and convey emotion. In noting these processes, Izard (1977, p.10) points out that:

> virtually all of the neurophysiological systems and subsystems of the body are involved to a greater or lesser degree in emotional states. Such changes inevitably affect the perceptions, thoughts and actions of the person.

Emotional states are, therefore, very important in terms both of our perceptions of the outside world and of how we respond to it. One indication of the importance of emotions is the fact that we have a very large number of terms which are used to describe emotional states. In one study Averill (1975) identified a total of 558 discrete emotional labels. Emotions are clearly of importance in interviewing. The emotional states of both the interviewer and interviewee will influence the way they communicate with one another. The interviewer needs to be aware of, and sensitive to, the emotional state of the interviewee. Yet there is firm evidence that in medical interviews practitioners tend to avoid emotional issues presented by patients, preferring to stay on the safer ground of factual matters (Dickson et al., 1989). In counselling interviews, of course, client feelings and emotions often form the core areas for discussion.

The nature of the relationship between cognitions and emotions is a matter for debate. Some theorists argue that a direct causal relationship exists between thought processes and emotions, with the latter being caused by the former (e.g.

Ellis, 1962). In this 'rational-emotive' perspective irrational beliefs are viewed as being the cause of fear or anxiety, and, it is posited, these negative emotions could be overcome by helping the individual to become more rational about his beliefs. This approach is regarded by others as being an over-simplification of the relationship between cognitions and emotions, since it is argued that emotional states can cause changes in thoughts (Forgas, 1983). The argument here is that a strong reciprocal relationship exists between the two, so that someone may be so worried they cannot 'think straight', and it is also possible to be 'out of your mind' with worry. As Forgas (1983, p.138) puts it:

> We not only differentiate between, and represent, social episodes in terms of how we feel about them, but mood and emotions also play a crucial role in thinking about and remembering such events.

Thus the way we feel can have a direct influence on the way we think, and vice versa. In this sense, both cognitions and emotions are core determinants of behaviour.

In addition to cognitions and emotions, there are other mediating factors which influence the way the interviewer will process information, and respond to the interviewee. Our values and beliefs will influence our perceptions, cognitions, emotions and actions. For example, a devout Roman Catholic would find it extremely difficult to advise a client about the procedures for obtaining an abortion. Other factors which will influence our responses to others include our knowledge and experience of interviewing and of dealing with particular types of interviewee, the personality and temperament which we possess and our attitudes towards specific groups (e.g. a selection interviewer who is a racist would find great difficulty being unbiased when dealing with an interviewee from the negatively perceived ethnic group).

All of these factors are operative at the decision-making stage during interviews. Just as we are usually not consciously aware of the goals which we are pursuing, so too does this mediating process between perception and action take place at a subconscious level. However, a knowledge of the role of these mediating factors is valuable for interviewers, since it can facilitate a greater understanding and awareness of some of the reasons for the behaviour of interviewer and interviewee.

RESPONSES

The third stage in this model of interpersonal interaction is the response phase. When a goal has been decided upon and a plan of action devised to achieve this goal, the next step is actually to carry out the plan in terms of overt behaviours. Judgements about skill are directly related to behavioural performance. We do not judge soccer players on their ability to discuss the game or analyse their own performance, but rather we regard them as skilful or not based upon what they *do* on the field of play. Similarly, we make judgements about social skill based upon the *behaviour* of the individual during social encounters. As Roloff and Kellerman (1984, p.175) point out:

> competence is a judgment that a person's behavior corresponds to certain standards of performance. In the case of communication competence, the focus is upon the evaluative judgment of a person's verbal and nonverbal behavior.

In like vein, Sypher (1984, p.109) argues that 'communication competence is dependent on certain skills that allow persons to achieve rewards and goals'. This is a perspective also taken by Hargie (1986) in his analysis of the nature of skilled performance when he defines a social skill as:

> a set of goal-directed, inter-related situationally appropriate social behaviours which can be learned and which are under the control of the individual. (p.12)

Thus, the essence of effective communication is appropriate social responses. In this way, interviewers will be regarded as competent or incompetent on the basis of how they actually respond to interviewees.

Social behaviour can be divided into three categories:

(i) Verbal. This refers to the linguistic content of a person's communication; in other words, *what* the person says.

(ii) Vocal. Here the emphasis is upon *how* something is said, as opposed to *what* is said. The meaning of an utterance can be radically affected by changes in pitch, tone, accent, volume and speed of delivery (Hargie *et al.*, 1987).

(iii) Nonverbal. In recent years, considerable attention has been devoted to the study of body language, in terms of the analysis of touch, proximity, spatial factors, posture, facial expressions, gestures and body movements, gaze, dress and physical appearance (Argyle, 1988).

The apposite use of these social responses is, therefore, the key to effective interviewing. This social skill dimension of interviewing is fully explored in chapter seven.

FEEDBACK

Once a response has been executed, feedback will be available to the interviewer. Such feedback allows the individual to monitor the effectiveness of his performance and alter subsequent behaviour, as necessary, in the light of this information. The importance of feedback for behaviour was highlighted by Bilodeau and Bilodeau (1961, p.250) who describe it as 'the strongest, most important variable controlling performance and learning'. Fitts and Posner (1973) identified three main functions of feedback. First, it provides the individual with *knowledge of results* with regard to the outcome of their actions. Second, it can serve as a form of *motivation* to continue a task, where the feedback indicates that goal attainment is close at hand. Finally, where the feedback is positive and conveys that performance has been successful, it may act as a *reinforcer* encouraging the individual to repeat that particular response in the future.

In order to execute any task effectively, it is vital to receive feedback, since we need to ascertain how successful or unsuccessful our initial efforts have been in order to gauge the extent to which change in behaviour is required. Thus, if we were blindfolded we would find it extremely difficult to ride a bicycle, make a cup of coffee or even walk along a straight line given the absence of visual feedback. Likewise, in interpersonal interaction we need feedback from others so that we can judge the effectiveness of our communications. Indeed we usually find difficulty in situations where we are interacting with someone who does not give us 'much feedback' since we are unsure how we are 'being received'. An extreme example of this occurs when we telephone someone and unexpectedly have to interact with a telephone answering machine! Interviewers must pay attention to the feedback received from interviewees, in terms of their verbal, vocal and nonverbal responses, so that they can evaluate the effectiveness of their behaviour.

During social encounters, however, we not only receive feedback from others, but also receive feedback from our own responses (see Figure 2.1). Thus, we hear what we are saying, and if we are highly skilled can also be aware of our nonverbal behaviour. Indeed it is important to take cognizance of our own behaviour so that we are aware of how we are 'coming across' to others. The skilled individual will have a greater capacity for what Snyder (1987) terms 'self-monitoring', which is the capacity to monitor and regulate one's own responses in relation to the responses of others. Effective interviewers will therefore be high self-monitors since they will be better able to control, adjust and adapt their use of skills and strategies to meet the requirements of particular interviewees.

In any social interaction the individual will be bombarded with a constant stream of stimulation both from the environment and from other people. These stimuli cannot all be consciously attended to since there is simply too much to cope with. To avoid overloading the system, this information must be selectively filtered into either the conscious or the subconscious (see Figure 2.3). Thus a selective perception filter is operative within the individual, and its function is to channel feedback into the conscious or subconscious. As a result, only a limited amount of information can be consciously perceived. During interviews there will be a variety of environmental feedback available to the interviewer, and this may include the ticking of a clock, the hum of a central heating system, noises outside the room and the pressure of one's feet on the floor or backside on the chair.

Such stimuli should be filtered into the subconscious during interviews, with the interviewer focusing primarily upon the responses of the interviewee. Unfortunately, vital information from other people is also quite often filtered out, so that for example important cues from the interviewee may be missed by the interviewer during interviews. Some such cues may be picked up subconsciously,

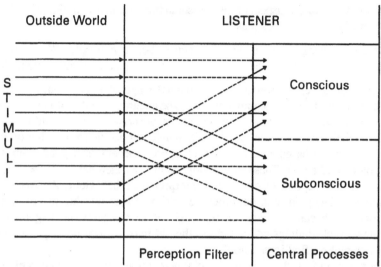

Figure 2.3 Selective perception process

and reactions such as 'I'm not quite sure what it was, but there was something about him I didn't like' may be based upon information which has been dealt with at a subconscious level.

However, in interviewing it is important actively and consciously to pay careful attention to the verbal, vocal and nonverbal behaviour of interviewees so that optimum use can be made of all social feedback available. On occasions this can be very difficult. For example, some medical interviews may take place in a hospital ward, where there will be a large number of impinging auditory and visual stimuli, including other patients and staff, visitors, bright lights and extraneous noises. Furthermore, it should also be remembered that, in interviewing, feedback is a two-way process since the behaviour of the interviewer is the source of social feedback for the interviewee. Attention must therefore be given to the feedback given as well as that received.

PERCEPTION

It is the function of the perceptual system to provide us with information about our environment through our five senses (sight, sound, touch, taste and smell). We use these senses to gather information both about the physical environment and other people. The latter type of perception is referred to as 'person perception' which as Warr and Knapper (1968, p.3) point out:

> not only involves the judgements we make about other people as objects (tall, bald, wearing brown shoes, etc) but is primarily concerned with the impressions we form of people as people (impulsive, religious, tired, happy, anxious and so on).

The importance of this aspect of interpersonal interaction is underlined by Forgas (1985, p.21) who describes it as:

the first, crucial stage in any interaction between people. We must first perceive and interpret other people before we can meaningfully relate to them.

This is often a very powerful and influential stage of interaction. Our initial impressions of other people may not always be accurate, but they do nevertheless affect our judgements. Although it is common wisdom that we should not judge books by their covers, we in fact do. When meeting people for the first time we make judgements based upon factors such as dress, accent, race, gender, physical appearance and so on. These initial judgements can then have a marked effect upon how we respond to others and interpret their behaviour. As Arvey and Campion (1984) point out, important decisions such as whether or not to offer someone a job can be made on the basis of first-impression judgements at interview. Such findings add weight to the old maxim 'You don't get a second chance to make a first impression'.

There are, in fact, three types of social perception. First, we can perceive our own behaviour (we hear what we say and how we say it, and we may also be aware of our body movements). Second, we perceive the behaviour of others. Third, there is the area of metaperception which refers to our perception of the perception process itself. Thus, when we interact with others, we attempt to ascertain how they are perceiving us and we also try to evaluate how they think we are perceiving them. This latter aspect is important since if person A likes person B, A is likely to judge that B feels likewise about A. A will therefore behave towards B accordingly, with the result that B will usually end up liking A. In this way, a self-fulfilling prophecy occurs.

One of the problems in this area is that our perceptions are not always accurate, and in fact our appreciation of many situations can be distorted. An example of this is illustrated in Figure 2.4. This impossible figure looks realistic when examined from any of the ends separately. Yet, when examined as a whole it can be seen that it is in fact an illusion. A similar phenomenon occurs in interviewing where an interviewee may be seen as having different and in-compatible 'sides'. Again, the overall picture will be difficult to relate to and come to terms with.

Another form of misperception is evidenced by the fact that people with physical disabilities are often viewed as being mentally less able (Herman et al., 1986). Thus, there could be the tendency for interviewees confined to wheel-chairs or otherwise physically incapacitated to be viewed as mentally, as well as physically, handicapped. A similar form of altered perception can occur where people are judged upon our previous experience of, or information about, them. In this way, we tend to select perceptions to suit our expectations or existing frame of reference. This was illustrated in an early study by Leeper (1935) who found that when shown drawings similar to those in Figure 2.5, subjects were likely to see an old woman in the ambiguous drawing (a) if they were shown (b)

Figure 2.4 Impossible figure

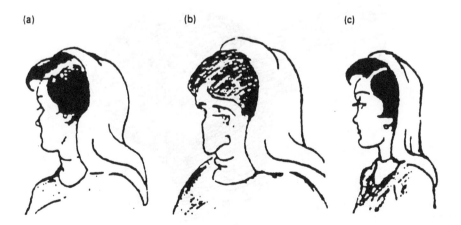

Figure 2.5 Old woman/young woman

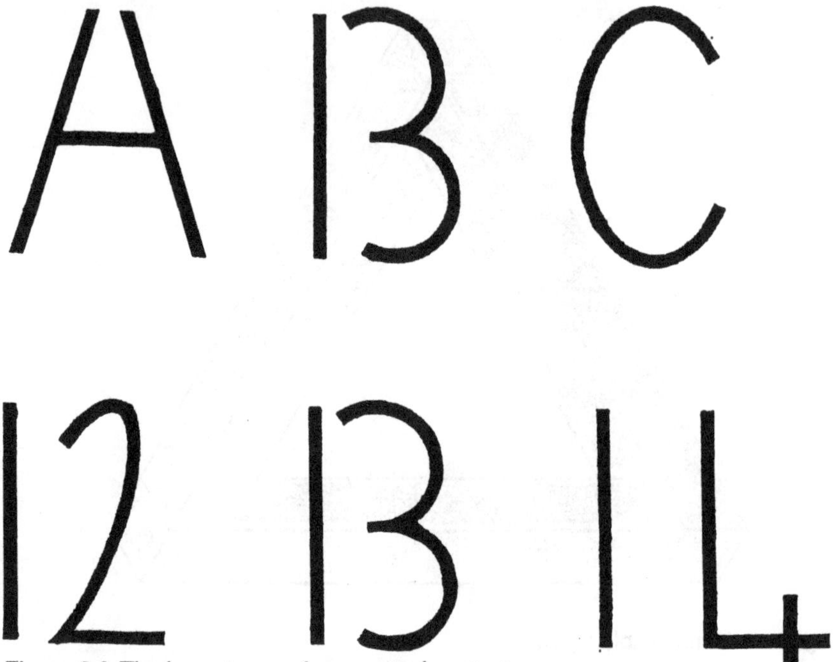

A B C

12 13 14

Figure 2.6 The importance of perceptual context

Figure 2.7 Different 'sides' to perception

first, but were more likely to see a young woman in (a) if they were shown (c) first. A similar process can occur in interviewing. For instance, in selection interviewing, an interviewer may be unduly influenced by a negative reference, or in medical interviewing the interviewer may be biased by what is contained in the interviewee's file.

The context in which we see people will also influence how we perceive them. Thus in Figure 2.6 the top line will be read as A,B,C, while the bottom line will be seen as 12,13,14. Yet, the middle figure in both is identical. Interviewers who deal with interviewees in only one particular context will, of course, have only one perspective on the person, but as Figure 2.7 illustrates there is often more than one side to many things (this figure can be seen as a duck or a rabbit). In other words, how we evaluate people can depend upon which side of them we prefer to focus on, as well as the situation in which the interview is taking place.

Our perceptions can also be inaccurate because some interviewees may, for varying reasons, be deliberately deceptive. As pointed out in chapter one, in research interviews respondents often give answers they feel to be most socially desirable, and so tend to overestimate activities such as voting, reading books and giving to charity, while underestimating illnesses, financial status and illegal behaviour (Bradburn and Sudman, 1980). A more extreme example in the medical sphere is known as Munchausen's syndrome, where a patient describes and enacts textbook symptoms of a disease state, but in fact has no such illness.

Person perception is clearly an important dimension of interviewing. The ability to perceive the cues being emitted by interviewees accurately, while also being aware of one's own responses and their likely effects, is crucial to effective interviewing. At the same time, interviewers need to be sensitive to the range of factors which can cause distortion or inaccuracy during the perceptual process. These issues are fully explored in chapter four.

Perception is the final central process in the interaction model presented in Figure 2.1 and, together with goals, mediating factors, responses and feedback, comprises the core of dyadic interaction. However, in order to gain a fuller understanding of the interactive process, it is necessary to consider two related aspects, namely situational and personal factors.

SITUATIONAL FACTORS

The situation in which any interaction takes place will influence the behaviour of the interactors, so in order to comprehend behaviour fully it is necessary to consider the effects of situational factors. Argyle *et al.* (1981) have identified eight main features of social situations.

   (i) Goal structure. As discussed earlier, skilled performance is guided by goals and no understanding of behaviour can be complete without a consideration of the goals being pursued by the interactors. Thus, in any analysis of interviewing the goals of interviewer and interviewee need to be taken into account.

(ii) Roles. In any situation people will play, and be expected to play, different roles. These roles carry with them sets of expectations about behaviour, attitudes, beliefs and values. In interviewing the interviewer and interviewee will have expectations about one another based upon their understanding of the respective roles. Problems can therefore arise if the interviewee holds mistaken views about the role of the interviewer, or vice versa. If interaction is to proceed smoothly, such misapprehensions will need to be rectified.

(iii) Rules. Every situation is rule-governed, in that there will be a range of (often implicit) rules which have to be adhered to in order to ensure effective communication. Fairly extreme examples of rule-breaking would be an interviewee refusing to speak at a selection interview, or a counsellor sitting with her back to a client throughout the interaction! It is important for interviewers to learn how to handle skilfully situations in which the interviewee breaks the generally accepted 'rules' of interviewing (e.g. by becoming aggressive or hysterical). Such rule-breaking may occur more often in certain contexts, such as in psychiatric settings.

(iv) Repertoire of elements. This refers to the types of behaviour displayed in any situation. There are four main categories of responses. The *verbal content* relates to the actual topics of conversation discussed; *verbal categories* are concerned with the classification of the linguistic content into areas such as questions, explanations, self-disclosure and so on; *nonverbal behaviour*, as has already been pointed out, focuses upon the analysis of areas such as touch, posture, gestures and facial expressions; while *bodily actions* refer to global movements including 'enters room', 'sits down' or 'takes notes'. All four categories are relevant to the analysis of interviews.

(v) Sequences of behaviour. The typical repertoire of elements in any situation usually occurs in a set sequence, and this sequence will be expected by the interactors. For example, in a restaurant the sequence would usually be:
(a) entering the restaurant
(b) going, or being shown, to a table
(c) asking for, or being presented with, a menu
(d) ordering the meal
(e) being served
(f) eating the meal
(g) paying the bill
(h) leaving the restaurant.
There may, of course, be some variations in this sequence, depending upon the type of restaurant or specific events (e.g. complaining about service or the meal).

Similar sequences occur in interviewing. Thus, in their study of doctor–patient interviews, Byrne and Long (1976) identified a six-episode behavioural sequence which involved:

(a) relating to the patient

(b) discussing the reason for the patient's visit

(c) conducting a verbal and/or physical examination

(d) considering the patient's condition

(e) detailing treatment or further investigation

(f) terminating.

To ensure a smooth interaction, both the interviewer and the interviewee should be aware of the expected behavioural sequence in an interview and this should be adhered to as far as possible.

(vi) Concepts. In any social situation there will be a range of concepts with which those involved must be familiar if they are to participate effectively in the interaction. In a restaurant one may need to be familiar with a range of concepts including 'waitress', 'menu', 'aperitif', 'hors-d'oeuvre' and 'à la carte'. Likewise a visit to the doctor will necessitate an understanding of concepts such as 'receptionist', 'prescription', 'capsules' and 'pharmacist'. A common error made by many professionals is to assume mistakenly that clients are familiar with the concepts being used. For example, doctors may assume that patients understand concepts such as 'blood pressure', 'cholesterol' or 'stroke', when in fact they do not fully comprehend these terms (Dickson et al., 1989). In interviewing, therefore, it is essential to ensure that the interviewee is familiar with all of the concepts involved.

(vii) Physical environment. The nature of the environment in which an interaction is taking place will influence the behaviour of the interactors. Factors such as the type, and layout, of furniture and fittings, the lighting and heating and the actual location of the room will all play a part in determining how individuals behave. People tend to feel more comfortable in their own environment than in an unfamiliar one, and this may be an important consideration in deciding where to conduct an interview. Likewise, people feel more relaxed and will self-disclose more in 'warm' environments (soft seats, subdued lighting, carpets, curtains, pot plants). Where the interview is taking place in the interviewer's office, consideration should be given to methods whereby this can be made as conducive as possible for the interviewee.

(viii) Language and speech. The final aspect of social situations relates to linguistic variations. There are changes in tone, volume, pitch, etc., of voice, as well as in the formality of language, across situations. For example, there are differing vocal patterns associated with barristers summing up in court, evangelical clergymen delivering sermons and sports commentators describing ball games. Similarly, there will be a more deliberate use of formal language when conducting a research interview as opposed to when having a chat with a colleague over coffee. On the other hand, the 'tone' of a counselling interview will be more akin to the latter than the former. Thus, the choice of language and speech needs to be appropriate to the context.

These eight features of situations are all of relevance to an understanding of the behaviour of interviewers and interviewees, and should therefore be borne in mind in any evaluation of interviewing.

PERSONAL FACTORS

The final element of the interpersonal interaction model (Figure 2.1) relates to personal factors, which refer to those features of the individual which are readily visible to others. As mentioned earlier, before we actually interact with others we make a number of judgements about them based upon their appearance, and these judgements can influence both how we interpret their behaviour and how we respond to them. Hargie and Marshall (1986) have identified four main personal factors which have a direct bearing on interpersonal communication.

(i) Gender. Although there is an increasing awareness of the importance of equal opportunities for females, we nevertheless still tend to respond differently to, and hold differing expectations of, others depending upon their gender. As Mayo and Henley (1981, p.3) point out:

> Sex as signaled by cues of appearance is a powerful force in human interaction; 'sex' is highly visible and often the first aspect to which we respond.

This differential is highlighted from an early age when female and male babies are dressed, and responded to, differently (Stewart and Ting-Toomey, 1987). These patterns of responses then persist into adulthood where differences can be found in the behaviour patterns of males and females (Mayo and Henley, 1981). For example, females tend to smile more frequently, require less interpersonal space, are touched more, use more head nods and engage in more eye contact than males. Linguistic differences have also been found, with females tending to use more intensifiers (e.g. 'It was *really* exciting'; 'This is *so* difficult'), more modal expressions (these convey doubt or hesitation, and include terms such as 'might', 'could', 'possibly') and more formal language (Ellis and Beattie, 1986).

The gender of interviewer and interviewee is therefore of relevance to an understanding of the pattern of communication in the interview. For example, generally we tend to disclose more to those of the opposite sex, but with certain topics (e.g. sensitive, sexual matters) may prefer to interact with someone of the same gender. In discussing gender issues in selection interviewing, Breakwell (1990) identifies a number of factors on which male and female interviewers differ depending upon the gender of the interviewee. She reports, for example, that female interviewers are more likely to show humour during interviews, and they place more value upon openness, honesty and enthusiasm on the part of candidates. Male interviewers, on the other hand, spend less time discussing the leisure pursuits or ambitions of candidates and are also less likely to express disagreements with them. Overall, she cautions that in attempting to understand the process of interviewing 'you ignore the sex of the interviewer at your peril' (Breakwell, 1990, p.31).

(ii) Age. Although some people go to great lengths to disguise their true age, this is an aspect of others which we can usually estimate fairly accurately, certainly within the main life stages of infancy, childhood, adolescence, adulthood, middle age and old age. We also hold expectations about the behaviour of people based upon their age, as exemplified by expressions such as 'Mutton dressed as lamb'; 'Act your age'; 'Still wet behind the ears'. In this sense, ageism is as much a feature of social encounters as sexism. This can have ramifications for interviewing, in that some interviewees may prefer an older interviewer who is seen as more experienced, whereas others may favour a younger interviewer who is regarded as being more up-to-date.

(iii) Dress. The importance of clothes as social signals is evidenced by the amount of money spent on fashion wear in western society. Clothes can serve to convey information about a range of factors including the wearer's gender, group membership, occupation, status, individual identity and personality. As well as clothes, other embellishments, including jewellery, watches, spectacles and make-up, are used to convey some of this information. The dress of the interviewer will be important in relation to the impressions being conveyed to interviewees. For instance, it has been shown that interviewees prefer counsellors who dress formally enough to portray an impression of competence and whose dress is in style rather than old-fashioned, to those who dress very formally and are thereby seen as 'stuffy' or unapproachable (Kleinke, 1986). In selection interviews there would appear to be a convention that the interviewers should dress in the manner they expect from candidates.

(iv) Physical appearance. This refers to body size, shape and attractiveness. Physique can influence how people are perceived, in that ectomorphs (thin figure) tend to be seen as clean, tidy, quiet and conscientious though nervous; mesomorphs (muscular) as strong, healthy and forceful; and endomorphs (fat) as lazy, untidy and sloppy though happy. Height is also important in that taller men in our society tend to perform better on occupational indices such as promotion and salary and social indices such as dating. Furthermore, higher status males (regardless of their actual height) are viewed as being taller in direct proportion to their status (Stewart *et al.*, 1979).

Attractiveness is an important feature in social encounters, in that those who are rated as attractive are also seen as being more popular, friendly and interesting to talk to, and thereby receive more eye contact, smiles, self-disclosures, body accessibility (openness of arms and legs) and closer bodily proximity (Kleinke, 1986). For this reason, interviewers should attempt to make themselves as attractive as possible to interviewees in order to encourage full and honest disclosures. It should, of course, be realised that attractiveness involves more than mere physical make-up, since dress, cleanliness, personality and competence are involved in judgements of attractiveness (Hargie *et al.*, 1987). Thus, less physically attractive interviewers may be 'attractive' to interviewees by adopting a friendly interactive style and ensuring they have a competent, professional approach.

SUMMARY

In this chapter we have presented a dyadic model of interpersonal interaction (Figure 2.1) which can be applied directly to the analysis of interviewing. This model highlighted seven main facets of the interactive process. These were: the goals of the people involved and their motivation to pursue them; a range of mediating factors including cognitions, emotions, beliefs, values and attitudes; the responses of the participants; the feedback available; the ability of the individuals to perceive this feedback; and the situational and personal factors which impinge upon the communication process. It will be apparent from this brief review of these facets that interaction between people is a complex process involving a myriad of variables, any, or all, of which may be operative in any particular encounter. Although, for the purposes of description, analysis and evaluation each of these have been studied separately, it will be realised that in reality these processes do not occur in isolation, but are inter-related and inter-dependent and are operative simultaneously. In addition, we are not usually aware that these processes are actually occurring, since we behave, for the most part, at a subconscious level. For this reason, it is very difficult to make judgements or interpretations about the behaviour of individuals during interviews.

However, the model as presented does provide a systematic structure for interpreting the interpersonal dimensions of interviewing. A knowledge of this model is therefore a very useful starting point for the study of interviewing, and so this chapter provides a necessary theoretical foundation for the remainder of the book. The following chapters provide in-depth analyses of the central elements of this model.

Chapter 3

Social psychological perspectives

The model of interpersonal interaction as outlined in chapter two provided the reader with a framework that could help explain human interaction across a wide range of social situations. In explaining such encounters the model emphasises both the situational and the personal variables and, furthermore, points out the importance of both intra- and inter-individual factors as contributors to complex social behaviour. For example, Benjamin (1981, p.35) suggests that 'everyone engaging in the helping interview brings along with him attitudes in terms of which he functions'. Such attitudes not only influence the interviewer's behaviour but must also substantially determine that of the interviewee. A somewhat similar view is taken by Brenner (1981) in his treatment of bias in the research interview. Furthermore, as Farr (1982) points out, the interview can be regarded as a particular type of social encounter, and so the interpersonal interaction model should prove helpful as both a descriptive and predictive paradigm. Indeed its usefulness as the basis of training in communication is well documented (Dickson *et al.*, 1989).

However, there are some aspects of the model, specifically those components which might be described as 'cognitive', that appear to have received less attention. To elucidate more clearly what comprise mediating factors (see chapter two) should prove most beneficial in attempting to explain why a certain type of behaviour was emitted or why a certain decision/judgement was reached. It is now widely recognised that significant intervening processes occur within the individual which mediate between perception of the stimulus and the execution of a response. (This holds except for those extreme behaviourists who regard the concept of intervening variables as neither necessary nor verifiable and therefore disregard them as insignificant.) Within the interview context the importance of searching for an understanding of the other person, to get to know him or to exert some influence over him in order to find something out, implies a thoughtful process arrived at by way of mainly conscious decision-making. That is, it is rarely the case that an interviewer *must* perform or respond in a certain way although many may have developed preferred 'styles' or have chosen to employ set strategies. This need not and possibly should not be the case. This is not to say that all such decision-making operates at the conscious level, a point made by

Forbes and Jackson (1980) when they identified subconscious information sources for interviewer attributions.

In our attempts to generate an understanding of others (and ourselves) we tend to seek out a range of different types of information upon which to form impressions and to make inferences concerning both current and future behaviour. These outcomes constitute the major objectives of the processes of attribution and will be more fully explored later in this chapter.

Before dealing with attribution processes it should also be noted that in the context of interviewing the responses or behaviours of the interviewee occur at least in part due to the presence of the interviewer. This dynamic interactive perspective is clearly incorporated into the interpersonal interaction model and suggests that each person engaged in the encounter may potentially exert some influence over the other. In certain types of interview a knowledge of the possible mechanisms through which social influence may be transmitted could be of immense value, e.g. the counselling or medical interview. The trend towards the professionalisation of interviewing across a number of contexts such as in personnel, medical, counselling or research fields may lead to an increased significance being attributed to such processes. The inclusion of the social influence model would seem justified on the grounds of it being 'the emerging theory of this part of the century' (Dorn, 1984).

To summarise, it is the intention of this chapter to clarify the appropriateness of attribution theory and social influence theory to a greater understanding of 'interviewing' and to conclude by outlining a number of errors which may occur in the process.

ATTRIBUTION THEORY

According to Shaver (1983, p.5) the objectives of attribution are

> to increase the perceiver's understanding of behaviour and the perceiver's ability to predict what the actor is likely to do in the future.

Based on observations of action the perceiver goes beyond such direct information and makes a number of inferences concerning other characteristics of the actor. The importance of the human activity of observation was stressed by Gorden (1987) as being a fundamental data collection activity in the development of an understanding of human behaviour. The process of observation enables the collection of overt information upon which inferences can be made of more covert psychological traits (Baron and Byrne, 1984).

According to Heider's (1958) psychology of interpersonal relations, individuals attribute causality of actions either to the environment (external attributions) or to something within the person observed (internal attribution). Deriving from the work of Heider (1958), the theory of *correspondent inference* was proposed by Jones and Davis (1965). Harvey and Weary (1981, p.12) define such an inference as being concerned 'about individuals' intentions and dispositions that follows directly from or corresponds to their behaviours'. When a person's behaviours are judged to reflect their internal personal dispositions then a correspondent inference has been achieved. According to Jones and Davis (1965), a correspondent inference is more likely when certain kinds of actions are observed, namely those perceived as intentional, those that produce unique (noncommon) outcomes and those low in social desirability. Therefore, although a wide range of behaviours may be observed, only those deemed to possess the above characteristics constitute attributionally valuable actions. It seems relevant to emphasise that behaviour which may appear to an observer to be 'out-of-role' will be much more informative than behaviour which is more 'in-role' and therefore more expected (Harvey and Weary, 1981).

This notion has immediate relevance to the interviewing situation with its prescribed roles and rule systems. How much can we infer about a candidate's personal dispositions where such a candidate 'plays the game' and indeed may be labelled a good interviewee? The implications of a proliferation of interviewee technique training courses suggest that interviewers will be faced with an increasingly difficult task of distinguishing one 'person' from another as more people become adept at playing the interview game. However, for the person who displays some behaviour which is judged to be 'out-of-role', the interviewer can with more confidence attribute stable characteristics. For example, the person who declines to speak during the interview (out-of-role behaviour) possibly tells the interviewer more about herself than does the person who speaks adequately (in-role behaviour).

In a refinement of Jones and Davis' (1965) theory, Jones and McGillis (1976) proposed that behaviours could be ordered in terms of the expected desirability of their effects with more unexpected behaviours conveying more information about the individual than behaviours which would have been expected in the given situation. It should be noted that the concept of expectation refers to what the interviewer (or observer) would expect most people to do in similar circumstances and is therefore a subjective judgement. Referring to the selection interview, Herriot (1981, p.166) suggests that

> attributions of dispositions will be made in two circumstances: when a party engages in behaviour which is unusual for interviews; and when these behaviours occur relatively infrequently within the interview.

The principle of correspondent inference (Jones and Davis, 1965) offers an account of how an observer arrives at inferences concerning stable dispositions of an actor. However, as Baron and Byrne (1984) point out, it will be important not only to develop an understanding of how causal explanations are generated but also to explore *why* they are necessary and *whether* they originate internally or externally (with respect to the person).

In an attempt to throw some light on the nature of causal explanations and to identify the types of information utilised in the making of such causal inferences, Kelley (1973) and Kelley and Michela (1980) articulated the principle of covariation between specified causal factors and observed effects. Kelley (1967, p.194) himself suggested that the

> effect is attributed to that condition which is present when the effect is present and which is absent when the effect is absent.

Effects are attributed to those causal factors with which they are perceived to correlate rather than to those from which no relationship is perceived. The crucial element in this statement emphasises the subjective nature of perceived co-variance; although there may indeed be an absolute correlation between cause and effect, it can influence the process of causal attribution only if it enters the observer's consciousness as a perceived element in her phenomenal world or forms a part of her personal theory (Herriot, 1989).

The social situations in which causal attributions may be made can be charac-terised along three dimensions which Kelley (1967) labelled Persons, Stimuli and Time/Modality. The task therefore becomes the attribution of cause for a person's (P) response to a certain stimulus (S) on a certain occasion (T). For example, what cause might be attributed to an interviewee who gives mono-syllabic responses to questions posed by a doctor during a medical consultation? In order to reach an answer to the question 'why?' three specific types of information are required by the attributer which Kelley referred to as distinc-tiveness, consensus and consistency. As Kelley and Michela (1980, p.462) sug-gest, the resultant causal attribution depends on:

> the perception of the degree of its consensus with other P's responses to S, its consistency with this P's response to S at other Ts and its distinctiveness from P's response to other Ss.

In terms of the example cited above, you (as observer) would draw upon informa-tion about how other patients (Ps) responded to questions posed by this doctor during their consultations (consensus), how this patient responded to questions during earlier consultations (consistency) and finally how this patient responded to other doctors' questions posed during their interviews (distinctiveness). Depending on the peculiar pattern of information processed, certain attributions will be made either to the person, to the situation or to a combination of both (Kelley and Michela, 1980).

What might these patterns be? Suppose, in the example you conclude that

(1) other patients also seem to be reluctant to talk freely to this doctor;
(2) this patient behaved in a similar fashion during the last visit; and
(3) after observation of other doctors you discover that they have no trouble in eliciting verbose responses from this patient.

This pattern of information where the behaviour displays high consensus, high consistency and high distinctiveness would lead to an attribution to the stimulus, i.e. the doctor. Taking a somewhat different pattern of data where the configura-tion might be low consensus, low consistency and high distinctiveness the resulting attribution will be made to the person; i.e. in the example above, to the patient. This clearly illustrates Kelley's principle of covariation of cause and effect. The causal factor that is always present in the first set of conditions when the effect is observed is the 'doctor', whereas in the latter case it seems to be the 'patient'.

The reader might well be thinking that in order to make an attribution along the lines proposed by Kelley, the attributer requires access to an enormous amount of information spanning a number of situations and ranging across time. Even if this information could be obtained, the task of mentally calculating an analysis of variance renders the model prescriptive rather than descriptive. However, despite the incomplete nature of the available information, causal attributions are made (Herriot, 1989).

Based on common-sense psychology, Kelley (1972) elucidated the Discounting and Augmenting Principles to enhance his explanation of external–internal attributions based on brief observation situations. According to Kelley (1972, p.8), the Discounting Principle is employed when the 'role of a given cause in producing a given effect is discounted if other plausible causes are also present'. This principle can be illustrated by reference to an interview situation where an interviewer attempts to persuade a high status person to divulge certain information. If the person complies and gives the information what plausible cause might be invoked by an observer? It would be plausible to assume that the high status person is stronger than the lower status interviewer and his compliance is unlikely to be due to external pressure; it is much more likely to be due to his internal disposition, i.e. he wanted to be helpful. Consider the situation where the interviewee is of lower status and complies with the interviewer's request for information. Attributions to internal states are inferred less strongly since the availability of plausible external causes for the compliance of the low status person leads to discounting. A major consequence of the operation of this principle is to introduce a degree of caution in making attributions of behaviour-correspondent dispositions as a result of a consideration of a number of possible plausible causes.

However, in certain situations the confidence with which a dispositional attribution is made can be enhanced. Some external causes may operate to suppress a certain effect. In cases where the effect occurs despite these external constraints, an internal attribution to the person is made more likely. For example, in situations where to express certain information or to act in certain ways carries a high degree of risk to the individual, an internal attribution is much more likely if such information is expressed or such actions executed despite the external pressures not to disclose or to act. This variation of the Discounting Principle was referred to by Kelley (1972) as the Augmentation Principle and both appear to make a useful contribution to the explanation of interview decision-making. According to Herriot (1981, p.167) these two principles:

applied in combination to the interview would suggest that behaviour is less likely to be attributed to the individual's dispositions when he behaves as expected in the situation than when his behaviour is contrary to expectations. Specifically, attributions will be situational in the former case and dispositional in the latter.

It was implied above that in many situations individuals are inclined to make attributions based on very limited amounts of information, certainly far short of the ideal amount implicit in Kelley's covariance model. However, in situations where inferences are made it seems reasonable to assume that such inferences are in part a product of the individual's past experience (Baron and Byrne, 1984). Therefore in the course of one's life causal relationships are observed, they are taught and are the product of empirical investigation which results in the mature individual building up a repertoire of explanatory frameworks with proven utility for generating sufficiently effective causal inferences based on limited amounts of relevant information. Such *causal schema* can be viewed as an assumed configuration of information like the completed jigsaw which allows one or two pieces to be recognised as pieces of the whole. Once this task is completed, the remaining pattern can be rapidly inferred and the causal network assumed, enabling attributions to be made as if the whole pattern of data were available. Jones (1982) writing from the health perspective documents a somewhat similar phenomenon evident in the medical interview. He asserts that doctors formulate, very early and often prematurely, 'hypotheses' concerning illnesses based on a very limited number of symptoms. In Jones' (1982, p.157) words:

> The presenting complaints...serve the physician as bases for inferring a host of additional concomitants of the hypothesized disease.

The operation of such premature inferential processes serves to reduce the likelihood of thorough and comprehensive case histories and/or medical examinations being conducted.

Like many other cognitive concepts, such causal schemata can display varying degrees of complexity although Kelley (1973) suggests that individuals may express a preference for simple rather than complex ones. The relevance of schemata at the simple end of the dimension can be illustrated by reference to what Kelley (1973) termed 'linear patterns'. A useful illustration of these linear patterns are so-called person schemata which tend to assume that persons with certain characteristics consistently (across time and situations) display corresponding behaviour and that importantly there appears to be considerable consensus among persons making such simplistic attributions. The observed consensus renders these schemata resistant to change even when shown to be incorrect. This phenomenon is more commonly known as stereotyping (well known to us all). Whatever label might be attached, the process acts to simplify the cognitive task by reducing the amount of information required to reach a conclusion. Behaviour–disposition links tend to operate without any appropriate reference to the situational influences hence omitting an important source of data for a more complete interpretation (Heider, 1958; Kelley, 1973). Furthermore, Brenner (1981) suggests that the operation of such stereotyping coupled with self-fulfilling prophecies enables research interviewers to 'fill in' more complete pictures of respondents' attitudes and attributes.

In a refinement of the basic internal–external attributional model, Weiner and his colleagues proposed an extended conception of causal categories employed within the achievement domain (Weiner et al., 1972; Weiner, 1985). According to Weiner (1985) the most salient categories are ability and effort both of which would characterise an internal locus of causality (as distinct from an internal locus of control). These two internal factors represent one of Weiner's other dimensions of causality, labelled stable–unstable. In this two-dimensional system, ability represents a stable internal factor while effort is an internal unstable one. Furthermore, Weiner (1985) introduced a third dimension called controllability. Using this three-dimensional taxonomy, ability represents an internal (locus), stable and uncontrollable factor whereas effort falls into the internal, unstable and controllable category. To complete the picture, those factors located as external to the individual deemed most salient by Weiner et al. (1972) were chance or luck and task difficulty. According to Weiner's (1985, p.549) findings there is a tendency for success to be 'attributed to high ability and hard work, and failure... to low ability and the absence of trying'. Weiner et al. (1972) note that we are more likely to attribute positive qualities to persons who overcome deficits of ability by expending maximum effort while, conversely, we tend to be much less impressed by the qualities of a person who fails to utilise her ability due to lack of effort. A similar phenomenon is outlined by Shaver (1983, pp.103–4) where:

> a person who fails because he does not try is held more morally accountable than is a person who fails because he does not have the requisite ability. Lack of ability is not under the actor's immediate control, and so is forgivable, but lack of motivation, especially when coupled with what would have been sufficient ability, cannot be excused.

The tendency to pass judgement and/or to judge harshly is strong. In terms of encouraging an interviewee to keep persisting, it makes sense to reward those elements which are internally controllable (i.e. effort) rather than those which are uncontrollable (i.e. ability).

An interviewer preparing to interview a job applicant who has a history of interview failures (and therefore job rejections) is more likely to attribute prior failures to a lack of ability or believe that succeeding at interviews is too difficult a task for this individual. The interviewer, therefore, carries with him a somewhat negative preconception into the interview which may severely disadvantage the applicant – she fails again and so the cycle continues. Even if the applicant has an occasional success to her credit this is more likely to be attributed by an interviewer to luck than to any enduring cognitive characteristic. It is important to recognise that the interviewer must share in the responsibility for breaking this vicious circle, particularly when the actual performance of the interviewee warrants a more favourable outcome.

Taking the perspective of the 'actor', Weiner *et al.* (1972) assert that self-attributions tend to be more likely for successful outcomes while attributions to luck or other external factors are more likely in failure situations. This pattern of causal attribution serves to maintain the individual's self-esteem and has been designated as performing an essentially ego-defensive function (Weiner *et al.*, 1972). We have had many discussions with student interviewers trying to consider all possible reasons for a poor interview performance rather than simply those which reside in the situation – usually a poor interviewee or the presence of an intrusive video camera. Even attributions to internal but unstable and controllable factors, such as effort, act in a more self-serving way than attributions to internal but stable and uncontrollable factors such as ability. Furthermore, Kelley and Michela (1980) quoting from Jones and Berglas (1978) invoke the concept of 'self-handicapping' as a potential means of managing self-attributions. In circumstances where an individual, being uncertain of the basis of past success, worries about the prospects of future repetition, Kelley and Michela (1980, p.492) suggest that:

> the introduction of a performance-interfering cause (alcohol, lack of sleep, underpreparation) during further endeavours makes it possible to excuse failure but take credit for success. Thus, the self-handicapper arranges causal conditions so that attributionally he cannot lose.

The deployment of such defensive attributions (Shaver, 1983) is operational in most human beings whether interviewers or interviewees and is a necessary weapon in the individual's armoury. Defensive attributions may be deployed in interviews as felt to be appropriate; that is, whenever the individual (interviewer or interviewee) experiences personal or ego threat. For example, in the context of the information-gathering research interview Gorden (1987) notes that the effect of ego threat can range from evasion or simple emphatic denial to elaborate subtle denial, depersonalisation or minimisation. Therefore, in addition to complete repression of information respondents can engage in a number of tactics which lead to incomplete or distorted patterns to be presented or indeed to complete fabrications of the truth. The potential for experiencing threat may be more likely in situations, such as appraisal interviews, where the interviewer tends to be searching for explanations for employee behaviour; that is, according to Makin *et al.* (1989, p.81), the interviewer, 'will attribute *causality* – who or what was responsible?' The appraiser searches for information that will enable her to locate the cause of the appraisee's successes and failures, either within the person (internal attributions) or outside in the situation (external attributions). Consequent attributions of responsibility will apportion 'blame' accordingly. The climate within which this search takes place can very easily be perceived by the appraisee as highly judgemental and evaluative. Perceptions of this kind simply serve to heighten tension, wariness and suspicion. It is difficult to relax and be open if you feel on trial. Therefore, the safer an individual feels (psychologically) the more likely he will be to communicate openly and honestly. Furthermore, as a consequence of this sense of safety/security clients can be challenged more effectively to develop new perspectives in the counselling context (Egan, 1982). If a variety of personal decisions are to be based on the information elicited, whether an appraisal, a job suitability decision, a clinical diagnosis or a research conclusion, the importance of attempting to ensure that the 'observed' information reflects as closely as possible the 'true' information seems axiomatic. In reality, however, it would also seem highly likely that such judgements will be prone to a number of human errors of a perceptual and a cognitive nature.

ATTRIBUTION ERRORS

Much of the research referred to above has sought to reveal the nature of the causal attribution processes; that is, how we go about making causal attributions, what types of information might be utilised and what short-cuts need to be taken to render the models descriptive rather than prescriptive, to explain attributions made in real rather than ideal situations. Throughout these accounts little is to be found which seeks to elucidate the accuracy with which attributions are made (Kelley, 1973; Kelley and Michela, 1980). Since attributions are based on perceptual and cognitive information-processing mechanisms it seems plausible to assume that they are (like their component processes) prone to error (Kelley, 1973).

Fundamental attribution error

Of all the biases reviewed by Ross (1977), the most significant appears to be that identified by Jones and Harris (1967), further explored by Jones and Nisbett (1972) and termed by Ross the 'fundamental attribution error'. The essence of this bias suggests that there is a general tendency for actors to attribute the causes of their personal actions to the demands of the situation but, when observing precisely the same behaviours exhibited by others, they attribute causality to stable personal dispositions (Kelley, 1973). In short, too much emphasis is placed on the individual's personality traits as the cause of behaviour at the expense of situational determinants. It would seem that important situational factors may be overlooked as we tend to focus our attention on the actions of the observed individual. Kelley and Michela (1980) assert that a large number of studies confirm Jones and Nisbett's hypothesis that actors tend to make more situational attributions and observers more dispositional ones.

Referring to the interview situation, the operation of the fundamental attribution error may lead to dispositional attributions being made when actions occur in accordance with the situational requirements. The candidate who knows or suspects that the successful interviewee will be the one who smiles appropriately, looks at the interviewer and responds to the interviewer's questions in sentences rather than in a word is attributed stable dispositional traits such as friendly, sociable, polite, etc. The patient who adopts the appropriately deferential and compliant 'sick' role may be inferred to be a cooperative, grateful and easy-going person – indeed, a 'good patient' (Taylor, 1979). Conversely individuals who display out-of-role behaviour are generally attributed negative personal characteristics; e.g. the patient who declines to act out the appropriate role behaviour may be termed troublesome, attention-seeking, selfish, stubborn, a griper or, as Bernstein and Dana (1970, pp.7–8) suggest, 'a scoundrel, un-motivated, recalcitrant to treatment or uncurable'. Herriot (1981, p.168) observes with respect to the selection interview that:

> out-of-role behaviour may be taken to indicate a bad applicant, rather than treated as valuable data appropriate to dispositional attribution in general.

We have often heard students, after interviewing school pupils, attribute to them dispositional traits such as unhelpful, uncooperative, difficult because they didn't play the expected role of good interviewee. Little influence is attributed to the stressful situation (which often includes some unhelpful, uncooperative and difficult student interviewers). This tendency to underestimate the influence of situational causes of behaviour may play a vital role in the appraisal situation where, ultimately, responsibility may be attributed, either to the person or to his situation.

The fundamental attribution error would suggest that a disproportionate amount of the responsibility for employee behaviour may be attributed to the employee – they will tend to be held personally more responsible for their successes and failures than the situation might warrant. There may be an implied unfairness or company bias communicated by the appraiser to the appraisee, a clearly detrimental aspect of the interview relationship.

Actor–observer differences

What is also clear is that causal accounts of an action proffered by the two participants may differ radically; on the one hand the interviewee may claim that his violent outburst was not 'typical' and that he was provoked by the circum-stances of the interview whereas the interviewer may attribute the violence to the interviewee being that 'kind of person'. Having characterised the interviewee in this way the interviewer's behaviour may continue in response to this 'aggressive person' by also displaying a degree of aggression. However, given the tendency to attribute our own behaviour to situational factors rather than to internal dispositional causes (Jones and Nisbett, 1972), the interviewer above is unlikely to conclude that he is an aggressive person. This confirms the cause of the aggression as residing in the interviewee – the 'it's not me, it's him' scenario. Once again this has important implications for appraisal situations (Makin *et al.*, 1989).

The implications of such discrepancies in causal attributions can also be seen in the context of the medical consultation where the nature of illnesses and their causes tend to remain implicit and often lacking in agreement (DiMatteo and DiNicola, 1982a). In an empirical investigation of diabetic patients and their doctors, Gillespie and Bradley (1988, p.68) suggested that if:

> causal attributions are not made explicit and discussed, misperceptions and biases on the part of either the doctor or the patient will go uncorrected.

Indeed this was found by Gillespie and Bradley (1988) with the doctor identifying the nature of the problem as the 'old insulin' whereas the patient identified the 'same' problem as 'pressures at work'. In the case of causal attributions for the diabetic problem, one doctor attributed the cause to 'poor control' on the part of the patient whereas the patient attributed the cause to 'inability to socialise'. These examples illustrate the low levels of both problem and causal congruence between doctor and patient particularly with respect to problem definition, the cause of the illness and treatment goals (DiMatteo and DiNicola, 1982a).

The existence of such 'false assumptions' has also been referred to by Herriot (1989) in the selection interview context. Employing Kelley's covariance model Herriot suggests that both participants may assume that the other participant holds similar attitudes and expectations about interview roles and role behaviours (that is, high consensus), that each behaves in a similar fashion outside the interview room (that is, low distinctiveness) and that each person's behaviour in *this* interview will be similar to their behaviour in others (that is, high consistency). The outcome of such beliefs and expectations will be to increase the likelihood of dispositional attributions being made despite the probability that all three assumptions are in fact likely to be false. As Herriot (1989, p.104) observes:

> If there is little agreement in expectations of interview behavior, little similarity between interview behavior and behavior in other situations, and little similarity in behavior across different interviews, then all that can be inferred is that behavior was a function of the specific occasion.

Under this pattern of covariation data, dispositional attributions would be unwarranted yet may be highly likely to occur. Of course such assumptions reduce the amount of covariance data required by users of Kelley's model for attributions to be made. However, false assumptions lead to false attributions. Given the assumption of falsely low distinctiveness, interviewers will tend to attach too much importance to behaviour witnessed during the interview as a predictor of behaviour expected to occur in the job to which in most instances it bears little resemblance (McHenry, 1981).

In terms of 'consensus', the inclusion within the interview process of an explicit statement or negotiated agreement as to role, content and procedural components within the opening phase should serve to increase participant consensus. Under such circumstances unexpected behaviours could with greater confidence be attributed to the person rather than to the situation. The senior author can clearly recall that during a selection interview with an undergraduate student, having explained what was to follow, during a silence midway through questioning him, he interjected with 'Come on, ask me another. Come on, anything!' Needless to say such a question was not expected, particularly as care had been taken to set out the rules at the outset. Under these circumstances more confidence was felt in making a dispositional attribution rather than a situational one. As the content of the consequent attributions tended to include such descriptors as arrogant, cocky, naive and possibly a little bizarre this student was unsuccessful.

Self-serving bias

It is also pertinent to include one further 'bias' at this point. In the examples cited above, the interviewer attempting to deal with the aggressive interviewee or the patient attributing the nature of the problem to pressures at work come out relatively unharmed, with egos intact. A similar 'self-serving bias' was found in the work of Gamsu and Bradley (1987) where, working with medical staff groups, they observed a tendency for them 'to rate themselves as having more responsibility over positive outcomes and to rate medical factors as less important in explaining negative outcomes'. When the diabetes becomes controlled both the patient and the medical staff are keen to take the credit for the success; they are both equally unwilling to take any blame for failure. Employing Weiner *et al.*'s (1972) causal paradigm suggests that ascribing failure to luck rather than to inability serves to preserve self-esteem and therefore may be termed a form of ego defence.

The potential information overload inherent in developing an understanding of our social worlds leads us to look for means of reducing the processing tasks to a manageable amount. For example, the utilisation of causal schemata, the discounting principle and the holding of covariance assumptions have enabled observers of human actions to reach decisions regarding the causes of such actions based on a much reduced quantity of information. These short-cuts are, however, not the only methods by which the complex information-processing task is rendered more manageable. Other important mechanisms for selecting out substantial amounts of information which are pertinent to the interview process are termed *primacy effects* and *saliency* of information sampled. Kelley and Michela (1980, p.468) comment on these processes as being those that rely 'heavily on the earliest or most salient information and [the interviewer settles] for the first adequate explanation consistent with it'.

A fuller account of these perceptual and cognitive processes as they impinge upon the processes of interviewing can be found in the next chapter.

SOCIAL INFLUENCE PROCESSES

Corrigan *et al.* (1980) begin their extensive review of social influence processes by observing that the very essence of relating to other human beings involves a process of influence. Indeed the concept of social influence assumes a substantial degree of prominence within the helping process (Egan, 1982). As indicated earlier, interviews being social encounters involve persons mutually influencing each other – this theme recurs throughout the literature on interviewing. According to Gorden (1987, p.126) writing about information-gathering interviews, the 'use of pressure to obtain information becomes more successful as the power and prestige of the interviewer increase'.

However, there are certain types of interview situations where, for example, personal change is an important outcome, in which a knowledge of the processes of influence might be of considerable benefit to both parties (e.g. the counselling or helping interview, the medical interview or negotiation contexts). In the context of interviewing, helping and counselling a large number of research papers (some 50 according to Heppner and Heesacker, 1982), inclusions in text books (Cormier and Cormier, 1985; Egan, 1982) and at least one major text (Dorn, 1984) have been published which implicate the notion of social influence process. Many cite Strong (1968) as the source of this theme of research, particularly in the USA where he proposed a two-stage model of counselling as a social influence process.

This model borrowed significantly from the theoretical concept of dissonance hypothesised by Festinger (1957). Whenever a counsellor enables clients to become aware of discrepancies between present modes of feeling, thinking and/or behaving and more appropriate versions, 'mental pain', discomfort or dissonance may be generated. Clients may attempt to reduce the dissonance by reducing the discrepancy employing a variety of strategies available. These strategies are listed by Corrigan *et al.* (1980) as:

1. changing in the direction advocated;
2. discrediting the counsellor;
3. discrediting the issue;
4. changing the counsellor's opinion; or
5. seeking others' support for one's own opinion.

It would seem reasonable to propose that the counsellor role might equally well be the GP or consultant role (Bernstein and Dana, 1970) and that irrespective of the role incumbent intervention objectives would primarily be directed at the achievement of (1) with a complementary reduction in the likelihood of (2) or (3) occurring. Corrigan *et al.* (1980, p.396) continue the story by noting that:

Strong postulated that the extent to which counselors are perceived as expert, attractive, and trustworthy would reduce the likelihood of their being discredited. By increasing clients' involvement in counseling, the likelihood of discrediting the issue would be reduced.

So, the counsellor attempts to influence the client by presenting herself in a particular way such that the client will perceive her as possessing significant 'relationship enhancers' (Goldstein, 1962). As Claiborn (1979) observes, this construal of counselling as a social influence process places considerable importance on how the counsellor is perceived. Once again, it is the subjective perception and processing of specific types of information by an individual (in this case a client) that determines outcomes rather than any notion of absolute presence. (A similar idea was emphasised during the discussion of Kelley's notion of the covariation principle.) Corrigan *et al.* (1980, p.398) conclude that:

> given some information about a counselor, the inferences a client draws from that information, not the information itself, are what determine the counselor's influence potential for that client.

There is an implicit emphasis on the 'influencer' managing his impression cues to establish a secure power base from which to exert maximum influence. If, as Kaul and Schmidt (1971) assert, counsellors perceived as being expert, attractive and trustworthy exert more influence over their clients, then the cues which lead to such impression formation assume substantial significance as means of establishing both credibility and attractiveness (Claiborn, 1979). The enhancement of these helper characteristics in the eyes of the client contribute to the formation of a power base which constitutes the first stage of Strong's model.

The generic term 'power' subsumes a number of different types of counsellor power, identified by Cormier and Cormier (1985) as legitimate, expert and referent. In the initial stages of the counselling process clients appear to be particularly influenced by what Heppner and Heesacker (1982) call 'the socially sanctioned role...associate[d] with a professional counselor', or 'legitimate power' (Strong and Matross, 1973). Therefore, simply being called a counsellor can, initially, contribute to an early influence base, irrespective of the role incumbent. Bernstein and Dana (1970) refer to a somewhat similar process when they indicate that patients tend to attribute substantial amounts of power, responsibility and even 'magic' to the physician and to a lesser extent to nurses, which initially endows the practitioner with immense influence. Beggs *et al.* (1970, p.19) further illustrate this point when they observe:

> Because of the qualities endowed on him by society the doctor may be used by the patient as a 'standard' and subtly tested as such during the course of the interview with remarks such as, 'Of course my wife shouting all the time in front of the kids is bound to be bad for them, isn't it doctor?'

With respect to vocational guidance Gothard (1985) suggests that interviewers possess role authority, which he cautions should be used with responsibility.

As the interaction progresses more and more cues become available to the client and more opportunities present themselves for the counsellor (or health professional) to demonstrate expertise and attractiveness. The perception (by the client) of behavioural competence endows the counsellor with expert power while client perceptions of interpersonal attractiveness, friendliness and client–counsellor similarity result in the attribution of referent power (Cormier and Cormier, 1985). It is the utilisation of these power bases that enables a counsellor to exert an influence on clients such that attitudinal and behavioural change is more likely to occur. This constitutes stage two of Strong's social influence model.

So, if clients perceive counsellors to be expert, attractive and trustworthy these counsellors are more likely to develop an influential power base whereby client change is greatly enhanced. However, as Cormier and Cormier (1985, p.44) comment:

> The influence base...seems to have the most effect on clients during the initial contacts, since that is when clients formulate their first impressions of counselors.

Expertness

Perceived expertness has been defined by Strong and Dixon (1971, p.562) as:

> the client's belief that the counselor possesses information and means of interpreting information which allow the client to obtain valid conclusions about and to deal effectively with his problems.

Egan (1982) expresses a preference for such counsellor qualities to be termed competence arguing that there may not necessarily be a high correlation between perceived expertness and competence (Egan, 1982). Cormier and Cormier (1985, p.46) summarise the various sources from which client perceptions of counsellor competence are developed as:

> level of skill, relevant education, specialized training or experience, seniority, status, type of setting, history of success in solving problems of others, and the counselor's ascribed role as a helper.

Initially the role incumbent may convey legitimate power supplemented by various descriptive 'competence' cues such as the setting, attire and observable evidence of qualifications (for example, diplomas or certificates) obtained testifying to knowledge and skills previously acquired - role competence (Egan, 1982; Heppner and Pew, 1977).

While in the early phase these visible cues of expertness may increase the likelihood of 'hooking' the client, it is unlikely that such cues will be sufficient to maintain a longer-term interaction. In order for the latter to develop, signs of behavioural expertise are necessary, that is, saying and doing things regarded by the client as competent and helpful in moving towards client goals. The concept of accomplishment competence attempts to draw a distinction between effective behaviours and behaviours which may initially appear to be competent but fail to achieve their goal (Egan, 1982).

Therefore professional helpers who make use of sophisticated aids such as psychological tests may convey early signs of behaviour competence (partly by 'beguiling' the client). This attributed competence may, however, disperse rapidly if such activities fail to assist the client in the resolution of his problem. Accomplishment competence implies behavioural competence but is a uni-directional relationship. In one of the few studies of real-life counselling Heppner and Heesacker (1982) demonstrated the potential for perceptions of expertness to change significantly (up or down) over the course of counselling, a feature that also points to the importance of focusing analyses at the dyadic rather than group level. Heppner and Heesacker (1982) observe that those counsellors who were rated as having increased in expertness, from the clients' perspective, were those who had facilitated more positive counselling outcomes. Those who, conversely, were perceived to be failing in expertness were defined by behaviours indicative of a lack of any clear direction and of a confused communicator. Perceptions of role and reputational competence appear to develop quickly (Heppner and Heesacker, 1982) but are superseded by behavioural and accomplishment competences as counselling proceeds. It will be to the counsellor's advantage to ensure that the various descriptive and behavioural competence cues display a high degree of congruence if maximum counsellor influence and maximum client involvement are to be developed.

In a similar fashion the centrality of expertise to the achievement and maintenance of power and influence has also been documented within the medical/clinical context (DiMatteo and DiNicola, 1982a).

Attractiveness

According to Schmidt and Strong (1971, p.348), perceived attractiveness refers to the client's 'positive feelings about the counselor, liking and admiration for him, desire to gain his approval, and desire to become more similar to him'. So, clients who perceive counsellors as being liked by, similar to and compatible with themselves tend to attribute attractiveness to the counsellor. As a consequence of such attributions the counsellor becomes 'an important source of referent power' (Cormier and Cormier, 1985, p.52). Supportive empirical findings from Strong and Dixon (1971) offered some confirmation of these components when they reported that counsellors engaged in attractive roles were more often attributed the labels 'likeable', 'similar to me' and 'trustworthy' whereas those playing unattractive roles were more often checked 'dissimilar to me'. Further evidence collected by Heppner and Heesacker (1982) suggests that such power may be enhanced in situations where the attractiveness (as defined above) is a mutually shared characteristic of the interaction.

What is it that clients perceive that leads them to infer attractiveness in their helper? Potential sources include surface features, such as physical characteristics/appearance, being in a helping role, reputational competence and behaviours (verbal and nonverbal) which enhance perceptions of attractiveness (Egan,

1982). In an early analogue study Strong and Dixon (1971, p.565) concluded that 'attractive' counsellors were described by clients selecting the following descriptors:

> more friendly, considerate, cheerful, warm, agreeable, understanding, interested, alert, sociable, responsive, interesting, happy, tactful, expressive, clear, optimistic, energetic, curious, motivated, excited, talented, poised, skilful, clever, outgoing, and active.

Conversely, those counsellors engaging in the 'unattractive role' were described in the following terms:

> more bored, dull, uninterested, tired, cold, humourless, unhappy, depressed, sad, blunt and retiring.

Social psychological research (e.g. Asch, 1946) has pointed out the importance of trait labels such as 'warm' and 'cold' as central inferential constructs (see chapter four). Although there appear to be clear distinctions in the attribution of descriptors to 'attractive' and 'unattractive' helpers, it has been suggested that such differences may be due more to the inhibitory effects of low attractiveness rather than to any significant enhancing effect of high attractiveness (Egan, 1982; Corrigan et al., 1980). Indeed, as a result of their analogue studies Kerr and Dell (1976) concluded that the relative effects of attire, setting and interactional behaviour favoured the salience of interviewer behaviour to the virtual exclusion of attire or setting. Research from the medical context tends to support the importance of physicians' interpersonal affective behaviour. According to DiMatteo and DiNicola (1982a, p.90), 'patients place interpersonal factors higher in importance than technical factors in their statements of what they wish to have from their medical care'.

Over the longer term, however, behavioural cues appear to exert more powerful, longer lasting effects on the social influence of the interviewer. Hence, whereas initially impressions may be formed on the basis of available visible data, sampling helper behaviour over time contributes more powerful determinants of helpee perceptions of helper attractiveness.

Trustworthiness

Of the three relationship enhancers trustworthiness has received much less attention from researchers, partly due to the ethical problems of empirically manipulating such a variable. Cormier and Cormier (1985, p.55), quoting from Fong and Cox (1983), suggest that:

> Trust is the client's perception and belief that the counselor will not mislead or injure the client in any way.

DiMatteo and DiNicola (1982a, p.84) observe that trust 'is often defined as the belief that one can rely on the support and affection of other people'.

It has been suggested that trustworthiness could be intrinsic to the helper role (Strong, 1968) and to other societal roles (Egan, 1982), irrespective of who the role player might be. Therefore, the mere fact that the helper is called 'dentist', 'doctor', 'priest', 'Samaritan', etc., is initially sufficient for people in need of help to attribute 'trustworthiness' to the individual role player. In support of this notion, Corrigan *et al.* (1980, p.432) note that 'expertness and trust-worthiness...may be integral parts of the socially defined role of the counselor'.

Indeed whether individuals seek professional help or help from friends, trust-worthiness seems to be a critical characteristic of both (Corrigan, 1978). The idea that participants commence with the assumption of a trustworthy helper and that such 'faith' may be tried and tested over the course of helping has a positive ring to it (Egan, 1982). However, for some individuals this may not be the way things are. On the contrary, for some people, particularly those in various minority groups, trust must be earned, and proof must be provided (LaFromboise and Dixon, 1981). It would seem to be important to decline the temptation to proceed on the assumption of anticipated initial trust based simply on one's role title and to employ an expectation requiring trust to be demonstrated and maintained on an ongoing basis. The lack of or an unwillingness to trust implicitly their physicians has been cited as one main reason why some patients attempt to take care of themselves, making only low risk informational demands on the prac-titioner (DiMatteo and DiNicola, 1982a). LaFromboise and Dixon (1981) point out the need for continuing helper vigilance on the grounds that trust is not always easily established but it can be much more readily destroyed.

So, what cues make a significant contribution to the establishment of inferences of trustworthiness? Strong (1968) suggested role, reputation, behaviours and the absence of self-centred motivation as possible categories. Furthermore, in situations where both verbal and nonverbal behaviours are expressed, it is important that a degree of congruence is evident between both 'messages'. Synchronisation of both channels of communication conveys a clear and unambiguous message which reduces any client suspicions or fears (that is, reduces unnecessary threat) and suggests a degree of openness in the interaction. The helper who avoids evaluative or judgemental responses communicates a degree of acceptance and respect for the client which again reflects a kind of openness. Whatever the helper does it appears to be important to respond in some way. For instance, a key behaviour in the development and maintenance of trust has been labelled self-disclosure and contributes substantially to a model of trust building described by DiMatteo and DiNicola (1982a) as moving through three major stages whereby:

1. the patient engages in risk-taking behaviour, primarily by self-disclosing personally sensitive information;
2. the helper greets the patient's self-disclosures with acceptance and under-standing; and

3. the helper returns the patient's trust by trusting the patient with helper self-disclosures signifying an open relationship.

The passive helper tends to reveal little of herself, remaining a closed book, and presenting a closed, secretive model rather than the desired model of openness. This passivity may also lead the client to question the helper's motives, all of which serve to erode any initial trust conferred by the role title. Generally these behaviours may serve to 'harm or injure' the client in a psychological sense and therefore justifiably comprise untrustworthy behaviour. In addition, there are more overt indicators of trustworthiness, where the helper engages in accurate listening and paraphrasing, observes confidentiality, carries out promised tasks and divulges accurate, appropriate and up-to-date information (Cormier and Cormier, 1985). Writing from an appraisal context Breakwell (1990) suggests that assurances and demonstrations of confidentiality, via the building of trust, will result in a greater degree of honesty developing within the interaction between the two participants. The evidence seems to suggest that actions speak louder than words.

SUMMARY

An attempt has been made in this chapter to set interviewing within a social psychological context. In particular, two main social psychological theories pertaining to attribution and social influence have been described. Their importance primarily as explanatory theories which serve to increase the interviewer's understanding of the processes which contribute to interview outcomes (whether process or product) has been presented. Indeed Dorn (1984) has suggested that an effective use of an established social influence base is to encourage interviewees to reconsider and restructure their causal attributions pertaining to their personal predicaments. More recently Weiner (1988) has discussed the applications of attribution theory to the process of counselling and therapy where more interest is currently emerging.

Therefore, interviewing is certainly more than a mere set of techniques or a collection of mechanistic skills. While such skills are important, it is also hoped that interviewers may develop a greater understanding of both their own personal psychology and that of their clients or fellow interactors such that they develop a more insightful context in which their developing skills may be more sensitively and effectively deployed.

Chapter 4

Social perception

Within the process of an interview there is an array of information available to the participants, which is used by them to form perceptions of the interviewee, the interviewer and the situation in which they find themselves. This information includes such factors as the nonverbal and verbal behaviour of the people involved and such features as the decor and layout of the environment where the interview takes place. Thus, for example, on observing the interviewee during an appraisal interview, the interviewer might note anxious facial expressions, body posture and excessive fidgeting. These perceptual cues would then be used by the interviewer to form an impression of the interviewee as tense, possibly due to feeling threatened by the subject being discussed. Similarly interviewers have available information or cues concerning their own behaviour. They would be able to hear their own voices and the content of their messages and also, to some degree, be aware of their own body language. Such cues may be used to assess the effectiveness of the interviewer's performance in, for example, a counselling interview. In this context a counsellor might decide that she was overly dominating in such a context through becoming aware of her many interruptions of the client's attempts to discuss his problems.

The environment also provides information which is used to form perceptions of the participants and the situation. Thus, on conducting an interview in a subordinate's office, the interviewer might note the untidy desk, lunch remains and cluttered notice board and form an impression of the interviewee as badly organised and unreliable. Clients also form impressions of the interviewer and interview climate based upon such cues (see chapter eight for a full discussion of the client's perspective). Hence the client in a counselling interview will use a variety of cues to form an impression of the interviewer as trustworthy or competent (see chapter three). The nature of the environment will also affect the client's estimation of the confidentiality or appropriateness of this situation for discussing personal concerns. For example, in an open plan office the client will be unlikely to form an impression of the situation as sufficiently private to disclose highly sensitive information.

However, perceptions in interviewing are rarely formed by a passive process of translating external cues into impressions. A variety of complex factors influences the formation of perceptions of both ourselves and others, including characteristics of the perceived individual, characteristics of the perceiver and situational cues in which the judgements take place. For example, in the context of selection interviews, the sex of the individual is likely to have an effect upon the judgements made. Many studies have shown that male applicants receive higher evaluations than females. However, judgements of specific interviewers may be influenced by a range of factors including their own personal theories on the type of person suitable for the job, their feelings at the time of the interview and their judgements of the attractiveness of the individual being interviewed. Characteristics of the interview situation may also affect judgements. For instance, when all applicants for a post are female, the sex of the applicant may be irrelevant to the impression formed. A female applicant may also be judged more favourably when the preceding interviewee has performed badly in the interview. It can be seen, therefore, that social perception is a highly complex activity. However, prior to discussing the part played by social perception within interpersonal interaction, it is necessary to outline briefly some of the main features of human perceptual processes.

WHAT IS PERCEPTION?

In our daily lives we are constantly being bombarded by a potentially bewildering array of stimuli. These include a variety of sights, sounds, smells, tastes and tactile sensations. Yet we do not live in a constant state of confusion and manage (at least for most of the time) to make sense of our world. This is achieved through a process known as perception. A dictionary definition of perceiving is 'to come to recognise or comprehend something observed through the senses' (*New Collins Concise English Dictionary*, 1982). Levine and Schefner (1981, p.1) offer the following definition:

> Perception refers to the way in which we interpret the information gathered by the senses. In a word, we sense the presence of a stimulus, but we perceive what it is.

Perception is, therefore, the process by which we come to detect and interpret, or give meaning to, the external world. Although we perceive the environment through our senses of sight, hearing, touch, smell and taste in what seems like a rather effortless manner, the ease with which this process occurs belies the complexity of the phenomenon. For example, it is quite an achievement to be able to move around a cluttered environment freely with only the occasional mishap, sometimes caused by 'a few drinks too many' rather than poor perceptual processes! The perceptual judgement involved in, for example, driving a car in rush hour traffic illustrates both the complexity and the usual efficiency of our perceptual processes.

An important feature of perception is that it is selective. We do not attend to all the available signals in any situation and consequently we rarely experience information overload. The first stage of perception is the filtering or selection of cues. This selection is influenced by many factors including the task being undertaken, the context, the observer's knowledge and experience of relevant cues and individual characteristics (for example, personal preferences or current physiological state) of the observer. For example, the reader currently has available to her senses a wide range of sensations. However, only some of these cues are attended to, such as the writing on the page. If the room is particularly warm or if a meal-time is approaching, then other cues such as the temperature of the skin or the sensation of hunger will be focused upon to the exclusion of other more salient stimuli. This process of selectively attending to cues also occurs in the social environment. In this way, an interviewer will attend to the responses of the interviewee rather than say the ticking of a clock, unless, of course, the interviews have run hopelessly over schedule or the interviewee is interminably boring. Under such circumstances, a clock can assume great significance.

The second stage of perception involves the simplification or organisation of the information gathered by the senses. In other words, meaning is assigned to the information cues received by a process of categorisation. In this way, objects in the environment which have flat surfaces and legs to raise them from the ground are categorised as tables. This process is also influenced by a number of factors. For example, the context in which the observations are made can influence perception (see Figure 2.6). In selection interviews, the interviewer's perceptions of a candidate can likewise be influenced by contextual features such as the performance of the previous candidate. Similarly, characteristics of the observer can have an impact upon perceptions, so that a keen birdwatcher may be predisposed to see the duck in Figure 2.7 rather than the rabbit. In other words, perception is not simply a passive process of observing and interpreting external stimuli, since other factors enter into the perceptual equation. The factors affecting social perception in interviewing will be explored in this chapter.

Finally, as Figure 2.4 illustrated, perception is not always accurate. In a similar way, we may make errors in our perception of ourselves and others. This chapter will: illustrate the factors in social perception which may bias our judgements; summarise the resultant errors in information processing; explore the question of perceptual accuracy; and examine ways in which interviewers can improve their perceptual abilities.

SELF-PERCEPTION

In an interviewing situation, as highlighted in the interpersonal interaction model described in chapter two, interviewers not only observe and receive feedback from interviewees but also have access to self-feedback in the form of their own responses, thoughts and feelings. Self-perception is therefore a significant feature in the process of interviewing. For example, an awareness of our own behaviour through self-monitoring can both positively and negatively affect our ability to operate within the interview situation. Additionally, people gradually form self-perceptions which have a degree of consistency, described as their identity, personality or character (Swann and Read, 1981). Such self-concepts can affect behaviour in interviews. Finally, some characteristics of self-perceptions will be more salient in interviews than others, and this will also have an impact on the interview process. Each of these areas of self-perception will be explored and examples will be drawn to illustrate how such self-perceptions can influence the interview process.

An awareness of their own behaviour can have beneficial outcomes for interviewers in achieving the goals of the interview. In many training programmes one of the main aims is to develop the participants' ability to analyse and evaluate their own actions and responses in interviews. Interviewers are thus encouraged to pay careful attention to and identify the responses which they make and to assess the effects of such responses in terms of the achievement of interview goals. Such awareness can lead to an ability to be flexible and purposeful in the interview. For example, interviewers can adapt their responses to be more effective in encouraging unresponsive interviewees. Thus, it may be that keen interest, demonstrated through intense eye contact and close proximity, is perceived as rather intimidating by a nervous interviewee and the perceptive interviewer may decide to move further back from the interviewee while maintaining moderate levels of eye contact. Ivey (1983) refers to this process of self-awareness and considered action as 'intentionality in interviewing'. Such self-monitoring of performance can thus lead to more effective interviewing because the interviewer is able to modify and adapt his behaviour in the light of feedback received during the interview.

However, self-awareness in interviewing is not always beneficial. At times the process of self-perception or of attending to self-feedback can lead to less effective action. This may occur for many reasons. For example, the interviewer may be at an early stage in her experience of interviewing and therefore may be unfamiliar with analysing and evaluating her own actions in this context. This process would therefore present a difficult task, leaving insufficient capacity to process cognitively information emanating from the interviewee. In training interviewers, the authors have often noticed how trainees will lose sight of the purpose of the interview in their efforts to ask the 'right' type of question. As Egan (1986) notes, further factors which lead to such overconcern with self-feedback may be a general self-consciousness or nervousness on the part of the interviewer, and an overeagerness in the counselling context to help the troubled client. Each of these factors can result in a preoccupation with the interviewer's own performance and feelings and less attention being paid to information relating to the interviewee, with resulting negative effects on the interview.

A further characteristic of self-perception which may affect the interview process is that once self-impressions have been formed they can then influence both the ways in which new information is approached and the salience of certain information during the interview. In interview situations we may, for example, become defensive or reject messages received when the information contradicts powerfully held views of ourselves. This view of ourselves may also affect the ways in which we interpret events during an interview. During our lives we develop consistent pictures of our own personality, which may be described as self-schemata. Self-schemata are cognitive frameworks relating to our own traits or behaviour (Markus and Sentis, 1982; Rogers *et al.*, 1977). Baron and Byrne (1984) describe the development of these self-schemata as occurring through opportunities to observe our own behaviour in a variety of situations and also by receiving feedback from others. While these self-schemata may be clear and well developed with respect to some characteristics, they may remain ambiguous in terms of others. Nonetheless, Baron and Byrne (1984) note that once self-schemata take shape they strongly affect the manner in which we perceive and process new information. Thus, interviewers may reject feedback from inter-viewees which is inconsistent with their self-concept. In this way, an appraisal interviewer who views himself as scrupulously impartial may deny an inter-viewee's claim that he is being biased in his judgements. Similarly, a counsellor who believes herself to be open and undefensive may mistakenly attribute the lack of progress in exploring sensitive issues solely to the client's hesitancy, rather than to any joint reluctance on the part of both individuals.

Our self-perceptions also affect the saliency of certain information during the interview. In an exploration of how we see ourselves and others, Jones (1986) notes that there is also a tendency in self-perception to be more conscious of features which are unusual in our customary environment than those which are usual. This was demonstrated in studies by McGuire and others (McGuire *et al.*, 1978, 1979) who examined the features which students chose to mention in a description of themselves. They found that subjects selected features which made them different within their environment. Thus, black students in a predominantly white college would mention this feature in their description, whereas the white students did not mention this characteristic. Similarly, males from a large family of females would mention this point. It would therefore seem that characteristics which make the person distinctive are more salient than characteristics which the person has in common with others. Indeed, this construct of uniqueness has been proposed as one of the key principles of identity formation (Breakwell, 1986).

This tendency can affect the interview in a variety of ways. For example, it may lead to a consciousness during the interview of differences between the interviewer and interviewee. Thus, female interviewers may be more conscious of this personal characteristic in an environment where the majority of personnel and interviewees are male. Such awareness may lead to a defensiveness on the part of the interviewer manifested in a certain aggressiveness towards male interviewees. A further effect of the awareness of unusual characteristics may be that the interviewer would choose to highlight such factors in information given to the client. For example, the interviewer might begin a counselling session by explaining how his approach differs from that of other managers whom the interviewee may have encountered within the organisation. Such information may be valuable as a means of allaying fears of the client who has perhaps had rather negative past experiences with management. Similarly, the interviewer may decide to make explicit reference to distinguishing features which otherwise might preoccupy the interviewee and lead to a less productive interchange of ideas. Hence, a pregnant interviewer may make reference to her condition in the friendly opening stages of an interview, rather than steadfastly ignoring this fact. It has also been shown that disabled interviewees who make explicit reference to physical handicap in interviews are rated more favourably by interviewers than those who do not acknowledge this characteristic (Stone and Sawatski, 1980). The presumption in interpreting these findings is that both parties are then able to accommodate to the heightened awareness of this factor. On the other hand, interviewers should be aware that their self-perception of unusual characteristics while potentially occupying their own attention is not necessarily of importance or interest to the interviewee. In other words self-perception, while remaining an influential process in interviewing, tends to play a subordinate role to the process of 'person perception' to which our attention is now turned.

Person perception

The term 'person perception' refers to the process of organising incoming stimuli from others in the interaction in such a way as to make this array of information understandable. When we are interacting with another person we are constantly receiving an array of stimuli. We see their clothes, hairstyle, facial expressions; we witness their gestures, hear their words and tone of voice; we observe their silences and note their movements. All of these signals are changing rapidly in response to our own behaviour, the internal processes of the other person and changes in the environment beyond the immediate dyad. Yet within this complex situation we manage for the most part to interact effectively in the pursuit of our professional and social goals. We can make some sense of the ever-changing stimuli that impinge upon us. In this section we will examine how we form perceptions of other persons in social and professional situations and the factors which affect these perceptions.

Several factors would appear to influence the way in which we perceive others. Arvey and Campion (1984), in a discussion of person perception in the selection interview, note that our perceptions are coloured not only by characteristics of the person observed, as one would expect, but also by various interviewer and situational factors. Thus, the sex, ethnic origin and behaviour of an individual can influence our evaluations of this person. Such additional factors as our personal stereotypes, attitudes and feelings will also play a part in the impression formation process. Finally, we may judge individuals differently depending on such situational variables as the order in which interviewees are encountered, the structure of the interview or prior information received concerning the person being interviewed. Each of these areas will be discussed in the following sections on the role of interviewee characteristics, perceiver characteristics and situational factors in person perception.

Characteristics of the person perceived

Person perception is partly determined by the characteristics of the perceived individual. A wide variety of cues is available concerning the interviewee including nonverbal behaviour, verbal behaviour, sex and features of general appearance including attractiveness and colour of skin. Various studies have investigated the relationship between these factors and how the interviewee is perceived. The studies have emanated mainly from the context of selection interviewing although they have general relevance to how individuals are perceived in appraisal, research, medical and counselling contexts.

Arvey and Campion (1984) reviewed a number of studies which investigated the influence of interviewee nonverbal behaviour on interviewer's evaluations, and concluded that the nonverbal responses of interviewees do influence the interviewer's assessment of the job candidate. For example, Young and Beier (1977) found that interviewees who demonstrated greater amounts of eye contact, head movement, smiling and other nonverbal behaviours received higher ratings on a hiring evaluation measure. This finding is supported by many other studies which have indicated the importance of nonverbal behaviour in the assessment of interviewees (e.g. Imada and Hakel, 1977; McGovern and Tinsley, 1978; McGovern et al., 1979). In a more recent study, Anderson and Shackleton (1990, p.74) found that interviewers' outcome decisions were dependent upon impressions of candidate personality which in turn were dependent upon candidate facial cues. They conclude that:

> interviewees would be well advised to maintain high levels of eye contact with the interviewer and to display frequent positive facial expressions so as to maximise their chances of success.

Baron (1989) also reports a study in which interviewers rated a female applicant who exhibited either high or low levels of positive nonverbal cues (e.g.smiling, leaning towards the interviewer) during the interview. He found that interviewers were more favourable towards the applicant exhibiting high levels rather than those exhibiting low levels of positive cues, on job related (e.g. motivation, potential for success) and personal (e.g. attractiveness, friendliness) characteristics. He does, however, report evidence of a 'too much of a good thing' effect, where the use of multiple strategies of impression management leads to a negative evaluation of the applicant. In this study, Baron (1989) also investigated the impact of two impression management strategies on interviewers' evaluations, namely, the use of positive nonverbal cues and the use of artificial scent. He found that male interviewers rated the applicant as possessing greater potential for success and as more intelligent when she either wore artificial scent or exhibited positive nonverbal cues than when she demonstrated both of these tactics concurrently. He consequently recommends that moderation may be the best course in adopting impression management tactics in interviews.

It would seem therefore that nonverbal cues are influential in interviewers' evaluations of interviewees. Some studies do, however, highlight that this effect may not be as influential as verbal cues. Hollandsworth *et al.* (1979) performed a discriminant analysis to determine the relative importance of verbal and non-verbal dimensions of communication in interviews. The results of this analysis placed the following factors in order of importance: appropriateness of verbal content, fluency of speech, composure, body posture, eye contact, voice level and personal appearance. More recent studies have also highlighted the importance of language proficiency on person perception (Bradac and Wisegarver, 1984; Wible and Hui, 1985; Hui and Yam, 1987). Therefore, interviewers would clearly seem to be influenced by the interviewee's verbal and nonverbal behaviour in the formation of evaluations or impressions of the interviewee. In other interview contexts, for example counselling, the importance of observing both verbal and nonverbal behaviour of clients is also affirmed (Ivey, 1983). There is evidence that the sex of the interviewee may be important in person perception. In their review of person perception in selection interviews, Arvey and Campion (1984) point out that many studies have indicated that male applicants receive higher evaluations than females. Heilman and Saruwatari (1979) investigated the impact of male and female applicant attractiveness on interviewer judgements. The results of this study revealed that attractive females were given more favourable evaluations than unattractive females when applying for clerical jobs, but were at a disadvantage when applying for management posts. Attractive males, by contrast, were always given higher evaluations regardless of the level of the job.

Certain characteristics of the person observed would appear to be influential. While the studies cited in this section have been conducted mainly in the context of selection interviews, the variables mentioned affect judgements in all contexts. However, as noted earlier, perception is not simply a mechanical process of interpreting cues otherwise everyone would evaluate people in the same way. The eventual perception formed is more an outcome of the interaction between characteristics of the perceived, characteristics of the perceiver and the situation in which observations take place.

Characteristics of the perceiver

A number of characteristics of the perceiver have been found to be influential in the formation of perceptions of others. When it comes to making judgements about people, the observer tends not to be unbiased and objective. Instead, a number of personal characteristics will play a part in the judgement process. These characteristics include the implicit personality theories which are held by the perceiver, the perceiver's stereotypes of groups of people, and personal feelings and attitudes towards the other person.

Implicit personality theories

Everyone has a set of beliefs about what people are like. In other words everyone has a range of categories which they use to describe others and certain beliefs concerning which categories occur together and which do not. These beliefs constitute an unspoken or implicit theory of personality. Hence, if we were told that a person was very open in his dealings with others and asked to predict what other characteristics this person possessed, a range of other characteristics might be listed such as honest, sensitive and intelligent on the basis of the respondent's implicit personality theory. Jackson (1972), using the term 'trait inference', suggests that in situations of limited information perceivers must infer a wide range of attributes from the direct perception of a few. By employing an inferential network perceivers are enabled to infer with confidence one trait from the existence of another closely related within the inferential network (Jackson *et al.*, 1980). Jackson (1972) offers the example of a target person displaying impulsive behaviour and a judge who might be prepared to attribute aggressiveness to this target person based on his implicit personality theory which associates impulsivity closely with aggressiveness within individuals. Evidence of the existence of one trait leads to an inference of the existence of the second.

The issue of trait centrality is also of relevance in considering interviewers' perceptions of others. Asch's (1946) now classical study on impression formation would suggest that some traits exert a disproportionate influence on trait inferences. For example, Asch identified warm/cold as a central trait and it has been found that simply altering the amount of this trait caused shifts in the ascription to individuals of both highly correlated and more distant traits (Ribeaux and Poppleton, 1978). The perceived location of an individual on the warm/cold continuum may by inference lead to attributing other traits of a socially desirable quality (Hamilton and Zanna, 1972).

Thus, the interviewer has implicit theories about what characteristics 'go together' in other people, and once the interviewer has categorised the interviewee on one attribute, she is likely to infer certain additional characteristics. Indeed, Rothstein and Jackson (1984) suggest that employment interviewers infer the existence of a number of traits from the occurrence of only 'a single act or statement' made during the course of an interview. In the circumstances of the relatively brief interview where only a limited sample of behaviour is viewed, the utilisation of such inferential networks becomes extremely functional as a means of assessing applicant personality traits. Yet, these judgements are based solely upon the interviewer's beliefs about what characteristics are likely to be associated, rather than on any direct evidence as to the inferred traits. As Nisbett and Ross (1980) highlight, the problem is that the interviewer then treats these inferences as facts, and believes that what has been inferred is the way things actually are.

Personal stereotypes or prototypes

A further feature of person perception is the tendency to categorise individuals as belonging to a particular group. Observers also tend to assign certain characteristics to their group categories. These groups may be gender-based categories, racial or ethnic categories, occupational categories or any group distinguishable by their activities, values or appearance. One interesting study indicated that people are willing to make inferences concerning others on the basis of their group membership, even at the earliest stages of the development of the other person. Rubin *et al.* (1974) conducted a study where parents of newly born infants were asked to rate their young (24-hour-old) sons and daughters. Objective measures established that the males and females did not differ in weight, length, colour, reflex irritability or heart and respiration rates. Yet, despite these facts, the parents rated their sons as firmer, larger-featured, better coordinated, more alert and hardier, and daughters as softer, finer-featured, more awkward, more inattentive, weaker and more delicate. On this occasion, stereotypes seemed to play more of a role in perception than the actual characteristics of the person.

In the context of selection interviews, some controversy exists over whether interviewers have distinct prototypes for particular occupations or a single prototype of the model candidate regardless of the job in question (Cantor and Mischel, 1979). There is some supportive evidence for the former view that interviewers have separate images of typical members of an occupation (Jackson *et al.*, 1982). However, a more recent study has supported the view that there is one prototype for suitable 'graduate' candidates (Anderson and Shackleton, 1990). In the case of graduate job candidates, for example, this prototype was of an interesting, relaxed, strong, successful, active, mature, enthusiastic, sensitive, pleasant, honest and dominant person. Anderson and Shackleton argue that since interviewers are attempting to cope with an overload of verbal, nonverbal and documented information, they will try to simplify their task by judging the candidates against a universally appropriate personality prototype regardless of the particular occupation in question. This may explain the contrasting findings of Jackson *et al.* (1982) who asked the interviewers simply to 'imagine' the typical employee in different occupations. This task would clearly present less of a demand in terms of information processing and hence may explain the tendency to describe diverse characteristics for each occupation.

In the complex situation of the interview, where the interviewer is presented with constantly changing information, simplification may be the only option. To an extent this is a helpful response to the problem of information overload which might occur were the observer required to make judgements based on the unique and varied characteristics of each individual encountered. This may help with attempts to remember candidates for later evaluations since there is evidence to suggest that people are better able to recall information about others when they form an organised impression than when they attempt to remember isolated facts (Hamilton and Rose, 1980; Wyer and Gordon, 1982). It is likely that in other interview situations, interviewers will likewise utilise stereotyping strategies in their perception of interviewees. In medical interviews, for example, doctors may stereotype patients in terms of their illness, such as 'the mastectomy patient'. The use of these labels can lead to the depersonalisation of care and trainees in the medical profession are therefore now encouraged to avoid employing these stereotypes (Dickson *et al.*, 1989).

Such prototypes or stereotypes therefore interact with the actual characteristics of the interviewee so that allocation to a group is achieved on the basis of only one or two features such as skin colour or sex. However, this tendency can also operate in reverse leading to the ascription of characteristics to individuals on the basis of their belonging to a particular group, when the individual in question may not actually possess these qualities. Arvey and Campion (1984, p.211) note that stereotyping can be differentially disadvantageous to certain groups through the operation of a variety of mechanisms:

(1) The stereotypes of minority groups may be essentially negative in nature (e.g. blacks are uneducated);
(2) The stereotypes of a candidate may not 'match' the stereotypes of the job. For example, the perception of females as passive, emotional, etc. may not fit the stereotype of a given job and its requirements;
(3) The stereotypes may shape the kinds of expectations and standards interviewers have of job candidates during the interview. For example, an interviewer may evaluate a female candidate on a different set of criteria, e.g. beauty, poise.

Effects of mood on perception

Schwarz (1984) conducted a study which examined the effect of the observers' mood on self-perception. In the study, factors such as being in a pleasant, relaxing room, the weather being good or unexpectedly finding a coin were found to be sufficient conditions to affect the mood of observers and to influence their judgements of, *inter alia*, their own level of happiness, satisfaction with life and work. There is also evidence that mood affects judgements of other people. Forgas *et al.* (1984) carried out a study in which subjects were videorecorded while taking part in interviews and asked on the subsequent day to make a judgement of both their own and their partner's level of social skill. It was found that subjects in a positive mood judged both their own and their partner's behaviour positively. Those subjects who experienced negative emotions judged their own behaviour negatively, although they were less critical of their partner's behaviour. This finding supports the evidence of earlier studies that mood affects our judgements of others (Clark *et al.*, 1984; Schiffenbauer, 1974). As a possible explanation of these findings, Forgas (1985, p.33) suggests that different categories of judgement seem to be activated depending on the mood of the person making the judgement, pointing out that:

when you feel happy, more positive happy thoughts, constructs and personal characteristics are activated, and consequently you tend to use these constructs to interpret the inherently ambiguous social behaviours of others. As a result, you will perceive positive happy instances in the behaviours of others and yourself.

Thus in an interview situation, the mood of interviewers can be important in their judgements of others.

A further factor which would seem to be influential in forming perceptions of others is the interviewer's emotional response to the interviewee. For example, in the selection interview candidates who have similar characteristics (i.e. biographical background, attitudes or personality) to those of the interviewer are liked more and judged more favourably than those who are dissimilar. This phenomenon has been termed the 'similar-to-me effect' (Rand and Wexley, 1975). Anderson and Shackleton (1990) found evidence for the pervasive bias of this factor in assessing job candidates, in that interviewers' overall evaluation ratings of interviewees were highly correlated with ratings of similarity-to-self. They point out that this 'clone syndrome' results in decisions being made without specified and valid criteria being selected. The employers get 'more of the same' regardless of whether these characteristics are useful for the recruiting occupation. Likewise a high correlation was found between overall evaluations and ratings of personal liking in this and earlier studies (Keenan, 1977; Graves and Powell, 1988). As Anderson and Shackleton (1990, p.64) point out, such findings contradict the common stereotype of the interviewer as 'the dispassionate observer who remains emotionally detached while carefully evaluating each candidate'. Such influences no doubt occur in other forms of interview where evaluation is necessary.

An extreme case of a positive attitude towards a person which affects judgements has been termed the 'halo effect'. In cases where the halo effect is operating, the observer is likely to attribute a range of positive characteristics to an individual whom he judges to be positive on an initial characteristic. Thus, if a person is judged to be kind because of an individual act of kindness, it would also be likely that this positive judgement would generalise to a number of other characteristics even though no evidence was available to support these judgements. Hence the kind person would also be more likely to be seen as honest, intelligent and attractive in the eyes of the perceiver. Similar biases occur for negative judgements, where the cruel person may also tend to be viewed as bigoted, unintelligent, rude and aggressive.

Physical attractiveness has been found to produce the halo effect. Furthermore, Forgas et al. (1984) found that smiling could also produce this effect. In their study, subjects were asked to decide about the guilt of and most appropriate punishment for a student who allegedly cheated in an examination. The information given to subjects included a photograph of the student when they were smiling or unsmiling. It was found that subjects who received the smiling photograph considered the student to be less responsible for the offence and gave a lesser punishment than those who received the unsmiling photograph. Such effects are likely to occur in interview situations where the doctor, for example, might feel that the attractive smiling patient will be more likely to follow advice than the unattractive patient. Indeed, there is some evidence for this effect in selection interviews as noted earlier in the section on interviewee characteristics.

Situational factors affecting the person

In terms of situational variables, one factor which is pertinent to person perception is the order in which interviewees are encountered. A number of studies have examined the effect of the quality of the preceding interviewee on interviewers' ratings in subsequent selection interviews. This influence is known as the 'contrast effect', and refers to the effect of a previous stimulus, in this case the previous interviewee, on the judgement of the current one. In reviewing these studies, Schuh (1978) indicates that interviewees when preceded by a poor applicant will tend to receive a higher rating than if preceded by a moderate to good interviewee. He points out that this effect can be quite dramatic during early interviews but that following several interviews the effects gradually diminish. Schuh consequently recommends that interviewers become aware of this possible biasing factor in early interviews, and that where possible interviews should take place in groups of more than four rather than in 'couplets' where the effect is most dramatic.

An important factor in the context of order is the phenomenon known as the 'primacy/recency effect'. It is common in our perception of objects for items at the beginning (primacy) and end (recency) of presentations to be more readily noticed and remembered (Hargie et al., 1987). This effect can also occur in interviews where the temporal placement of information during the interview can affect interviewers' perceptions. Farr and York (1975) found that initial impressions based upon positive or negative information were influential in making judgements of applicants. They also found that negative information presented after positive information had a greater impact than positive presented after negative information. It would seem, therefore, that negative impressions are more influential than positive in making judgements. Rowe (1989), in an examination of the impact of unfavourable information on interview decisions, points out that this may be due to a 'positive test strategy' which is used by interviewers in selection interviews. In such a strategy, the interviewer would test whether the applicant was a good candidate for the job. In assuming the positive, favourable information would not represent proof of the competency of the applicant but negative information would prove the assumption false, and hence lead to the rejection of the candidate. The interviewer, therefore, may actively seek negative information. This may have a beneficial effect in counterbalancing the effects of the perceiver's biases which lead to focusing on confirmatory data.

Prior knowledge or information concerning a person can also affect person perception. What we hear or learn about a person can affect our judgements of that individual whenever we eventually encounter them. This information may be informally given to interviewers through expression of the opinions and attitudes of colleagues or may be presented in a formal manner such as work reports, medical case notes or, in the case of selection interviews, through application forms and test results. In many settings, interviewers will attempt to be rather more systematic in their efforts to acquire information about the interviewee prior to conducting an interview. Breakwell (1990), in discussing appraisal interviews, highlights the value of appraisal pro formas completed by the interviewee in advance of the interview. This document provides prior information for the interviewer concerning what the employee has been doing over the specified period and a personal evaluation of performance. Selection and, to some extent, career counselling procedures have made considerable use of pre-interview information in forming impressions of interviewees and indeed in selecting candidates to proceed to the interview stage. This information might include application forms, psychometric test results, school reports and independent references.

Extensive research has been conducted regarding the effects of prior information on judgements of interviewees in selection interviews. Dipboye (1989), in a review of studies in this field, concludes that pre-interview impressions are highly related to post-interview assessment. For example, Phillips and Dipboye (1989) asked 34 interviewers to assess the qualifications of candidates for stock-broker positions before interviewing on the basis of their applications and a test score. They were then asked to make a second assessment following an interview. A strong relationship was found between pre-interview and post-interview assessment. Of those interviewers who would recommend or strongly recommend hiring the applicant before the interview, 80 per cent said that they would select one of these options following the interview. Of those who would not recommend hiring the applicant on the basis of pre-interview information, 54 per cent indicated that they would make a similar decision following interview. It would seem therefore that post-interview assessment is strongly correlated with the interviewer's evaluation of pre-interview information. Phillips and Dipboye also found that the more positively interviewers assessed interviewees on pre-interview information, the higher they evaluated the applicant's performance in terms of answering questions in the interview. There is some evidence that this effect can operate in both directions, so that interview performance is also highly related to post-interview assessment of paper credentials (Powell, 1986). Interviewees, of course, can also obtain prior information on interviewers, and there is evidence to suggest that such pre-information affects their judgements of interviewers.

The studies discussed so far have shown that situational variables can produce biasing effects in person perception. However, situational variables may also reduce the biasing effects of other variables. For example, Heilman (1980) conducted a study where interviewers were asked to assess a female candidate's application form as well as interviewing seven other candidates. The proportion of females interviewed was either 12.5, 25, 37.5, 50 or 100 per cent. It was reported that when women represented 25 per cent or fewer of those interviewed, the female applicant was rated less favourably than when there were more women interviewed. These findings were interpreted as indicating that situational factors can reduce the adverse influence of sex stereotypes in selection interviews.

IMPLICATION FOR INFORMATION PROCESSING

As social perceivers we engage in a process of labelling ourselves and others through classification or categorisation. This action of categorisation is influenced by a number of factors relating to the person perceived, the perceiver and the situation in which they find themselves. Because we are influenced by factors other than simply the person perceived, there is considerable scope for misperception of others in interviews. Indeed, it has been argued that our perceptions of others say more about the perceiver than they do about the perceived. Gage and Cronbach (1955), in a now classical critique of research into accuracy in person perception, suggest that social perception is a process dominated far more by what the judge brings to it than by what he assimilates during it. The main effects of these biasing influences on our ability to process information need to be recognised. Such biases include a tendency when making judgements of others to 'misrepresent the past' by perceiving more consistency than is warranted, ignoring inconsistent information, and even recalling 'imaginary' information which was not actually presented. Further effects on perception relate to 'shaping the future' by actively searching for information which confirms our impressions, closing our minds to new information and inducing others to behave in ways consistent with our expectations.

The processing and recall of information concerning others are influenced by biases in social perception, such that we tend to note and remember information which is consistent and ignore or not remember information which is inconsistent with our impressions. In other words, we attend to information which confirms our biases and filter out information which would require us to confront them. Therefore, when we stereotype someone as a 'yuppie' we are more likely to notice characteristics which are consistent with this stereotype, such as an interest in health food, and fail to notice or recall inconsistent information such as modesty. Retrieval of information would appear to be influenced by the way in which the material is stored in memory. Once information has been stored by organisation around a particular trait or theme, then information consistent with that organisational focus tends to be better recalled than inconsistent information (Cantor and Mischel, 1979; Lingle et al., 1979). Indeed, it has been shown that we may even recall information which was never presented, if this is consistent with our impressions. Snyder and Uranowitz (1978) conducted a study in which subjects were asked to read a detailed description of a woman, Betty K., which included details of her education, friendships, childhood and so on. After reading this information they were told that Betty K. was either heterosexual or lesbian. Their findings indicated that subjects 'recalled' information which was consistent with their stereotypes of heterosexuals and homosexuals, even though this information was not in the descriptions. In other words, subjects imagined that there had been information consistent with their perceptions in the absence of any evidence. In this way, social perception shapes the manner in which we recall the past and reconstruct reality.

Future information processing is also to some extent 'shaped' by our perceptions (Jones, 1986). This occurs because there is a tendency for social perceivers not only to notice information consistent with their impressions but to search actively for such information; to ignore new information; and to induce others to behave in line with their expectations thus creating a self-fulfilling prophecy. For example, in a medical interview the doctor may form a perception of a patient as a 'malingerer' on the basis of a number of biasing factors such as comparison with the previous seriously ill patient, unfavourable prior information or a personal disliking for this individual. Once this perception is formed, future information is likely to be shaped by the interviewer's active search for confirmatory information. Thus, the questions the doctor chooses to ask will seek to confirm this 'diagnosis' and other questions which may have changed her views of the patient will remain unasked.

As Jones (1986) notes, new information concerning others is often ignored following the formation of initial impressions. Once a label has been placed upon someone, on the basis of often superficial and biased information, the perceiver acts as if this is all there is to know about the person. These premature judgements can then result in the perceiver ignoring further pertinent information. In other words, our perceptions can cause us to be blind or to close our minds to new information. Hence, in the medical example, even if the patient volunteers significant information, this may be ignored by the doctor and not followed up because of initial impressions and premature diagnosis. At times we can also behave in ways that induce others to confirm our expectations of them. For instance, if we expect certain individuals to be cold and unfriendly, we may not be warm and welcoming towards them and as a result they may indeed behave in a cool, hostile manner towards us. In this way, a self-fulfilling prophesy is created. There is a range of studies which provide evidence for this phenomenon where we define the situation through our perceptions of others and hence leave the other person little option but to conform to our expectations (Jones, 1986).

The ability to organise, categorise and interpret stimuli concerning ourselves and others is clearly most important for our social functioning. Whether in social conversation or the interviewing context, we need to be able to cope with the ever-changing information picked up through our senses. The factors affecting information processing as outlined in this chapter are largely the consequences of our need to simplify the information which we receive. For professionals who encounter a wide range of clients the short-cuts of labelling and categorisation are necessary in dealing with the overload which would occur if each individual had to be assessed as a unique entity. However, perceptual processes can also lead to considerable distortion of information, thus placing in doubt the accuracy of our perceptions.

HOW ACCURATE ARE SOCIAL PERCEPTIONS?

Cook (1984, p.161) points out:

> whether people can or cannot, or should or should not, pass judgements on each others' personalities, the fact is that they do, and many such verdicts have far reaching effects.

Therefore, it is important to attempt to estimate the extent to which such evaluations are accurate. A wealth of evidence suggests that accuracy of perception is rather poor (Arvey and Campion, 1984). Early reviews of studies which specifically attempted to measure accuracy by assessing the correlation between different interviewers' evaluations of the same interviewees found that reliability among judges was typically low. Carlson *et al.* (1971) also found that experienced interviewers were no more reliable than inexperienced interviewers and in so doing presented a rather dismal picture of our ability to form accurate perceptions of others. However, there have been critiques of these studies which have questioned their conclusions, and which present a less pessimistic picture.

McArthur and Baron (1983), in a methodological critique of accuracy studies, argued that the experimental context in which accuracy of perception was investigated was not representative of typical human judgement situations. This experimental context was typically asking subjects to make judgements based only on verbal descriptions of people. It would not be legitimate, they suggested, to draw more general conclusions about our ability to perceive others accurately on the basis of such restricted methods. Arvey and Campion (1984) also criticise the accuracy studies for their tendency to use 'paper people' rather than actual interviewees. As Kenny and Albright (1987, p.393) point out:

> person perceivers in everyday life do not view their targets through one-way mirrors. They touch, yell at and interact with each other.

Accuracy studies therefore need to consider the interaction between individuals and the consequent effect on person perception.

Kruglanski and Ajzen (1983) further argue that in many accuracy studies the process of human inference has been confused with specific instances of inference. In other words the researchers have generalised from single instances of misperception to person perception in general and have often overestimated the extent of misperceptions, especially since:

most tests of bias take as the null hypothesis that people are totally accurate and show, not surprisingly, that indeed they are not perfectly accurate.

(Kenny and Albright, 1987, p.392)

Making an interesting comparison with high levels of achievement in other fields, Kenny and Albright also note that:

an excellent tennis player double faults, makes unforced errors, and allows his or her opponent to make passing shots. (p.392)

But such occurrences do not make this person less than excellent in their sport. They simply do not play tennis perfectly. Likewise, they argue, observers make errors, but mistakes mean only that person perceivers are not perfect. They may still be highly accurate. It would seem, therefore, that the studies on accuracy of person perception may have overestimated the problem. On this basis perhaps we need not be quite so sceptical about the ability of interviewers to perceive interviewees accurately. There is nevertheless ample scope for improvement in the judgemental process and it is useful to examine ways in which accuracy in perception might be improved.

TOWARDS MORE ACCURATE PERCEPTIONS

In interviewing, the perceptions of the interviewer are often used to determine important decisions. For example, the doctor's diagnosis of illness and consequently the course of treatment adopted depend upon judgements made during the interview. Likewise the perceptions of the interviewer determine whether or not an interviewee will get a job or promotion. Therefore, interviewers need to be as accurate as possible when making judgements about interviewees.

A possible first stage in improving the accuracy of our perceptions is the realisation of the potential inaccuracy in our perceptions. Forgas (1985) argues that recognition of this reality is the first and necessary step towards improving our own person perception skills. He points out that accurate assessment of people is much more difficult and fraught with problems than is commonly believed. Awareness of these difficulties and recognition that observers are often mistaken and biased can lead to greater care and more accuracy in person perception. Interviewers should therefore recognise that their perceptions may be wrong and hence that they should be cautious in their judgements.

Second, interviewers should be aware of the various factors which affect their judgements so that they can expect possible biases under these conditions. In a selection interview, an understanding of the potentially biasing effects of a similarity between interviewer and interviewee, of the performance of the previous job candidate, of a personal liking for or attraction towards the candidate, may enable interviewers to adopt a more objective stance in their assessment of each individual interviewed. Kruglanski and Ajzen (1983) suggest that interviewers should become aware of their personal tendencies in assessment of others. For instance, the interviewer may tend to see women as overly emotional or less capable. Certainly a knowledge of personal stereotypes would alert the interviewer to possible sources of bias in their judgements.

In addition to an awareness of the many factors which bias our judgements, a knowledge of the mechanisms by which these biases are formed will also be helpful. Thus, an interviewer who is aware that he may be looking for too much consistency will be more cognizant of the danger of ignoring information which does not match existing perceptions of a particular individual. Interviewers need to develop an openness to information presented. They need to question their judgements, particularly initial impressions.

Finally, there is evidence that the actual procedures adopted in interviews may affect the accuracy of judgements made, so that a change in operation of interviews may improve accuracy. Latham (1989) notes that the use of a 'situational interview' procedure has been shown to reduce the halo effect in person perception. This involves conducting a systematic analysis of situations which would be encountered by the successful job applicant and constructing questions which would examine what the candidate would do in the given situations. Similarly, improved skill and tactics in interviewing (Schuler and Funke, 1989) may allow interviewers to explore interviewee responses more effectively and hence get a clearer picture of the person encountered (see chapter seven).

SUMMARY

The process of perception involves interpreting or giving meaning to the information which we receive through our senses. In the context of interviews, this information includes visual cues such as the facial expressions, gestures and appearance of the interview participants, and auditory cues such as the speaker's rate of speech, intonation and accent. However, our perceptions involve more than simply receiving information available at the time of interview. Other factors relating to characteristics of the perceiver and past experience come into play in forming impressions of ourselves as interviewers and our perceptions of interviewees.

This chapter has examined the process of self-perception and the ways in which this affects our responses in interviews, our perceptions of others and the problem of biases in our judgements. Finally, ways in which perceptual accuracy can be improved were suggested.

An important part of the process of interviewing involves forming perceptions of the other parties involved. Perceptions of interviewees are influenced by many factors including characteristics of the perceived individual, characteristics of the perceiver and of the interview situation. Each of these factors helps to shape the ways in which we interpret the behaviour and character of the person observed (Bayne, 1977).

Chapter 5

Goals, goal setting and feedback

It was pointed out in chapter two that one of the key elements of all socially skilled behaviour was its goal-directedness. Much human behaviour has been construed as goal-directed and purposeful (von Cranach *et al.*, 1982) whether viewed at the macro- (e.g. life goals) or micro-level (e.g. putting someone at ease). Indeed, an understanding of human actions can be elusive or confusing in the absence of a clear knowledge of the actors' goals. Furthermore, confusing behaviour can often be related to a lack of a clear purpose or to vague goals. The authors have witnessed some extremely meandering tortuous interviews where the purpose seemed to elude both participants and observers.

Operational definitions of socially skilled behaviour (Hargie *et al.*, 1987) and specific definitions of the 'interview' outlined in chapter one have implicated the purposive nature of competent action. Human behaviour has been construed as 'naturally' goal-directed (Locke and Latham, 1984) or, in Maslow's terms, need-reducing (as outlined in chapter two). Human beings tend to like to know where they are going and experience varying degrees of anxiety when they do not have a clear direction.

WHAT ARE GOALS?

The dictionary definition of a goal is 'an end that one strives to attain; aim' (*Collins Concise English Dictionary*, 1978). In a similar vein Locke and Latham (1984, p.5) suggest that a goal is 'the object or aim of an action'. It is something yet to be achieved. Von Cranach *et al.* (1982, p.17) define goals in a similar fashion when they state that:

> By goal we mean the condition at the end of the action, imagined before or during the action... the goal is the objective of the action.

Locke and Latham (1984) draw no distinctions between goals and objectives on the grounds that both concepts can be characterised in terms of both a directional and a quantitative/qualitative component. However, a goal may serve to motivate an individual only if it holds, for that particular individual, some value.

Hierarchical nature of goals

Von Cranach *et al.* (1982, p.7) propose that a major characteristic of goals is their hierarchical structure and furthermore:

> The goal hierarchy is theoretically unlimited, but higher and highest goals in it may be of a more general nature, and, in life, are almost impossible to distinguish from 'values'.

Goals can, therefore, be conceptualised at a variety of levels ranging from higher order needs down to micro-behavioural actions. At the highest level goals can comprise the ultimate, developmental aims reflected in Maslow's (1954) self-actualisation need or in Rogers' (1951) fully functioning person. At a hierarchically lower level, Havighurst (1972), for example, conceptualised human development as progressing through a series of life stages, each of which presents the individual with a number of key developmental tasks. Mastery of these behavioural tasks represents goal achievement at each successive stage. Strong expectations are held regarding what individuals (in our culture) should have achieved at specified life stages. For example, adolescents are expected to have developed more mature relations with peers of both sexes, achieved emotional independence from parents, whereas adults in the early years of adulthood should have selected a spouse, started a family and begun their occupational career. In order to have attained these developmental milestones individuals need to have acquired the requisite life skills as 'means' to the above 'ends' (Hopson and Scally, 1981).

The reaching of such long-term goals can be a daunting, distant and possibly meaningless prospect and may, in fact, lead a person to seek professional assistance. However, the concept of substituting distant long-term goals with a number of more immediate shorter-term goals tends to render the ultimate goal more attainable in the same way that a general aim may be accomplished by working through a number of more specific objectives, each taking the individual a step nearer the achievement of the ultimate aim. For example, the individual whose longer-term life goal is to become a happily married family person and who experiences anxiety because he has not found a partner, at a time when it seems as if *everyone else* has, may demand (of himself) that he finds one. In order to achieve this ultimate goal the individual may establish a number of mediational or intermediate goals which, if reached, will increase the likelihood of attaining the ultimate goal. Such intermediate goals (or subgoals) may include a number of social and life skills (Hopson and Scally, 1981) such as getting out of the house and going to locations where members of the opposite sex are present, trying to talk to members of the opposite sex, developing a degree of self-confidence and assertiveness, learning conversational skills and content, taking a more active interest in one's appearance and coping with disappointment or rejection (or acceptance). Individuals who perceive themselves as 'failures' on the 'achieving married status' criterion may seek professional help to assist them to clarify goals and to establish explicitly a number of sub-goals which can be identified as steps taking them closer to their ultimate goals (Nelson-Jones, 1982). Therefore, the achievement of mediating goals may require a range of helping interventions, such as teaching/training, advice-giving, information-giving or counselling, most of which may be delivered via the dyadic interview situation.

Types of goals

Goals have also been viewed as relating to different spheres of the individual. The major dimensions along which 'people' develop can typically be represented by categories labelled educational, personal, social, medical, leisure/recreational and vocational (National Development Group, 1977). In stating these categories we would not wish to convey the impression of discreteness but rather would wish to emphasise the integrative nature of these areas. Career development theories have clearly emphasised this holistic perspective where career goals have been conceptualised in terms of the number and variety of life roles (one of which could be the role of worker) taken on by an individual throughout her life (Super, 1980). Another application of this integrated concept can be found in the field of care, particularly care of the handicapped and elderly where, according to Balthazar (1973), programmes can be devised to assist individuals to develop as 'fully as possible as people'.

Similarly, in the medical context the doctor has been urged to consider patients as human beings rather than as medical cases requiring only the doctor's technical medical expertise. DiMatteo and DiNicola (1982b) suggest that medical practitioners need to develop an understanding of their patients as integrated and dynamic individuals with a range of feelings and unique cognitions. A meaningful understanding of illness makes sense to the practitioner (and patient) only when viewed within the cultural and family context of the patient. This type of understanding is, therefore, a major objective for medical interviewers. This holistic philosophy towards helping people in need reflects a belief that goals identified in one area of life tend to be influenced by, and themselves influence, goal achievement in other concurrent and sequential life stages. However, it creates major difficulties for practitioners who may regard themselves as possessing specific expertise in assisting individuals who express problems (and goals) within finite life areas, such as medical, educational, marital, vocational, etc. The impermeable boundaries established by various professions may require a shift towards more permeability. This, of course, raises a number of important professional issues which will be discussed more fully in chapter nine.

Level of awareness of goals

At this point a brief note should be included regarding the extent to which goals act in one's consciousness. During everyday life it seems evident that many goals which motivate the tasks of living are not always clearly in our thoughts, particularly those that relate to the more habitual action patterns. Indeed, in social encounters it may not be very functional for the participants to be continually juggling with a stream of conscious goals as it would be unlikely that any coherent behaviour would result. Although it is by no means inevitable that goals will be consciously set by an individual a lack of purpose may bring a person to a counsellor, motivate a call to the Samaritans or lead a supervisor to question work motivation. Indeed, Trower *et al.* (1978) have offered explanations of chronic schizophrenics' irrational and meaningless behaviour in terms of an absence of social goals. Therefore, individuals may fail to select appropriate goals, may choose not to establish any goals or may choose from any number of possible alternatives. Implicit in this view is the notion that goals tend to have an internal quality; that is, they belong to or are owned by the individual who chooses to adopt them. However, it can be the case that goals are stated for individuals by society, as developmental tasks or expectations, or be required of employees by their employers and are, therefore, external. External goals can become internalised, an outcome clearly of benefit to goal accomplishment. Interviewers, like any other social actors, tend to behave, for a large part of the interview, habitually, without much conscious goal setting. In training interviewers, we are constantly reminded that goals, at least initially, seldom play a prominent part in the trainees' thoughts. It is only at specific times that trainees become acutely aware of their lack of clear goals, or lack of effectiveness of their habitual actions as a means of goal achievement. In simple terms, this is when the interview is perceived as not going well and something needs to be done or a decision needs to be made (von Cranach *et al.*, 1982).

Before moving on to outline the process of goal setting it seems pertinent at this point to remind the reader that the concept of goals particularly in terms of owning and setting goals applies equally to both parties engaged in the interviewing process (Wicks, 1982). Indeed, Maier (1958) cites discrepancy between the appraiser's and the appraisee's goals as an important influence on the outcome of the appraisal.

This chapter will continue by making reference to goals and goal setting as they relate to both interviews/interviewers and to interviewees. However, the reader is also referred to chapter eight for a fuller discussion of the interviewee's perspective.

GOAL SETTING

It may be deduced from the previous section that goals can be set for virtually any aspect of life, and if set they tend to motivate and move the individual forward. As suggested earlier, individuals may not always be entirely aware of precisely what their goals are (Trower *et al.*, 1978) or, even if aware, goals may be vague, conflicting or simply unrealistic (Locke and Latham, 1984). The idea of naturally establishing explicit goals is generally alien to most individuals in pursuing their daily chores. However, individuals who possess goal-setting skills may be in a position to make wiser choices (Egan, 1982). Once goals have been tentatively set, individuals find the need to engage in planning. According to von Cranach *et al.* (1982, p.8), 'a plan is the totality of the deliberations and notions as to how this goal can be achieved'. In this sense, plans set out the range of routes, the chosen route and subsequently enable the effectiveness of the plan, as a means of moving nearer to the selected goal, to be evaluated. Furthermore, Egan (1982) regards the process of goal setting as pivotal within the overall helping process, while Locke and Latham (1984) note its centrality (both implicit and explicit) within most major theories of occupational motivation. This is an important element, since goal-directed actions tend to require an effort of will, particularly in situations where obstacles present themselves and must be overcome if goal attainment is to be the outcome (von Cranach *et al.*, 1982).

GOALS AND INTERVIEWING

Wicks (1982, p.311) asserts that one of the major problems encountered with interviewing is the 'absence of a shared common aim'. Schweinitz and Schweinitz (1962, p.10) state that interviews conducted within the social services should 'have known and established purposes'. Giving advice to would-be selection interviewers Breakwell (1990, p.10) says with respect to informal interviews, 'Know the objectives'. A similar view is expressed by Beggs *et al.* (1970, p.10) who assert that speech therapists 'must have a clear idea of the purpose of the interview'. It seems safe to say that interviewers must know what they are trying to achieve. Furthermore, Heron (1976) has included awareness of purpose as a dynamic component of interventions as one of his main criteria of professional helpers.

Interviewing involves an exchange of information between its participants (Wicks, 1982) whereby, irrespective of the content, interviewers generally aim to gather information, the precise nature of which tends to vary depending on the situation (Richardson *et al.*, 1965). In the interview context information-gathering is simply a means to a variety of ends rather than the end itself. Gorden (1987) emphasises the importance of the information-gathering function when he notes that the success of the interview is strongly dependent on the interviewer's repertoire of interpersonal skills and data collection tactics. Stewart and Cash (1988, p.103), also writing about research interviewing, state its purpose as establishing 'a solid base of fact from which to draw conclusions, make interpretations, and determine future courses of action'. This information-gathering function can be construed as the main task to be accomplished by the research interviewer. However, as a means towards task completion, interviewers should also keep in mind the importance of developing and maintaining optimal interpersonal relations with the interviewees. Successful interviewing depends on both tasks being accomplished (Gorden, 1987). The generalisability of these dual objectives for interviewing seems highly appropriate.

The specific purpose of the research interview is to collect research-relevant information (Brenner, 1981) which will throw some light on the research hypotheses. Obviously, in order to increase the confidence with which the research objectives can be met, information collected by interview must be as relevant, reliable and valid as possible (Gorden, 1987). It is the duty of the research interviewer to strive to maximise these outcomes and, in fact, Gorden's (1987) three criteria seem equally applicable to all interview contexts and might always permeate or guide interviewer objectives. Indeed they should inform the information gatherer as to whether interviewing would be the most appropriate method to adopt for collecting information. This makes sense, given the information dependence of decisions reached within the interview situation.

Arguing from a more counselling perspective, Hopson (1982) has suggested that the ultimate goal of all approaches is to enhance the individual's personal effectiveness or to 'empower' the person. Particular theoretical models tend to focus initially on changing different psychological components of the individual; for example, actions, feelings or thoughts. Ultimately, however, it is hoped that the person will behave differently and more effectively, the impetus for which may derive from more positive thinking, the development of a more positive self-concept or simply by re-learning more effective ways of behaving (Nelson-Jones, 1982). In more eclectic counselling models the counsellor's focus may, at different times throughout the process, focus on feelings about the self, thinking about the self and acting out action plans. Once again the counsellor works towards identifiable goals which, in Egan's (1982) model, may be summarised with respect to three main stages. Each stage has its own main counsellor objectives which according to Egan (1982) are:

Stage One   'to help the client explore, define, and clarify the problem situation' (p.84).

Stage Two   'the counsellor helps the client develop new and perhaps more objective perspectives or points of view on the problem situation, the kinds of perspectives that enable the client to set reasonable goals' (p.39).

Stage Three   'Determining how to implement goals and then actually going out and initiating goal-achieving programs' (p.44).

Cormier and Cormier (1985) summarise six important functions of goals in counselling which focus on the establishment of a direction for counselling, towards specific goals by means of selected counselling interventions which the counsellor feels are both appropriate in meeting this client's needs and within his individual competences. In the absence of goals, Cormier and Cormier (1985) caution that counselling may have no direction, save that determined by the personal preferences of the interviewer.

Counsellor behaviours are intended to work towards meeting whichever objective seems appropriate in the hope that meeting his objective will enhance the probability of clients reaching theirs. Counsellor objectives are simply means to client ends. In this sense, the interviewer's goals may serve as mediational with respect to the achievement of client goals. This seems to be especially appropriate with helping interviews such as vocational guidance, counselling or within the medical context. In more competitive situations it may also be of paramount importance for information to flow, as a failure here makes it unlikely that a candidate would be successful in her selection interview as attribution for the failure is unlikely to be made by the interviewer to himself (see chapter three). Information transmitted in the medical interview enables the doctor to reach a differential diagnosis (Jones, 1982), while in the vocational guidance context this information comprises the basis on which a vocational assessment may be undertaken (Kline, 1975) and appropriate action agreed upon.

Writing from the perspective of selection interviewing, McHenry (1981) suggests that the main task of the interviewer is to enable the candidate to self-disclose relevant information upon which the interviewer can make predictions concerning the candidate's future work performance. As Eder *et al.* (1989, p.18) advocate:

the employment interview provides the organization with the opportunity to infer whether the applicant possesses the critical knowledge, abilities, and interests to be successful in the targeted position.

The information collection function is confirmed by Goodale (1989) who further adds the provision of information to prospective candidates and the checking of personal chemistry; that is, will the candidate 'fit in'? However, emphasis is clearly focused on the information collection objective pertaining particularly to whether the candidate can do the job and is willing to do it (Goodale, 1989).

Finally, the overall purpose of interviewing within the appraisal context has been stated by Lawson (1989, p.3) as helping 'improve individual performance, realise potential and achieve better results for the organisation'. Appraisal attempts to encourage individuals by recognising and rewarding effective performance and planning future actions of projected benefit to both the individual and the organisation (Maier, 1958). So, the purpose of encouraging the free flow of information is to agree objectives, negotiate performance goals, monitor performance against agreed criteria and agree action (Breakwell, 1990). Furthermore, Makin *et al.* (1989) suggest that a major function of the information-gathering process in the appraisal context may be to check out the accuracy of causal attributions made pertaining to personal versus situational responsibilities. In other words, the greater the sampling of interviewee behaviours the less the risk of making attributional errors (see chapter three).

Any significant deficits in the data base will inevitably feed into poorer selection decisions, less effective staff development/motivation, premature research decisions or less than helpful counselling. Implicit in all interviewing situations is the idea that information is not simply collected but it is processed, sifted, selectively weighted and utilised (or rejected). The authors are reminded of the computing maxim: garbage in, garbage out.

However, for set goals to act as effective motivators of human performance, whether in one's personal, educational or occupational world, or as effective determinants of interview outcomes, they should be formulated with specific features in mind. A substantial consensus exists as to what features constitute an effective goal (Egan, 1982; Locke and Latham, 1984; Nelson-Jones, 1982; Trower *et al.*, 1978). In summary, effective goals tend to be (1) clear, specific and stated in behavioural units; (2) measurable or verifiable; (3) realistic or achievable; (4) internal rather than external; (5) in keeping with the client's values; and (6) appropriately time-scaled. Adherence to these criteria serves to increase the likelihood of effective goals being set for interviews by both interviewers and interviewees.

Clear, specific and stated in behavioural units

Goals couched in clear and specific language convey precisely what is to be achieved, what is to be aimed at or for. It is not uncommon, during the initial phases of helping, to seek from clients what Egan (1982) calls a 'statement of intent' or what Trower *et al.* (1978) call an 'intention statement': a declaration that the client/patient wants to take some action to alleviate his problem. The process of goal setting seeks to specify more precisely what the goal is to be by moving from a vague statement of 'I want to do something about my low self-esteem', through an aim which might be stated as 'I must do something about my weight', and culminating in the agreement of a specific goal such as, 'I will lose 12lbs by the next interview in three weeks' time' (because this will make me feel much better about myself). This shaping process moves clients from the general to the specific and renders the goal workable. Generally, specifically defined goals are more likely to motivate and act as guides to action than are nebulously defined goals (Cormier and Cormier, 1985; Locke and Latham, 1984). Vague goals such as 'do your best' leave unspecified just what expectations are implied whereas specific goals stated in actual tasks or concrete behaviours result in the individual holding clear and unambiguous expectations concerning what constitutes successful goal achievement.

The principle outlined above might equally be expressed with respect to interviewers in the sense that, just as interviewees should be assisted to identify clear and concise goals, so interviewers should have formulated specific goals for their interviews. To approach a forthcoming interaction with vague notions of having a cosy chat would probably fail to meet the needs of either party. It is incumbent upon the interviewer to have clear formulations of potential interview objectives, a sort of menu from which particularly appropriate goals may be mutually selected. The degree to which interview objectives are negotiable in this way depends substantially on the particular context. While a personnel officer would tend to conduct the employment interview primarily to meet her employer's needs (i.e. to make an effective selection decision), she may adopt a somewhat more egalitarian approach for an appraisal or counselling interview.

Nevertheless, a sound conceptualisation of what might be achievable (and what might not) is an essential prerequisite for effective interviewing. The goals of interviews might be construed as ultimate, chosen by either or both parties, as a focus for their joint activities. The nature of the particular activities derives from the numerous subgoals adopted by the interviewer/interviewee in their attempt to move forward towards the selected ultimate goal (Cormier and Cormier, 1985). For example, in order to assist an individual who is experiencing difficulties in making a career choice (i.e. the ultimate goal) the interviewer may isolate more specific mediational goals which comprise more manageable steps in the desired direction. Any particular careers guidance interview may, therefore, have a variety of possible goals specifically identified to increase the likelihood of meeting a particular client's needs. An amalgamation of the range of possible goals for vocational guidance interviews (Gothard, 1985; Shackleton and Spurgeon, 1982; Wicks, 1982) can be seen in Table 5.1.

The identification of specific and unambiguous performance indicators has been implicated in appraisal by Breakwell (1990) when she advises that any appraisal objectives should be 'clearly formulated' and explicitly described in terms of concrete performance indicators. The process of moving towards such criteria can be conceived in a fashion similar to that indicated in Table 5.1, where goal achievement may be enhanced by subdividing the ultimate goal into a series of smaller subgoals. Breakwell (1990) offers such a step-wise approach for would-be appraisal interviewers when she suggests three such subgoals: (1) establishing objectives and negotiating performance indicators; (2) reviewing performance against previously established indicators; and (3) deciding what changes in performance are needed and the subsequent plan of action required to achieve them.

It is crucial that goals specify precisely what success entails. For the individual who is ultimately trying to obtain a job, an intermediate goal might be to secure an interview for a wanted job or for the individual trying to overcome a respiratory illness an intermediate goal might be to reduce the number of cigarettes smoked from twenty to five per day. The individual who secures a wanted interview or who manages to reduce his smoking to five cigarettes a day *knows* that he has succeeded in accomplishing his set goal. The importance of this criterion led Locke and Latham (1984) to include, as one step in their goal-setting procedure, the need to specify the standard or target to be reached and in so doing corroborate Egan's (1982) and Cormier and Cormier's (1985) suggestions of stating goals in terms of overt behavioural accomplishments and/or in terms of more covert thoughts and feelings.

The interviewer, by attempting to meet a sequence of process subgoals, increases the likelihood of an ultimate product or outcome goal being achieved by the client. This idea of coordinating, in a rational and coherent manner, the objectives of both client and interviewer has been elegantly presented by Egan (1982). It will be recalled that for each stage Egan (1982) specifies counsellor objectives which are related to more specific counsellor behaviours which in turn

Table 5.1 The range of possible goals and subgoals for vocational guidance interviews

	Goals		Subgoals
*	Enable the client to make realistic self-assessments	* * * *	develop self-awareness develop informed self-discovery encourage an exploration of aims, goals, attitudes and values provide accurate and current information relating to the client's individualism (e.g. testing)
*	Enable the client to make realistic occupational/further education/higher education/ training assessments	* * * * *	provide relevant information encourage critical evaluation of all available information increase the client's awareness of all potential opportunities promote a thorough exploration of opportunities organise any activities deemed of assistance to the client (e.g. work visits, experience)
*	Assist the client to make realistic decisions	* * * *	develop an awareness of the decision-making process including goal setting enable the client to explore the costs and benefits of all possible options (i.e. the implications) facilitate reality testing of any tentative decisions made note any interim or final decisions made by the client and act as agreed
*	Stimulate the client to act upon decisions reached	* * * *	provide necessary information (e.g. addresses, names, telephone numbers, etc) set goals for completion of subgoals help increase the likelihood of action being taken by strengthening the facilitators and reducing the inhibitors undertake any action promised as part of the agreement

are deployed with the intent of facilitating certain client outcomes. This synchrony characterises Egan's (1982) problem management model. A somewhat similar account (in principle) has been presented by Maier (1958) for would-be appraisal interviewers. Each of his three approaches to appraisal implicates the deployment of a different array of interview skills and the holding of somewhat different attitudes and values both towards the process and the appraisee.

Measurable or verifiable

In keeping with the scientific behaviourist tradition goals should be open to measurement or at least to what Egan (1982) calls 'verification'. Procedures based on a medical type of model tend to stress the importance of the diagnostic phase where a base-line picture can be compiled of the individual. It is against this base line that goals are set and goal achievement subsequently ascertained (Balthazar, 1973). In a somewhat common-sense vein, Egan (1982, p.213) states quite simply that:

> Clients can't know whether they are making progress if they do not know where they started.

The athlete striving to secure her place in the Olympic team knows precisely the 'qualifying standard' required if she is to be eligible for consideration. A series of competitive events provides the athlete with evidence as to whether progress towards the goal is evident or not and, furthermore, how far from or near to the goal she is. The idea of performance standards is clearly important within the appraisal context, for, in order to be in a position to be able to meet some of Maier's (1958) purposes of appraisal, both yardsticks and measurable behavioural indices must be communicable. For instance, to be able to tell appraisees where their strengths and weaknesses lie, it is imperative to be able to measure and norm their performances against known performance indicators (Breakwell, 1990).

Vocational guidance models have also been proposed which attempt to account for client progress by basing such evaluations on an initial diagnostic phase followed by appropriate interventions (or, in medical terms, treatment) terminating in a review phase to establish whether any progress has indeed occurred (Bedford, 1982). The model depends on the extent to which vocational guidance needs can be ascertained or measured in the same way as a doctor prescribes a certain course of treatment based on his earlier conclusions reached in the diagnostic interview.

In the event that goal-related behaviours cannot be subjected to some form of measurement or at least verification then subsequent evaluations of goal attainment are futile both for the interviewer and for the interviewee. How much change has occurred and in what direction will remain a mystery.

Realistic or achievable

The extent to which a goal can be judged to be realistic or achievable is a relative decision which can be ascertained only with reference to the particular individual under consideration. With this in mind it appears unlikely that practitioners will find themselves in a position to be able to set realistic goals *for* clients. A more appropriate approach would be to enable individuals to set goals for themselves having given due consideration to all the potential factors present. Factors may be located within the individual as personal resources or may reside outside the person in the environment as facilitators or inhibitors of goal attainment (Egan, 1982).

Establishing a realistic goal often requires that the client focuses on outcomes that can be achieved without a reliance on other people or society somehow changing (that is, within his control). Goals of this type are often expressed in terms of 'wishes'. For example, 'I wish my boss wasn't so obnoxious', or 'I wish my parents wouldn't nag me so much', or 'I wish that it wasn't so difficult to get around in the community' or 'I wish my A-level results had been better'. Of course, some of the more environmental obstacles might be modifiable but to focus energy on and develop high hopes for a quick solution might be an unrewarding exercise in the short term.

Interviewers need to assist their clients to explore any obstacles that might interfere with goal achievement while also seeking to identify the range of resources likely to facilitate goal achievement. For instance, Cormier and Cormier (1985, p.242) cite the following factors as of potential significance as inhibitory and/or facilitatory influences:

> the absence or presence of certain feelings, or mood states, thoughts, beliefs and perceptions, other people, and situations or events...could also include knowledge or skills.

The importance of agreeing to goals that are achievable has clear psychological implications for the individual. Locke and Latham (1984, p.39) state the implications clearly when they note that:

> Nothing breeds success like success. Conversely, nothing causes feelings of despair like perpetual failure. A primary purpose of goal setting is to increase the motivation level of the individual. But goal setting can have precisely the opposite effect if it produces a yardstick that consistently makes the individual feel inadequate.

Goals set too high can reap a high psychological cost. To experience a sense of achievement goals also need to be set such that they act as a challenge to the individual (Locke and Latham, 1984). Therefore, easy goals, set at too low a level, rarely act as performance enhancers. From the perspective of appraisal, goals should be set such that the individual is 'stretched but not snapped' (Breakwell, 1990, p.66).

However, it should be noted that some clients often set very high goals due to their irrational, 'musturbatory' thinking which tends to impose on the individual idealistic, perfectionist self-demands (Dryden, 1987). Such demands tend to be self-defeating and therefore represent dangerous levels for goal setting (Cormier and Cormier, 1985).

Of particular relevance is the notion of acceptance or internalisation of the goal. A personal goal is likely to command a greater degree of personal commitment. However, a person who takes on board such a goal which turns out to be beyond his reach (possibly due to acquiescence or irrational thinking) will 'sabotage' his efforts (Egan, 1982). Cormier and Cormier (1985) further summarise a number of points which comprise the main reasons why failures occur with respect to goal achievement. These include making the steps between subgoals too large, not ensuring that the interviewee really owns the goal or not taking enough care to ensure that the interviewee has the personal resources to attain the goal, while Trower *et al.* (1978) add that conflicting goals can lead to a failure to take any actions at all.

Realism from the interviewer's perspective is also very important for effective interviewing. Gorden (1987), for example, outlines a number of facilitators and inhibitors with respect to the effectiveness of research interviewing. Indeed, the main objectives of the research interviewer may be construed as seeking to increase the facilitators of, and to decrease the inhibitors of, the flow of relevant, reliable and valid information. The generalisability of this notion seems self-evident and appears to be of considerable significance where decisions are likely to be made based on the calibre of the information gathered.

Realism might also refer to 'how much' is expected from the interview in terms of both quality and quantity. For instance, it seems unlikely that one interview could realistically include all the goals/subgoals listed in Table 5.1 as potential components of the vocational guidance process. Gothard (1985) notes this point and suggests a somewhat more realistically truncated list more amenable to one interview intervention. Maier (1958) makes a similar plea on behalf of the appraisal interview when he notes the fallacy of attempting to meet most or all of his eight appraisal objectives in a single interview.

So, just as the client is encouraged to set targets that are realistic, the interviewer should seek to apply similar considerations to his own interview practice.

Unrealistic expectations for the interview may also relate to the specific purposes for which the interview is employed. One of the major tasks for which interviews are employed is for carrying out assessments of individuals. This is particularly appropriate in selection, medical and counselling settings where a diagnostic phase tends to constitute a distinguishable part of the process. However, the extent to which the interview is suited to undertake such an assessment task is arguable. Some authors have severely criticised the interview on technical grounds within both occupational selection and vocational guidance (Kline, 1975), claiming high unreliability and consequent low predictive and concurrent validity. It would appear, therefore, that to collect certain types of information by way of the interview violates Gorden's (1987) criteria of reliability and validity. Nonetheless, Shouksmith (1968) asserts that interviews can be employed for the purpose of assessing a limited number of critical job requirements ascertained for each vacant position. The realism relates to the acknowledgement of human limitations in that to ask an interviewer to assess more than about six factors is unrealistic (Shouksmith, 1968). The outcome of maintaining realism serves to limit the scope of the interview to a specified number of specific types of human attributes which, according to Shouksmith (1968), might include certain aspects of a candidate's personality, expressed interests and attitudes.

It would appear that a great deal of faith has been invested in interviewing as a generic data-gathering method without any significant choices being made to enhance reliability and validity – it has been widely misused (Millar, 1979).

It should be noted finally that there is a relatively fine line between a realistic and an unrealistic goal. As a consequence, it becomes crucial to monitor carefully the individual's progress with respect to the agreed target. New evidence may require goals to be modified (making them either easier or more difficult, or more appropriate) to maintain motivation and self-esteem. Bearing in mind the importance of setting challenging goals, caution should be exercised in lowering targets frivolously without careful consideration.

The concept of goal modification is, however, extremely relevant to practitioners who employ interviews where objectives can alter rapidly as circumstances change. Adherence to initial objectives should be viewed as temporary or tentative as any notion of goal permanence may render the interview at best irrelevant (Cormier and Cormier, 1985).

Interviewer vigilance and flexibility assume great importance if the interview is to continue to meet the needs of its participants throughout its duration (Gorden, 1987).

Internal rather than external

A brief reference has been made to individuals accepting goals and acting as if they owned them. To maximise the likelihood of individuals 'owning' goals, practitioners should encourage full participation in the choice process. Goal-setting responsibility lies with the individual not with the practitioner. In the former case the individual will tend to work harder for goal achievement whereas in the latter situation individuals can legitimately blame others for their failure to reach an externally imposed goal. It boils down to a question of responsibility (Egan, 1982). Makin et al. (1989, p.85) summarise the position when they note that:

> When people are committed to a course of action they adopt it as their own and will make efforts to ensure that they succeed, without the necessity for continual monitoring by others....[and when they are not] they will take advantage of any loophole or excuse that presents itself in order to avoid doing what is required.

The individual's commitment to the interview process and motivation to work towards successful outcomes has been referred to as 'inclusion' (Stewart and Cash, 1988, p.15). This concept is applicable to both participants and suggests that an effective interview is a cooperative venture. The impact of participative goal setting, according to Locke and Latham (1984), has led to increased performance and the generation of feelings of competency among employees. However, participation appears to exert its effect not on more effective goal setting but on an increased likelihood of action being implemented in an attempt to achieve goals (Locke and Latham, 1984). Egan (1982) simply notes that clients tend to 'work harder' for *their* goals.

The appropriateness of such participation has a substantial application to interviewing of all types and tends to be particularly important during the opening phase (see chapter seven for a fuller discussion) where objectives can be on the agenda. For example, the negotiation of appraisal interview objectives seems preferable to an impositional style (Breakwell, 1990). However, it should not be concluded that such participation is confined to this opening phase. Work on the appraisal process, reported by Nemeroff and Wexley (1979), suggests that:

> allowing subordinates some degree of control over setting goals and giving them the opportunity to participate are both effective ways of increasing the success of the feedback interview process.

Similarly, the notion of the medical consultation being considered as essentially a process of negotiation, previously discussed (chapter six), is of relevance here. Rapport between patient and physician has been viewed as a'mutuality of goals' (DiMatteo and DiNicola, 1982a, p.82). The ultimate mutually shared goal of both participants is to restore the patient to a healthy condition by eliminating the illness. The outcome of such mutuality of goals, coupled with shared definitions of patient–physician roles, brings about rapport (DiMatteo and DiNicola, 1982a).

The importance of participation has also been stressed by Cormier and Cormier (1985) who go so far as to suggest that, however well meaning, in the absence of active participation by the interviewee, the dictatorial counsellor has a slim chance of reaching successful outcomes.

In keeping with the interviewee's values

Within the sphere of human action behaviours are often guided by personal value systems. Behaviours or actions which compromise a strongly held value tend to create a degree of psychological tension which may be experienced as anxiety, guilt or dissonance. Individuals left to their own devices tend to seek consistency or congruence between their values and overt behaviours. However, when actions are demanded of an individual by another, personally held values may be endangered. For example, the individual who holds positive respectful values of her human peers is likely to suffer psychologically if 'ordered' to manage her peers in a way that implies a value system that views such contemporaries as basically lazy, sneaky time-wasters who need constant supervision (perceived as a checking-up-on function) and frequent threats.

Within the counselling context the significance of human values, both those of the client and those of the counsellor, assumes substantial proportions. Attempts by practitioners to impose alternative value systems on clients remain unethical. To impose a value system which permits a mother to work full time or which allows a young unmarried woman to consider having an abortion, despite the client's strongly held contrary values that suggest that either of the goals would be totally unacceptable, raises grave issues and may in all probability lead to further problems. This is not to say that helpers must accept or internalise their clients' values but rather that they should attempt to understand and respect such value systems and encourage clients to engage in further exploration of a range of alternative value systems. Egan (1982, p.217) sums up the situation when he suggests that:

> Although helping is...a process of social influence it remains ethical only if it respects the client's values. Helpers may challenge clients to re-examine their values, but they should in no way encourage clients to actions that are not in keeping with their values.

Imposing alternative value systems by way of endorsing certain actions tends to suggest that your values are more worthy, more appropriate or more acceptable than those of the interviewee. It is quite likely that these judgemental overtones will be perceived by the interviewee as preaching, pointing the finger or simply as dismissive of the interviewee's perspective as unimportant, unworthy or incorrect.

Messages conveying the relative values of courses of action need not be communicated verbally but can be clearly conveyed by nonverbal signals. An example was witnessed by the senior author in an interaction between a careers officer and a young client where options after school were to be explored. In response to the useful open question 'What could you do at the end of your fifth year?', the careers officer noted down the ideas expressed by the client on a blackboard as indicated in the storyboard depicted below (Table 5.2).

The message, although never explicitly verbalised, seemed clear and un-ambiguous: the careers officer had communicated her values clearly regarding which was the best option to go for and conversely which was the most un-acceptable. The message was further pressed home by having enough time to discuss fully only how the 'best' option of 'finding a job' could be attained. The fact that the client had mentioned two educational options first was subtly disregarded. The careers officer was, however, unaware that her values had leaked out in this manner.

Reasonable time scale

Specifying an appropriate time span constitutes step four in Locke and Latham's (1984) seven-step goal-setting process. Goals to be realistic need to be time-scaled in such a way that accomplishment has a reasonable chance of occurring. An initially realistic goal, in terms of client resources, could be rendered un-achievable simply because not enough time is afforded the individual in which to

Table 5.2 The leakage of values

First idea	Second idea	Third idea	Fourth idea	Fifth idea
			Find a job	Find a job
	Further education	Further education	Further education	Further education
Stay at school	Stay at school	Stay at school	Stay at school	Stay at school
				Youth training
		Sign on	Sign on	Sign on

reach the target. The client who has never been able to perform some task is unlikely suddenly to be in a position to achieve complete performance within a short period of time. The chronically indecisive person is unlikely to be able to make several important decisions by the next session the following week. The shy, unassertive adolescent is unlikely to be in a position to go and confront an aggressive teacher immediately because you, the interviewer, feel that it would be the best course of action, the quickest route to a solution or maybe what you would do. In these cases, the setting of subgoals or steps would, if attained, gradually lead the individuals to their ultimate goals by making reasonable incremental demands on their resources.

Second, time scales should be agreed in specific terms. It was unlikely that Mae West received much response to her famous quip 'Come up and see me some time' in the same way that Egan (1982) admonishes helpers for establishing imprecise time scales for goal accomplishment. It is equally important within the appraisal context that appraisees know how long they have to reach agreed behavioural targets (Lawson, 1989).

However, in our complex society time scales are often imposed on individuals. Examination anxiety needs to be alleviated by the date on which the examination is to be held, application forms need to comply with submission dates and research data are required by specified deadlines. An awareness of just what can be achieved within such imposed time scales will make a substantial contribution to the realism of the goals agreed and consequently to the likelihood of ultimate success.

Given the purposes/objectives set for the interview it is imperative that the participants evaluate the appropriateness of such goals with respect to the time available for the interview (Schweinitz and Schweinitz, 1962). It is generally agreed that somewhere within the opening period of any interview interviewees should be told what length of time can be allocated to them on this occasion. This knowledge enables the interviewee to contribute to a more valuable use of what is often a limited period of time and will tend to reduce any anxiety generated by not knowing how long the commitment will be (Stewart and Cash, 1988).

Once a certain time limit has been agreed it is then essential to stick to it. It is very easy indeed to get so carried away in what might be regarded as crucially important interview content that the tendency just to carry on for a little while longer is strong. While this may be quite acceptable to some interviewees, this cannot be assumed. It is interesting to speculate upon how many young people being interviewed in school have missed out on their much looked-forward-to football match during breaktime or even sat on through increasing anxiety at the thought of missing their school bus at the end of their school day. Overrunning in this way tends to act in a way similar to one of Gorden's (1987) eight inhibitors of communication, which he termed 'competing demands for time'. Under these conditions, Gorden (1987) cautions interviewers to be aware of the possibility that captive interviewees may be very unwilling to engage in any meaningful interactions since this would only serve to prolong matters. To keep individuals under such conditions fails to meet the needs of both participants. Obviously, under these circumstances, arranging a further interview seems to be the obvious outcome especially if the information needed is regarded as an important component in goal achievement.

The impact of time restrictions has been referred to previously when discussing the realism of interview objectives – particularly how much ground can be covered within the purview of a single interview. In addition, however, time factors can diminish the quality and depth as well as the quantity dimensions of the interview. Schweinitz and Schweinitz (1962, p.46) express the influence when they say:

> Time often threatens to outweigh purpose. The necessity for an expeditious finish may loom so large in the mind of the interviewer that he may centre his attention upon speed, skimming over and through the essentials.

Such brevity of coverage tends to reduce the comprehensiveness and reliability of the data collected and leaves clients less than satisfied with their interview experience. Jones (1982), in exploring the medical interview, cites a further difficulty encountered when incomplete data are collected – a not uncommon occurrence in the medical context. In the absence of detailed case histories, Jones (1982) asserts that the way is open for the medical interviewer to bring into play a number of inferential processes which essentially construct a picture of the whole (i.e. the syndrome) on the basis of having identified only some of the parts. When only a few pieces of the jigsaw are available then the interviewer tends to employ a range of implicit processes, including implicit personality theories, stereotyping, etc. (see chapter four), to construct the total picture. The likelihood of interviewer prejudices and biases influencing the inferential process and outcomes of the interview is considerably greater where the depth and range of information collected are superficial and narrow respectively.

Most interviewers find themselves struggling to complete their tasks and reach their objectives within the stringent time constraints usually imposed. This state of affairs serves to elevate the importance of the relevance of the interview content with respect to interview purposes (Gorden, 1987; Rodger, 1970). The interviewer takes the responsibility for maintaining relevance and not wasting interviewees' time (Shouksmith, 1968), making the most effective use of the limited time by working competently towards meeting the objectives for which the participants have come together. The interviewer's objective, according to Schweinitz and Schweinitz (1962, p.45), is a double one – 'purpose and time'.

It would, however, be an error to assume that longer interviews are necessarily more effective or competent than shorter ones. The plea 'if only I had more time' is no guarantee of improved effectiveness or competence. Schweinitz and Schweinitz (1962, p.46) summarise the dangers of such an argument:

> Because, however, time can easily be measured, while it is exceedingly difficult to appraise quality, speed and numbers can become in and of themselves a goal, a way by which a person can justify himself in a tendency towards slipshod performance.

Limited available time suggests that interviewers need to prepare and plan to make the most effective use of what contact time they have by considering the use of various interview guides, levels of structuring and to consider participation by the client in the process of prioritising what particular goals will guide the content of the forthcoming interview.

PRIORITISING GOALS

Locke and Latham (1984, p.33) include as step five in their goal-setting model 'prioritize goals' because:

> as jobs increase in complexity, the number of different goals is also likely to increase. When more than one goal is set it becomes important to rank the goals in terms of their relative importance.

In the complexities of life individuals tend to juggle with several goals, some important, other less so, some critical, others more long term, some mediational, others ultimate. Failure to achieve goals within a certain time scale and/or to attain the requisite standard may contribute to a feeling of crisis (e.g. missing deadlines, getting electricity cut off, etc.). Therefore, in a situation where the ascertainment of needs suggests a number of potential goals a process of prioritising or targeting may be necessary where the selected goal would tend to:

* be highly desired or valued;
* be short term with high likelihood of success (motivational);
* be within the anticipated level of personal competence;
* be within the person's control rather than under 'others'' or environmental control;
* alleviate or prevent a crisis situation;
* be a central goal the achievement of which may reduce the need to set or address other goals; for example, where goal achievement in one domain may enable the individual to achieve goals in other directions (social confidence, social-educational knowledge, physical health).

Failure to prioritise or target specific areas for attention may result in few effective actions ensuing and low goal accomplishment (Trower *et al.*, 1978). Locke and Latham (1984) refer to situations where goal overload may contribute to the formation of varying degrees of stress. The resulting anxiety, panic, fear or helplessness symptomatic of trying to work with too many goals at the same time may be such as to lead the sufferer to seek professional help.

So it seems to make sense to focus one's attention and resources on clearly identified goals selected as instrumental in maintaining motivation, reducing anxiety, avoiding a crisis or moving the individual towards some highly valued, ultimate and agreed goal which may be rather longer term.

Feedback

Reference to feedback in chapter two suggested that it plays a significant control function in social interaction. In the context of this chapter, feedback constitutes a crucial regulatory component in goal-directed action (Locke and Latham, 1984; von Cranach *et al.*, 1982). Indeed, Locke and Latham (1984, p.66) note the necessity of feedback within their goal-setting model, and further suggest that without adequate provision of feedback:

> the effectiveness of goal setting is minimal. The goal or target is practically useless if there is not enough information to keep performance on track.

With respect to interviewing, Stewart and Cash (1988) emphasise the pivotal role played by feedback in successful interviews, the main functions of which have been summarised by Egan (1982) as (1) confirmatory; (2) corrective; and (3) motivating. It is important to let individuals know that they are on the right lines and moving, as planned, towards agreed goals. However, it is equally important to provide information which encourages individuals to explore why they seem to have strayed off course. Through effective use of feedback individuals are provided with, or are encouraged to generate, more alternatives, to have more options (Egan, 1982; Hopson and Scally, 1981).

It was suggested in chapter two that feedback was continually available, and in the context of social interaction was available to all participants. Within the interview context feedback provides potentially available information for both participants virtually all the time (Stewart and Cash, 1988). For example, counsellors may perceive data evident within the counselling relationship as it happens, as they interact. These data can be openly and explicitly introduced into the counselling process by the counsellor for consideration by the client. This type of 'cueing' feedback (Locke and Latham, 1984) offers the interviewee feedback as the interview proceeds. Quite often this type of feedback in counselling is managed by sensitively and respectfully deploying specific skills termed reflection, immediacy and confrontation (Egan, 1982). So, in order to help the client to engage in self-exploration, a counsellor may pick up, say, a lack of social confidence from the client in the interview, and *choose* to reflect this perception on hearing the client claiming a high degree of social confidence as an element of the self-concept. This kind of 'formative' feedback is relatively infrequently witnessed compared with the second type of feedback termed by Locke and Latham (1984) 'summary'. This tends to be given on completion of the performance, at the end. Summative feedback in the form of knowledge of results has been the traditional means of evaluating progress or attainment. However, there is currently a greater recognition of the relative ineffectiveness of being informed of a poor performance at the end of a task (being too late) and a greater utility in providing guidance in the form of formative or cueing feedback throughout.

So, given that the provision of feedback is crucial to the effectiveness of goal-directed action, the interviewer needs to take care to handle the situation as skilfully as possible. A number of 'rules' have been proposed precisely for this purpose and the following brief summary is based substantially on Hopson and Scally's (1981) six key rules.

Feedback should:
1. be offered rather than imposed.
It is important to be aware that feedback should not be forced on a client. We all have the right to accept or reject information about ourselves provided by others (including interviewers) – it is the individual's choice (Hopson and Scally, 1981). The important point is to attempt to create a climate whereby the interviewee will feel able at least to consider the feedback rather than immediately reject it out of hand.
2. be descriptive rather than evaluative.
What interviewees need is a chance to consider what behaviours they display, how they 'come across'. What appear to be less helpful are attempts to present analyses of underlying meanings, interpretations or evaluative statements (Egan, 1982).
3. be specific and refer to features or behaviours that can be changed.
Interviewees are more likely to be able to assimilate feedback when it refers to specific and concrete behaviours rather than relating to personality labels which tend to become overgeneralised. Global types, such as 'handicapped', 'weak', 'unemployable' or 'failure', provide little meaningful feedback and tend to focus attention on some vague totality rather than on specific overt behaviours, thoughts or feelings. Psychologically, a weak person is quite different from a person with specific weaknesses which are manifest only in a specific situation. Stewart and Cash (1988, p.179) recommend that interviewers 'attack the problem not the person'.
4. emphasise the positive rather than the negative.
This rule emphasises the importance of offering the interviewee supportive, rewarding feedback and is of considerable importance in situations where only partial goal attainment has occurred. The significance of rewarding positive achievements cannot be overstressed, even in the context of an overall failure to

reach the desired outcome. Such feedback serves Egan's (1982) motivating function, giving credit where credit is due.

However, the rule does not suggest that only positive feedback should be given. The significance of a balanced feedback has been documented, for example, in the appraisal context. Fletcher and Williams (1976, p.81) write:

> the interviews which included a balanced discussion of both strengths and weaknesses in performance achieved the greatest positive effects overall... Where only the particularly good work done by the appraisee was reviewed, the encouraging effect of the interview and the favourable attitude toward it appear to be offset in some cases by the tendency to get too rosy a picture of the assessment given, and perhaps to feel in consequence that further improvement is neither possible nor desired.

Establishing a picture where successful feedback can be offered creates a stronger, more secure base for offering more negative data for the interviewee to consider. The distorted outcome of negatively skewed feedback was clearly witnessed by the senior author on visiting a student on a professional fieldwork placement. On reaching the placement office, the student immediately made an interception in order to prepare the ground for an anticipated negative report from the fieldwork supervisor. To both our surprises, the dreaded report was overwhelmingly positive. The negative impression had arisen because from day-to-day the *only* feedback offered to the student (such as 'we don't do things like that here', 'look you're in the real world now', or 'don't they teach you anything at that university?') was perceived as negatively critical, contributing to a very distorted and overly negative self-image and consequent lowered self-esteem.

5. include positive suggestions, particularly when it is negative.

The emphasis is on the potential of all feedback to be constructive (Breakwell, 1990). Simply giving negative feedback is likely to result in rather destructive outcomes, particularly if such feedback is not linked to more positive suggestions for improvement (Egan, 1982). Given that, in attempting to reach desired goals, a number of alternative courses of action are usually possible, feedback is more constructive where it questions the particular ineffective course of action by providing alternative options which might offer additional hope, be more positive and be motivational.

6. be owned by the person giving it.

The responsibility for any feedback given lies with the giver. It is his or her perspective that is reflected in the feedback. One thing is sure – it is not an incontrovertible fact that is contained in such feedback and therefore it should not be stated or asserted as if it were. Feedback offers the interviewee another perspective, no better or no worse than their own but in all probability different. The interviewer's hope is that the interviewee will, at least, consider it. As a consequence, feedback will probably contain a higher proportion of 'I' statements than would normally be recommended in interviews.

7. be appropriately timed.

The importance of providing feedback at the appropriate time has long been recognised by learning theorists. Feedback consequent upon desired performance is most effective when only a short period of time has elapsed since the performance because the longer the delay the more likely it will be that the relationship between the performance and the reward will become obscured. Feedback overly delayed will act in a less motivating manner, may motivate individuals to pursue the wrong courses of actions or may thwart the resolution of performance deficits.

The task of reviewing progress forms an essential evaluative stage for interviewers and interviewees. Jones (1982, p.161) suggests that:

> The ideal situation for diagnosis and treatment evaluations is one in which the physician has continuing or, at least, periodic contact with the patient so that repeated observations can be made over time to assess the course of treatment.

Locke and Latham (1984) and Balthazar (1973) also stress the value in reviewing action plans to check progress towards goals so that both parties can assess the extent to which changes are necessary and, if so, where they might be made. Interviewers operating in the selection context should carry out reviews of objectives to establish the reliability and validity of their procedures. Professional interviewers should, indeed, be reviewing the extent to which their interviewing strategies and interpersonal skills are contributing to the attainment of both their objectives and those of their clients.

SUMMARY

The content and character of goals and the principles of goal setting have been set out with respect to interviews, interviewers and interviewees. The key criteria that, if adopted, result in effective workable goals being set have been summarised as being clear and behaviourally specific, measurable, achievable, owned by the goal-setter, congruent with his or her values and appropriately time-scaled. The effectiveness of goals and the goal-setting process needs to be reviewed in order to provide feedback, which may confirm or correct the situation and/or act in a motivational capacity. It was, finally, suggested that giving feedback (and indeed receiving it) constitutes a skilled element in the process and adherence to a number of basic rules will increase the likelihood of a forward moving, positive outcome resulting, for both interviewee and interviewer.

Chapter 6

Interviewer tactics

The story so far has suggested that interviewers, engaging in a form of social interaction, perceive their interviews in individual ways and process available information to reach conclusions about what specific goals might be realisable (and which might not) within the context of their interviewing. Once realisable goals have been identified it becomes important to consider what particular form of interviewing would carry the highest probability of success. As was indicated in chapter four, there are a plethora of routes to a goal, with the result that considered choice needs to be exercised by the interviewer about how to conduct the interview to maximum effect. According to Wicks (1982, p.311):

> content must be tailored to the particular aim in mind, each interview requiring careful planning with preparation related to desired outcome.

It is incumbent on the interviewer to work towards the achievement of an agreed aim while ensuring that professional competence is at all times maintained (Wicks, 1982).

In addition to a careful consideration of interview structures and overall tactics, interviewers must also make choices regarding the deployment of appropriate interpersonal skills, which, in turn, facilitate goal attainment. The focus of this chapter will be on the variety of methods for planning and organising interviews, followed, in chapter seven, by an account of the range of behavioural responses potentially available to the professional interviewer. Therefore, the focus of these two chapters will be on the interviewer rather than the interviewee.

WHY PLAN?

In the previous chapter, a number of brief references were made to the potential benefits of considering a well-planned and structured interview. It may be helpful at this juncture to outline briefly some of the main reasons for considering planning an interview in this way. In essence, interviewers should consider their 'tactics' (Gorden, 1987, p.44) in order to increase the likelihood of gathering information that is relevant, reliable and valid. The typical situation of operating within stringent and often inadequate time limits suggests that interviewers need to plan to use the interview to maximum effect and certainly need to avoid wasting interviewees' time (Schweinitz and Schweinitz, 1962; Shouksmith, 1968). One means of maximising effective use of contact time is to ensure that interview content is *relevant* to the purpose of the interview (Breakwell, 1990; Gorden, 1987; Kline, 1975; Munro Fraser, 1971; Rodger, 1970; Shouksmith, 1968). Prior planning can ascertain the main topic areas that meet the criterion of relevance – indeed, Rodger's seven-point plan was developed with relevance as one of the four research criteria (Rodger, 1970). Furthermore, Munro Fraser (1971, p.207) identifies one of the main tasks of interviewers as steering:

> the candidate over the ground to be covered, so that the essential facts appear as quickly as possible and the irrelevancies are cut down to a minimum.

Second, interviews that have clear, realisable objectives and specified content tend to reduce the influence of a variety of interviewer subjective biases and prejudices; that is, interviewer errors are reduced (Jones, 1982; Shouksmith, 1968; Wicks, 1982). A number of interpersonal perceptual errors, as discussed in chapter four, are proposed as one of the main reasons for the reported poor predictive validities commonly held for selection interviewing (Anderson and Shackleton, 1990; Ribeaux and Poppleton, 1978). A lack of adequate sampling of interviewee behaviours coupled with a lack of a clear plan creates ample opportunity for interviewers to sample whatever they think might be important (e.g. Taylor and Sniezek, 1984), to whatever depth they wish, all of which tends to be strongly influenced by interpersonal perceptions of liking, and/or similarity, saliency of information and the application of stereotypical information processing. In fact, such distortions may begin before the candidate has even engaged in the actual interview, in circumstances where pre-interview documents are available. According to Eder *et al.* (1989, p.28):

> Cognitive schemas developed by the interviewer after a brief review of the candidate's resumé and application materials likely guide the interview process and predetermine its outcome.

The outcome of this array of potential human errors serves to reduce the accuracy with which human attributes are measured; that is, the errors reduce the reliability of the information collected and, therefore, distort the outcome. The potential significance of estimates of interview reliability has been explored recently by Wiesner and Cronshaw (1988), who report that about 23 per cent of the variance in interview validity is explained by differences in interview reliability. In concluding their meta-analysis on selection interviewing, Wiesner and Cronshaw (1988, p.288) reported results that:

> supported the contention that reliability and interview structure affect the validity of interviews. First, improved reliability was invariably associated with higher interview validity. Second, interview structure was associated with a considerable increase in predictive validity.

However, the automatic assumption of validity given high reliability cannot necessarily be made. Within the context of research interviewing, Gorden (1987) issues such a warning and goes on to caution that decisions as to whether to employ interview schedules or not cannot be made by taking into account only these technical criteria.

The concept of validity, for example, can be evaluated only in relation to purpose. This theme is commented upon by Hetherington (1970, p.167) when, discussing the clinical interview, he points to the intricate relationships between reliability, validity and structure:

> Highly structured interviews based on standard questions may be more *reliable* in that similar results may be obtained by different interviewers or on different occasions; but less structured topic-interviews may be more *valid* in that the real problems of patients are more likely to emerge.

The research context has always focused attention on the criteria of relevance, reliability and validity as key determinants of the method of interviewing adopted, particularly with respect to interview structuring (Fowler and Mangione, 1990; Gorden, 1987).

More recently, attention focused on the validity of selection interviews has led to a number of developments which have contributed substantially to improvements in the predictive validities reported for interviews by structuring the interviewing process (Eder *et al.*, 1989). These developments, such as situational interviewing, will be referred to later in this chapter.

Within the guidance and counselling field the role of the interview seems generally to have been less threatened, although Kline (1975) has presented a strong challenge to vocational guidance interviewers. Notwithstanding his primary attack which focuses on the 'assessment' function of the interview within the overall vocational guidance process, Kline (1975) himself, in a vein similar to Shouksmith (1968), has suggested that there may be some aspects of both the assessment and guidance functions where interviewing may be appropriate, if planned. This function might relate to the amplification or verification of psychological test scores or to generating a more dynamic, holistic image of the person. The problem of 'asking too much' of the interview has been referred to in the previous chapter (Millar, 1979; Shouksmith, 1968).

In the sense that all counselling theories stress the importance of the relationship dimension (Hopson, 1982) the appropriateness of the interview seems axiomatic. It is difficult to envisage such relationships being possible without two human beings being in contact with each other. However, the extent to which these encounters are structured or controlled and by whom is very much dependent upon the theoretical inclination and/or personal style of the counsellor. For example, on video, one is struck by the striking degree of control exercised by Albert Ellis (1966) in his cognitive approach to counselling while being similarly aware of Carl Rogers' (1966) much less interventionist style – both are proponents of counselling and both claim to be effective.

DIRECTIVE–NONDIRECTIVE DIMENSION

Implicit in the preceding paragraph is the concept of a dimension which reflects the degree of direction and control introduced by the interviewer into the interview. This directive–nondirective continuum has been proposed as a major style dimension particularly with respect to interviews in the guidance and counselling field (Stewart and Cash, 1988). According to Stewart and Cash (1988) a directive interviewer assumes complete responsibility for imposing a chosen interview structure, determines the topics to be discussed and those to be avoided, and decides on the general pace and duration of the interview. In contrast, nondirective interviewers act out a less dominant nonexpert role where the interviewee assumes a more powerful role in determining the direction, topic content, duration and pace of the interview, all with the interviewer's blessing (Benjamin, 1981). It will be evident that the commitment of time may be considerably greater in nondirective interviews which are usually more time-consuming than directive encounters. Indeed, interviewers who find themselves operating within limited periods of time tend to adopt more directive styles of interviewing (McKitrick and Gelso, 1978). In a study of 29 careers officers (from the time-pressured Careers Service) interviewing 114 clients, Reddy and Brannigan (1982) concluded that careers officers essentially control or direct their interviews.

This dimension is also clearly evident in Maier's (1958) three approaches to appraisal interviewing. On the one hand, the 'Tell and Sell' method, described by Fletcher (1988, p.60) as 'bossed-based', adopts as its objectives to present the appraisal evaluation and then to sell both this and the derived action plan for improved performance to the appraisee. In a slightly less directive mode, the 'Tell and Listen' method introduces an element of appraisee reaction, although the decision-making power and control remain with the appraiser. Third, and operating along more egalitarian principles, is the 'Problem-Solving' approach where control is much more equally shared and, as a consequence, responsibility for evaluation and future action planning falls on both the appraiser and appraisee. This approach of joint problem solving requires a sufficient level of trust between both participants if it is to be effective (Hodgson, 1987). A similar explanation could be made for research interviewing, which, depending on purpose, could range from a highly structured 'oral' questionnaire to a more in-depth phenomenological type of interview particularly useful at the exploratory stages of research or for case study approaches. However, selection interviewing tends to be typically more directive with the power residing quite definitely with the interviewer. The extent to which this is necessarily the most effective style has been questioned, where the deployment of more counselling type skills has led to the collection of more valid data and to the increased likelihood of successful applicants accepting subsequent job offers (Harn and Thornton III, 1985).

Fowler and Mangione (1990) paint a rather directive picture of the medical interview when they assert that physician interviewers, by way of their considerable social status, technical expertise and knowledge, make it difficult for patients to do anything other than agree with their diagnoses, explanations or advice even when patients may not be satisfied with the conduct or the outcome of the consultation. However, the medical consultation has also been viewed as a process of mutual influence or negotiation where the patient does not relinquish control or delegate decision-making power to the physician (DiMatteo and DiNicola, 1982a). According to DiMatteo and DiNicola (1982a, p.75):

> An important general goal of each party to the practitioner–patient negotiation process is this: the practitioner seeks to feel that he has done what he believes to be professionally appropriate while the patient wishes to receive what he feels is in his own best physical and psychological interest.

The balance of mutual influence may be disturbed when acceptable compromises cannot be negotiated. For example, the physician may attempt to exert coercive power over the patient whereas the patient may resort to sabotage, fabrications or total rejection of the physican.

Whatever relational outcome is achieved, Banaka (1971, p.9) invokes the concept of inclusion when observing that:

> Each person has to find his degree of involvement in, and commitment to, the proposed action, be it an interview or a trip to the beach. Inclusion issues are unresolved when one person is unable to participate freely in the proposed action.

The idea that interviews are necessarily either directive or nondirective fails to reflect what often appears in practice. Interviews may display different control characteristics on different occasions or at different times within a single interview. This is very much a product of the view that interviews generally progress through a number of identifiable stages, which themselves contribute to structuring the interview process and enable movement to be detected (Benjamin, 1981).

INTERVIEW STAGES

Although noting differences in specific interview characteristics, Stewart and Cash (1988) suggest that all interviews move through three stages; namely, the opening (which includes rapport building and orientation), the body and the closing. This level of analysis, while of some interest, appears to have a relatively low utility for would-be interviewers. However, a number of theories have been proposed which identify discernible stages in the interview process. These various approaches are summarised in Table 6.1 and span a range of interview contexts. Each stage more readily represents the subgoal(s) which comprise the interview process; they suggest to interviewers what they are supposed to be aiming for at various points in the process, whether this be establishing a relationship, gathering information, processing the information, giving information or closing the interaction.

Table 6.1 Stages in the interview process across different contexts

Stewart and Cash (1988)	McHenry (1981)	Gorden (1987)	Echterling et al. (1980)	Egan (1982)	Benjamin (1981)	DiMatteo and DiNicola (1982b)	Rae (1988)	Fletcher (1988)	Hewton (1988)
All contexts	Selection	Research	Counselling	Counselling	Helping interview	Medical	Basic interview	Selection	Appraisal
Opening: 1. Rapport 2. Orientation	Rapport		Rapport and trust	Establishing a relationship	Establish purpose, roles and time commitment		Introductory	Beginning	Welcome, put at ease / Explain purpose
Body	Biographical	Collect information	Basic problem discovery	Problem clarification	Statement of the matter	Complete case history of the problem / Physical examination; information collection	Investigatory – information gathering	Collect information – probes	Asking for information for clarification
	Questioning	Make valid inferences		Develop new perspectives					
			Decision making		Development and exploration	Diagnosis	Generation of possible solutions	Give information	Deal with positive areas
		Behaviour modification		Develop action plans		Treatment recommendation	Consideration of possible solutions		Deal with more problematic areas
							Decision making		Agree ideas for further development (new targets)
Closing	Applicant queries / Parting			Review and termination	Closure		Concluding or summarising	Invite questions / Ending	Bring to a close

The opening phase

Table 6.1 displays the considerable amount of similarity between interviews conducted in different contexts. Most models include, early in the process, a relationship-establishing phase where rapport and, according to Echterling *et al.* (1980), trust should be established. In essence, this comprises an introductory stage where the type of relationship can be agreed in a relatively social and affective climate, prior to getting down to the more cognitively based business. Egan (1982) stresses the importance of establishing an appropriate relationship which then permeates the helping process throughout its duration, and, indeed, may be subject to change as the helping process changes. For this reason, Egan (1982) does not list this as a stage one goal.

In addition to the social aspects of the opening, Stewart and Cash (1988) also implicate 'orientation' which seems to reflect a process similar to Hargie *et al.*'s (1987, p.121) 'cognitive set', which serves to:

> induce an apparent cognitive set in the participants, so that they are mentally prepared in terms of the background to, and likely progression of, the main business to follow, which should as a result flow more smoothly.

Within this phase Breakwell (1990) identified a major factor in her outline of the appraisal process which she labelled 'setting objectives', while Hargie *et al.* (1987) specify ascertainment of interviewee expectations, potential interview function and possible goals as significant components. Benjamin (1981) adds that some indication of the amount of time available should be stated so that the interviewee will be in a better position to decide how best to use it. A further important element in the opening phase is included by Banaka (1971) and concerns 'ethics'. Interviewees should be completely in the picture regarding such issues as confidentiality, anonymity, recording the interview, note taking and what the information collected in the interview might be used for. More on these ethical issues will be included in chapter nine.

The body of the interview

Once both a social and cognitive set induction have been achieved the interviewer is ready to move into the 'body' (Stewart and Cash, 1988) of the interview. As was indicated earlier, one of the main goals of most interviews relates to the collection of information. It is, therefore, not surprising to find that most interviewing processes include a stage concerned with data collection, relevant to the particular context in which the interview is being employed. The extent to which the outcomes of interviews are realised or not is clearly dependent on the calibre of the information collected (Keenan and Wedderburn, 1980), which in turn is dependent on what Gorden (1987) termed interviewer tactics (that is, the use of interview guides, schedules, structure) and techniques (that is, the deployment of appropriate interviewing skills). The former category will comprise the remainder of this chapter.

Moving on to the next phase of the process, one notes that information collected is subjected to processing, to attach meaning to it so that a variety of types of decision can be derived from it. The outcome of most interviews implies some form of decision making, by either the interviewer or interviewee or jointly by both. In some contexts, such as selection, interviewer decisions may occur on completion of the interview in the absence of the interviewee whereas in many counselling and appraisal contexts decisions tend to be made within the interviews based on more egalitarian principles involving a shared responsibility. In Benjamin's (1981, p.20) words, the central part of the interview will be concerned with 'mutual looking into the matter trying to examine all its aspects and reach certain conclusions'.

The image of 'mutually looking into the matter' in a responsible partnership has been referred to by Bernstein and Bernstein (1985) in the medical interview when they employ one of Veatch's four relational models termed 'contractual' to describe their preferred doctor–patient relationship as one that resembles a respectful and concerned attitude towards the patient. Bernstein and Bernstein (1985, p.22) summarise their views by concluding that physicians:

> must assume responsibility for the conduct of the interview, but avoid the kind of control or rigidity that will inhibit or intimidate patients and limit patients' verbalizations regarding the problem. Professionals should keep the content of interviews in focus while maintaining flexibility so that relevant material is not inadvertently excluded.

However, in the 'Priestly' model control is attributed to the doctor by patients who invest in the practitioner both technical expertise and more widespread wisdom. According to Bernstein and Bernstein (1985) this paternalistic view diminishes patient participation and shifts the decision-making power entirely to the practitioner. The future direction of the patient is determined by the practitioner rather than by the individual patient and is therefore quite contrary to the 'contractual' model. The danger of this asymmetrical distribution of power is captured by Fowler and Mangione (1990, p.17) when they suggest that:

> It is not uncommon for physicians to suggest words to describe respondent feelings so that they can translate respondent experiences into a medical framework.

In this sense the patient's medical history, as presented, is simply the raw data and requires a transformation by the doctor so that diagnostic meaning may be attached and a medical conclusion reached pertaining to prognosis and prescribed treatment.

In specific interview contexts it may be necessary not only to collect information but also to provide relevant information for the interviewee's consideration. In the selection context applicants may need to find out more detailed information (than those particulars sent out prior to the interviews). Given the limited amount of time, the interviewer needs to be selective in those job details that are explained to the interviewee. In selecting details the interviewer should be extremely careful to select and present what is considered of crucial importance to all candidates and to be aware of the possibility of employing such selectivity to encourage 'good' candidates and/or to deter 'poor' ones (Fletcher, 1988). The presentation of vacancy details enables the potential employee to decide whether the job is suitable or not, in the same way that the information collected by the interviewer facilitates a selection decision. Furthermore, the provision of more information may provide the interviewee with material from which additional questions may emanate – this is useful only if the interviewer offers the interviewee a chance to pose these questions and is prepared to provide helpful answers.

Within the helping context giving or providing information has always been regarded as being potentially very helpful. Most people can recall a time when they were helped by someone making available crucial pieces of relevant information, which enabled the individual to proceed independently towards making a decision or taking some action. Generally, information should assist interviewees to find answers to *their* questions rather than those of the interviewer. This can be achieved only if the information is presented at the right time and in the appropriate medium (that is, written, pictorial, experiential or oral) such that the interviewee can make sense of it and therefore assimilate it. Providing information that is to be helpful is a very complex process requiring a considerable amount of informed thought and an in-depth understanding of the needs and capabilities of each interviewee.

The precise sequencing of the information-collecting and information-giving phases varies from one type of interview to another and in some cases within types. For example, some selection interview structures suggest that information gathering precedes information giving whereas other proposals proffer a reversal. This reversal is argued on the grounds that applicants, having considered the more detailed account of the job, may select themselves out and therefore not waste any further interview time (Rae, 1988). Interviewers need to take care not to dominate the interview by monopolising interview time presenting vast amounts of information about *their* jobs (or courses). Although this may facilitate the interviewee's decision making it can hardly enable the interviewer to reach an effective decision outcome (except by basing such a decision on somewhat superficial impressions highly prone to error). Nonetheless, an individual who possesses such specialised and desired information may be in a position to wield considerable 'informational power' over those who need access to it (Yesenosky and Dowd, 1990).

The closing phase

In the final stages of the process, a number of models make explicit provision for a stage whereby interviewee questions are dealt with (Banaka, 1971; Breakwell, 1990; McHenry, 1981). Traditionally, counselling, appraisal and medical interviews have required a higher degree of interviewee initiated communication throughout and, therefore, have tended not to set out explicitly a particular stage devoted to this function. However, selection interviewers have delineated periods in their interviews where interviewees are 'allowed' to question them, where the roles are somewhat reversed (Fletcher, 1988). This is clearly illustrated in Table 6.1.

Given that interviews are social encounters it is evident that all interviews should include closure as a final step. Some models explicitly include closure, parting or termination as a discernible stage, whereas others tend to include it by implication only. A number of skills can be identified as contributing to meeting the various goals of closure and tend to comprise means of summarising what has been achieved and an orientation towards the future. The appropriate skills will be more fully discussed in the next chapter.

Overall, therefore, the interview would appear to move through a number of identifiable phases or stages which can be summarised as (1) establishing both a realisable purpose and a working relationship; (2) the collection of relevant, reliable and valid information; (3) the evaluation of the information collected with respect to purpose; (4) decision making, making recommendations or for-mulating action plans: (5) giving appropriate information; and (6) responding to client questions and closure.

The remainder of this chapter will concern itself with the range of interviewer 'tactics' (Gorden, 1987) which, if employed, will make significant contributions to the reliability and validity of interview outcomes. Of course, the stages outlined above set out the various subgoals for interviewers to strive for (and in so doing establish purpose) but offer little or no concrete assistance as to 'how' these subgoals might be achieved; that is, which interviewer tactics (and tech-niques) will make a substantial contribution to goal attainment.

INTERVIEWER TACTICS

Gorden (1987, p.44) describes tactics as:

> those decisions the interviewer must make about the chronological order of topics, subtopics, questions and probes. Some of these decisions are part of the advance planning and some are made on the spot in the give-and-take of the interview process.

The question of what topics should be included (that is, relevance), in what sequence and in what way they should be sampled, pretty much defines the resultant structure that the interview will have. It will be recalled that the main objective for considering tactics was to increase the likelihood of reliable and valid interview outcomes being achieved based on the collection of relevant information, within a fairly short period of time available for sampling inter-viewee behaviour. The relating of tactics to purpose cannot be overstressed.

Structuring the interview

The idea of approaching an interview without any preconceived notions about what topics might be significant enough to include or by merely encouraging the client to talk about whatever springs to mind at the time seems today to be unacceptable (except for some forms of counselling). The problems of failing to adopt a more restrictive agenda have been referred to with respect to the 'Life Story Interview' approach as comprising principally the immense length and scope and the interpretative difficulties of the resultant interview protocols (Tagg, 1985).

The notion of possessing a plan which helps focus on topic areas high in relevance carries much support (Beggs *et al.*, 1970; Breakwell, 1990; Fowler and Mangione, 1990; Hetherington, 1970; McHenry, 1981; Munro Fraser, 1971; Rodger, 1970; Shouksmith, 1968; Stewart and Cash, 1988). The employment of an interview guide or plan, while reducing the subjective biases introduced by interviewers (Shouksmith, 1968) will, in the words of Stewart and Cash (1988, p.44), help them:

> develop areas of inquiry (rather than a random list of questions), remember areas of information, record answers, recognize relevant and irrelevant answers, and determine which probing questions to ask.

It has been argued, however, that such plans should not be so specific and predetermined as to preclude the inclusion of other topics when deemed of specific relevance by either the interviewer or interviewee (Rae, 1988). Indeed, this flexibility has been expressed as a major strength of interviews (Shouksmith, 1968). An initial intention to follow a particular interview plan should be open to modification, as required by interviewee initiations and responses. Indeed, the senior author recalls an interview where an overly rigid adherence to a plan severely reduced the effectiveness of an interview (from the interviewee's perspective). In the aforementioned interaction the interviewee responded to the question, 'What are you doing at school at the moment?', by saying, 'I've been thinking of trying to become a nurse'. As this response did not answer the interviewer's question she decided to defer dealing with the interviewee's response until later when it fitted into her preconceived plan. Her response, therefore, was 'Could we leave that until later – after we have covered your school work?' Such rigidity of approach may fully meet the interviewers' needs by obtaining answers to all of their questions but in so doing may fail totally to meet the interviewees' needs by not helping them find answers to their questions. It is important, at the outset, to come to some mutual agreement concerning the agenda for the forthcoming interview.

The likelihood of topic guides being available is increasingly possible within the employment, vocational counselling and clinical/medical interviewing contexts. The task of producing such a generic guide within the research context would be impossible, as the specific purpose of the research interview would determine the exact topics to be included. Nonetheless, such a specification stage is an essential prerequisite of effective research interviewing (Brenner, 1981; Fowler and Mangione, 1990; Richardson et al., 1965). The extent to which interviewers exert 'topic control' (Gorden, 1987), in terms of the determination of topic content, sequencing and topic changes within the interview, makes a substantial contribution to the degree of structure imposed on the interviewing procedure.

Structural dimensions

Within the field of interviewing there are three major dimensions along which interviews may be ordered with respect to their structure. These are (1) structured–unstructured; (2) standardised–nonstandardised; and (3) scheduled–nonscheduled. Basically, varying degrees of standardisation and scheduling contribute to the overall degree of structure the interview possesses. So, what characteristics determine the location of any interview on the structured–unstructured continuum?

The main criteria are displayed in Table 6.2. These criteria tend to relate to the degree of interviewer flexibility with respect to the content of the interview, what is included, how it is sampled, in what sequence and how much freedom is offered to interviewees with respect to their answers (i.e. open ended or multiple choice formats).

In the research context, the importance of collecting data which are both comparable and classifiable (Richardson et al., 1965) has led to the use of more standardised interview tactics, especially where the same or similar information is required from each interviewee (Fowler and Mangione, 1990; Gorden, 1987).

Table 6.2 Structuring criteria

Highly structured	Criteria	Highly unstructured
High	Topic control	Low
Fixed wording	Question content	Variable wording
Closed	Question type	Open
Fixed	Number of questions	Variable
Fixed	Sequence of questions	Variable
Fixed	Probes	Variable
Fixed	Response alternatives	Variable
Extensive	Interviewer training	Absent

However, it should be noted that not all interviews conducted within a single study need of necessity to be standardised (Gorden, 1987). One such case may include interviews conducted in the early exploratory stages of research where the interviewer's purpose is to clarify further the research domain and to elucidate any major areas or constructs which may require a more precise treatment, possibly by means of a more standardised approach in the later stages (Fowler and Mangione, 1990; Richardson *et al.*, 1965). The temptation to judge either highly structured or unstructured interviews as superior is, once again, not an absolute decision but must be related to purpose.

The degree of scheduling

The degree to which standardised interviews are characterised by structure is dependent to a large extent on whether an interview schedule is employed or not. In the case of highly scheduled standardised interviews the interviewer is totally straitjacketed by the introduction of a schedule which seeks to specify exactly what topics will be included, their sequence of coverage, the main and secondary questions and the precise nature of the response alternatives. This degree of standardisation is reminiscent of the procedures adopted in the administration of many psychological tests. In the sense that both 'tests' and interview are predominantly carrying out a measurement function such similarities may not be too surprising (Dijkstra *et al.*, 1985). However, there are varying degrees of scheduling (Gorden, 1987; Stewart and Cash, 1988). For example, Stewart and Cash (1988, p.47) describe highly scheduled interviews as containing:

> all the questions to be asked and the exact wording to be used with each interviewee, allowing no unplanned probing or deviation from the schedule.

Nonscheduled interviews tend to be much less defined and, indeed, may simply be a list of topics or subtopics.

Therefore, although the collecting of similar information may be the objective, the interviewer may adapt to the respondent by employing a greater variety of questions posed in varying, more natural sequences which are more dependent upon the characteristics of each individual respondent. For example, within the medical context, Fowler and Mangione (1990, p.17) state that:

> While the physician may start out with the same protocol for all patients, he or she will also feel free to digress and explore idiosyncratic avenues of inquiry if answers given by respondents seem to warrant it.

Furthermore, it has been argued that presenting questions to different persons using the same words may not automatically imply that each individual attributes the same meaning to the question (Dillon, 1990; Hetherington, 1970; Mishler, 1986; Richardson *et al.*, 1965). This led Richardson *et al.* (1965, p.45) to summarise the position by observing that:

> the schedule standardized interviewer asks the same question of each respondent and hopes this will have the same meaning, whereas the non-schedule interviewer formulates the classes of information he is seeking and hopes he can formulate the questions in such a way that they will have the same meaning for each respondent.

The idea of attempting to formulate standardised questions which can be presented to interviewees has been described as 'unrealistic' (Brenner, 1985a) and strongly criticised by Mishler (1986, p.21) who asserts that the outcome of his review:

> makes it clear that the idea of a standard stimulus is chimerical and that the quest for 'equivalence of interviews in terms of interviewer–respondent interaction' is misdirected and bound to fail.

While to some extent concurring with the view that the construction of questions that always have the same meaning for all potential interviewees is an unlikely outcome, Fowler and Mangione (1990) and Brenner (1985a) argue strongly for rigorous pretesting of 'items' coupled with a thorough training of interviewers both in adhering to the standardised procedures and in the deployment of non-directive probing techniques whenever appropriate.

Interestingly, the history of (employment) interviewing also tends to illustrate this continuum where the recent trends are away from the rather unsystematic biographical approaches (Wicks, 1982) towards much more structured schedules based on detailed job analyses, critical incident analyses, the generation of job-relevant questions and scenarios, and the provision of rated response alternatives (Eder and Ferris, 1989).

It would, however, be unfair to suggest that the field of selection interviewing has only recently become aware of the value and importance of employing more structured interviewing tactics. In Britain, two of the most influential selection and/or vocational guidance interviewing guides are the Seven Point Plan (Rodger, 1970) and the Five Fold Framework (Munro Fraser, 1971). The influence of both, particularly the former, is still evident today (Rawling, 1985; Wicks, 1982). In an unpublished survey of 120 careers officers, undertaken in the early 1980s, we found that just over one third made exclusive use of the Seven Point Plan in their careers guidance interviews with a further one third being directed by an *aide-mémoire*, which bore a striking resemblance, at a 'headings' level, to Rodger's (1970) 'Plan'. None made use of Munro Fraser's (1971) Five Fold Framework. Both plans were introduced basically to assist interviewers who employed a biographical type approach, usually in a rather unsystematic and undisciplined manner (Wicks, 1982). The task of trying to collect and make sense of a wealth of life story and life history data without any means of ordering or prioritising the categories *known* to be relevant seemed to be in desperate need of an organising framework.

Interview content

A number of systems have been proposed covering a wide range of interview contexts and are summarised in Table 6.3. Rather than leaving interviewers to decide what to include within the purview of their interviews, each proposal

Table 6.3 Topics specified in interview guides/plans

Rodger 1970	Rawling 1985	Munro Fraser 1971	Munro Fraser 1971	Hetherington 1970	Beggs et al. 1970
Selection/ guidance	Selection	Five Fold	Bio-graphical	Clinical	Medical
Physical make-up	Physical characteristics	Impact on others		Attitude to illness	History of present complaint Previous medical history
Attainments	Attainments	Qualifications	School life Further education and specialist training		
General intelligence	General intelligence	Innate abilities			
Special aptitudes	Special aptitudes				
Disposition	Personality	Adjustment or emotional balance		Relating to others Attitude to past and future	
Interests	Interests (Motivation)	Motivation	Spare-time life	Interests, likes and dislikes	
Circum-stances	Circum-stances		Home and family background in childhood Work history Service life Present circum-stances		Social history Family history

attempts to focus attention on aspects of interviewees which have been found to be highly relevant within each specific context. Rodger (1970, p.5) describes his Seven Point Plan as:

> a short-list of 'influences' (or 'conditions' or 'determinants') which, in our personnel selection and vocational guidance activities particularly, we shall neglect at our peril, because thorough enquiry has shown them to be the most generally important.

Biographical life histories can also be managed more adequately by considering them as comprising a number of phases. For example, Munro Fraser (1971) suggests that most individuals' lives can be covered satisfactorily by seven categories whereas Wicks (1982) suggests just four (Table 6.3). In particular situations, the general life history categories may fail to ensure that the interviewer focuses on relevant topics within each of the broad phases of life identified by Munro Fraser (1971) or Wicks (1982) simply because the biographical perspective excludes nothing. However, by focusing the discussion on particular points within a person's phases of life, such as discontinuities and transitions or high and low times, the interviewer may, as Munro Fraser (1971) advocates, utilise this wealth of data to formulate an assessment of the interviewee along a specified number of individual attributes. His Five Fold Framework, derived from life history data, purports to represent interviewees in terms of five general graded measures, assumed to be normally distributed and labelled: Motivation, Impact on Others, Qualifications, Innate Abilities and Adjustment or Emotional Balance (Table 6.3).

As indicated above, Rodger's (1970) occupational research suggested that a seven category system would more adequately accommodate significant individual attributes (labelled: Physical Make-up, Attainments, General Intelligence, Special Aptitudes, Interests and Disposition) and the circumstances in which these mainly psychological characteristics develop. Interviewers, making use of this system, are required to focus their attention on the assessment of each individual on each of the seven dimensions, each of which is further defined by means of a number of supplementary questions affording greater prescription and clarification for the interviewer.

It will be evident that the employment of these plans will impose some degree of structure on the interviewing process by specifying those categories of information high in contextual relevance rather than by stating the actual questions to be asked (Hetherington, 1970). With respect to life story interviewing, Tagg (1985) cites strategies which help focus attention on specific aspects of the 'story' relevant to the research in question. For example, surveys of social mobility have employed 'Life-History Charts', on which, Tagg (1985, p.171) notes, the interviewer documents:

full details of a respondent's occupational history from his first full time employment to date and, in conjunction with this, further details of changes in the composition of his family and household over the same time span.

In the same chapter, Tagg (1985) cites another type of life story grid on which information is arranged in a temporal sequence under four major headings of migrational, occupational, educational and family history. Ultimately, the goal is to assimilate a similar array of information about each interviewee such that an effective selection decision can be made, informed vocational guidance can be offered or an accurate clinical diagnosis agreed. In this sense these systems serve to standardise the process but do so in a very unstructured or nonscheduled way. Procedural issues relating to topic sequence, question types, question sequence, number of questions and response alternatives are left entirely to the discretion of the interviewer who, as a consequence, possesses a substantial amount of flexibility. This can be extremely important from the interviewee's perspective, where a more personalised made-to-measure interview can exert strong motivational forces on individual interviewees (Hetherington, 1970) and, furthermore, may be absolutely essential where, for instance, interviewees suffer from failing memory (Gorden, 1987).

The important point is that interviewers must be thoroughly knowledgeable about what information is needed from each interviewee rather than how it will be collected (Hodgson, 1987; Richardson et al., 1965).

Of course, systems such as the Seven Point Plan can be utilised as if they were extremely prescriptive, highly structured schedules – this, however, would seem to be more of an abuse than a use. Therefore, what these frameworks offer is a relatively simple, flexible yet *systematic* coverage of areas high in *relevance* for selection, appraisal, careers or clinical interviewers.

When interviewers are left to their own devices it would appear that they tend to express little agreement concerning the importance of specific content areas nor do they include adequate topic coverage of those factors that they do regard as important (Taylor and Sniezek, 1984). In a study of vocational guidance interviewing by careers officers, Reddy and Brannigan (1980) identified relatively rigid patterns of content coverage with a number of the sample consistently failing to include certain categories (e.g. health). Apart from interviewer embarrassment or reluctance to invade the interviewee's privacy, Taylor and Sniezek (1984) further suggested that noncoverage may be related to the degree of task complexity. Recruiters were simply unable within the time available to sample all prescribed areas adequately – some had to be briefly covered or omitted entirely in order to complete the overall task.

Where to start?

As indicated above, these systems do not prescribe the sequence in which the categories are to be covered. Interviewers will, therefore, need to decide where to start the data collection process with each individual interviewee. There are, naturally, no hard and fast rules concerning this issue. However, it seems plausible to assume that in order to generate a climate where the client is encouraged to self-disclose as early as possible in the interview it may be conducive to begin with categories that are most familiar to interviewees, such as previous job experience or interests. Such a topic area as interests is not only familiar to most interviewees but also tends to be an area of achievement and carries with it less personal threat. Interviewees are less likely to develop defensive postures given such a start. Furthermore, Banaka (1971, p.10), when discussing relational issues, notes that:

> An initially unfavorable impression may be changed when one finds that he and the other share a strong interest in some activity.

Topic sequence

The sequence of topics that follows is then solely determined by the interviewee's prior contributions – that is, structure is an interviewee-determined feature of such interviews. Kline (1975) conveys the theme when he suggests that by skilful interviewing we can ultimately include all the topic areas over the course of an interview where the sequence is determined by careful attention to client responses rather than by adherence to any rigid, predetermined interviewer schedule of topics.

The appropriateness of the sequencing of topics may also make a substantial contribution to interviewee perceived relevance. For example, McHenry (1981, p.7) recommends two plans that can be used to sequence selection interview topics to optimise relevance:

> If the candidate is young and has a short job history it is best to work chronologically *forward* during the interview, starting at his or her school career and working up to the job held at present. Otherwise, it is preferable to work chronologically *backwards*. Older candidates often fail to see the relevance of anything but their present job to the job to be filled.

The use of such 'chronological sequencing' (Stewart and Cash, 1988) serves to impose minimal structure on the interview in an attempt to increase relevance and interviewee motivation. The ground will be covered in a manner partly dependent on the amount of participation and on the specific content preferences brought to the interview by the interviewee. However, the style in which this journey is undertaken may fall anywhere along the directive–nondirective dimension previously discussed. It does, however, seem reasonable to assume that interviewees will enter interviews having decided to (at least initially) make certain contributions or to seek answers to predetermined questions – interviewers who deny them the opportunity to make those contributions or decline to respond to their questions (even unintentionally) are likely to generate high levels of frustration, considerable irritation and be less effective (Hodgson, 1987).

The plans above represent the relatively nonscheduled end of the structural continuum but are distinctly more structured than a completely *laissez-faire* approach. Indeed according to Goodale (1989) very few selection interviewers, nowadays, employ a completely unstructured approach; those who do, he claims, are doomed to failure. Schuler and Funke (1989) advocate a rather more multi-modal approach to the task of selection interviewing.

THE ISSUE OF VALIDITY

One further issue is raised which relates to the criterion of validity. For instance, in vocational guidance and selection the Seven Point Plan is not simply an interview plan but, in the words of Rodger (1970, p.3):

> It aims at providing us with a simple but scientifically-defensible assessment 'system'.

Interviewers who find themselves in the position of having to compile an assessment of an individual's occupational strengths and weaknesses are encouraged by Rodger (1970) to employ whichever methods possess the best credentials for the job. Therefore, Rodger (1970), being greatly influenced by psychological thinking in the 1930s and 1940s, suggested that the 'points' pertaining to General Intelligence and Special Aptitudes would be more reliably and more validly measured by employing psychological tests. It will be recalled that the plan takes account of all three criteria relating to data collection – relevance, reliability and validity. To continue to strive to meet these laudable criteria it will always be necessary to attempt to keep up to date with advances in cognate areas. For example, Rawling (1985) in an update of Rodger's plan suggests that, in order to keep apace with current advances in, for example, the measurement of personality, a substantial revision of the original category termed 'Disposition' is called for, both to update the nature of the construct and to consider the relative merits of assessment by psychological questionnaires versus assessment by interview. In a similar vein, Herriot (1985, p.35) advocates that:

> What needs to be avoided is the use of the interview as a quasi-personality test with interview behaviour being used as evidence of personal characteristics.

Unfortunately, this seems to be precisely what graduate recruiters employ their interviews for (Anderson and Shackleton, 1990).

Structure and validity

Moving towards the more structured end of the continuum a number of approaches can be identified, particularly within the research context (Breakwell, 1990; Fowler and Mangione, 1990; Gorden, 1987; Richardson *et al.* 1965; Stewart and Cash, 1988) and, more recently, within the selection situation (Eder and Ferris, 1989). As Fowler and Mangione (1990, p.14) state, the goal of standardisation is that:

each respondent be exposed to the same question experience, and that the recording of answers be the same, too, so that any differences in answers can be correctly interpreted as reflecting differences between respondents rather than differences in the process that produced the answers.

The advantages of employing highly structured, scheduled interviews can be summarised as ensuring uniform topic coverage, precision and reliability of measurement (quantification), comparability across interviewees, replicability of data collection (consistency), less time-consumption and more interpretability (Breakwell, 1990; Fowler and Mangione, 1990; Gorden, 1987; Stewart and Cash, 1988). In situations which depend centrally on the measurement of constructs and consequent statistical analysis, the highly scheduled interview tends to be more suited than the less scheduled variety. As indicated above, the price paid for this standardisation is a reduction in the procedure's flexibility and adaptability, giving no space or opportunity for deviation, interviewer initiative or the development of new insights (Breakwell, 1990; Gorden, 1987; Stewart and Cash, 1988). The inflexibility is derived from the application of the structuring criteria (Table 6.2) which suggest that all aspects of the interview must be built into the schedule at the planning and/or piloting stages (Fowler and Mangione, 1990; Stewart and Cash, 1988). Given the fact that the research interview tends to be part of a set of ideally identical interviews, Stewart and Cash (1988) indicate that the most commonly employed research interview is the highly scheduled standardised variety. However, the reader is reminded that such levels of structuring may not always be an appropriate interviewing tactic to employ within the research context.

Earlier, it was suggested that during certain stages or types of research the inflexibility of the highly structured approach would limit rather than enhance data collection. Therefore, with certain interviewees flexibility would be essential (for example, those with poor memories) and/or, as Breakwell (1990, p.79) observes, when the objectives of the researcher are:

> to understand the meaning of what is said...it is done through immersing yourself in the data until you think like your respondents, you see the world as they do and find you understand them.

It will be evident that Breakwell's rationale could have been extracted straight from accounts of helping interviews, which themselves tend to be low in structure, rarely employing any form of scheduling (Benjamin, 1981; Egan, 1982). Once again, purpose assumes paramount importance in the determination of interview tactics.

The emphasis on the comparative measurement function inherent in many research contexts is transferable to the selection situation, where candidates are 'measured', compared to other candidates and a selection decision made. The importance of collecting data that are relevant, reliable and valid is of major concern to both the organisation and the applicant. A good deal of research has been conducted over the last decade in pursuit of higher levels of, in particular, predictive validity for the selection process as a whole, and specifically for the part played by the interview. Where selection decisions are based on data collected during the interview, the basic assumption being made suggests that how an interviewee behaves in the interview will, in large part, reflect the way he or she will behave if employed. Of course, how the interviewee behaves is very much influenced by how the interviewer behaves, especially in terms of what types of question are asked. It is in response to such questions that judgements are made regarding the interviewee's prospects for future work (Feild and Gatewood, 1989). In interviews where the interviewer has total responsibility for whatever is asked (often on the spur of the moment) in a rather unstructured manner, Feild and Gatewood (1989, p.146) caution that:

> The lack of systematic coverage of job-relevant information and the impact of nonjob-relevant factors on interviewer evaluations are two factors that appear to contribute to the low validity of the interview.

Again, of crucial significance is the ascertainment of what is relevant and what is not relevant to the specific purpose of job selection. Current research suggests that a key component is the determination of relevant, job-related interview content, derived from a thorough job analysis (Breakwell, 1990; Eder and Ferris, 1989). The structuring of actual interview content follows by establishing those particular behaviours that distinguish effective from ineffective performance (that is, critical incidents) and then converting these incidents into a number of selected job questions, scenarios or situations. In the resultant situational interview (Latham, 1989) interviewees are presented with a number of 'standard' situations and are asked what they would do if they were in the predicament. In this sense, from the interviewee's perspective, the situations are hypothetical but from the interviewer's viewpoint they are highly representative of real occupational situations. Once presented with the situation, interviewees are required to make a response which reflects their intention to behave (Latham, 1989). Evidence suggests that where interviewers are left to decide, entirely by themselves, how to judge the calibre of interviewee responses, then the situational interview fares no better than other interview techniques (Latham, 1989). The structuring of situational interviews, therefore, extends beyond interview question content to the provision of a scoring guide which enables interviewers to rate interviewee responses (Janz, 1989). Latham (1989, p.179) summarises the key features of this highly structured approach to selection interviewing when he writes that:

> the questions are based on a job analysis and are hence job-related, the questions are sufficiently abstruse that applicants cannot determine the desired answer, and hence must state their true intentions, the interviewers have a scoring guide for each item, and the predictors and the criteria are similar so that one is using 'apples to predict apples rather than oranges'.

The outcomes of this highly structured approach seem to be fairly significant increases in both reliability and validity (Wiesner and Cronshaw, 1988; Wright *et al.*, 1989). Latham (1989) quotes internal reliability coefficients ranging from 0.61–0.78, inter-observer coefficients of 0.76–0.96 and predictive validity values of 0.14–0.45.

Although alternative means of structuring the job-related interview content have been developed (Feild and Gatewood, 1989; Janz, 1989) these methods are fundamentally based on similar principles. For example, Janz (1989) questions the use of hypothetical job-related content and argues for a more historical, experientially based structure, while Feild and Gatewood (1989) suggest a more adequate coverage of the critical knowledge, skills and attitudes required for effective job performance. Both structures are, however, derived from the isolation of critical incidents which define the specific demands of the job in question. The need to generate unique job-related content for each occupation is implicit in the principles elucidated and is seen as essential for effective prediction. Nonetheless, the degree of structuring is very high and the opportunity for the interviewer to respond to the interviewee by varying the questions and by introducing a variety of secondary probes is severely restricted. Any such freedom would, of course, serve to reduce the structuring and create the opportunity for interviewer biases to encroach into the decision-making process.

As a result of the high degree of structuring, interviewers are focused on only relevant content, are required to sample this content in highly prescribed ways and, with respect to situational interviews, are provided with a means of scoring interviewee responses. This sounds rather like the administration of an oral psychological test with its highly standardised characteristics. For this reason Goodale (1989, p.320) observes that:

> highly structured interviews can appear to the applicant a bit like an interrogation, and may place too much emphasis on the *selection* objective at the expense of the *attraction* objective.

This rigid standardisation with its focus on task completion tends to subordinate the importance of the interpersonal relationship aspect between interviewer and interviewee. Indeed, Fowler and Mangione (1990, p.34) suggest that one of the major reasons for research interviewers not adhering to strict interviewing schedules is their attempt to reduce the formality of the situation by personalising some of the questions. The senior author has certainly experienced the very strong urges to personalise the administration of psychological tests in the face of stiff opposition urging him to maintain standardisation. Arguing very strongly, Brenner (1985a, p.17) advocates that:

> The interviewer's role cannot possibly be restricted to its quite rigid measurement aspects, as interviewer–respondent interaction is social interaction nevertheless....Thus, the interviewer's role, while necessitating the precise

command of a fairly complex repertoire of interviewing techniques, does not include impersonality of performance.

Interviewers are again reminded of the importance not only of getting the job done, but of doing so in as personable and humane a manner as possible within the constraints of the interviewing context. Interviewing is not a mechanised set of activities but is clearly perceived as a social encounter by both participants.

SUMMARY

This chapter has outlined a number of potential interview tactics that illustrated the structured–unstructured dimension. It has emphasised that decisions relating to the degree of structure or scheduling can only be made with reference to the purpose for which the interview is to be employed. When employed appropriately, structure has been shown to ensure the relevance of and improve the calibre of the information collected, especially where measurement is required, primarily in research and selection contexts. However, a number of specific circumstances were cited which warranted the employment of tactics low in structuring, where flexibility and adaptability were essential if the purpose of the interview was to be realised (Schuler and Funke, 1989).

Readers will recall that, in addition to interviewer tactics, interviewer techniques were also identified by Gorden (1987) as substantial contributors to effective interviewing. It is to this topic that we now turn in chapter seven.

Chapter 7

Social skills and interviewing

Many definitions of what has been termed social or interpersonal skill have been offered in the communication literature. The definition adopted in this text is that 'a social skill is a set of goal-directed, inter-related situationally appropriate social behaviours, which can be learned and which are under the control of the individual' (Hargie, 1986, p.12). This definition provides a skeleton for the identification of actual ways of responding which might be considered skilled in any professional context. However, as the definition states, skills are situation-specific and consequently the skilled interviewer must be alert to the effects of his behaviour in professional settings and with different interviewees. In an interviewing context, skills are purposeful and synchronised ways of responding in an interview in order to achieve the aims of the interview. The novice interviewer must learn these skills and use them in a flexible and adaptive manner in response to the demands of the interview situation.

Skilled behaviour may be verbal or nonverbal in nature (Hargie *et al.*, 1987). Verbal behaviour refers to the actual words or language used by the interviewer. Nonverbal behaviour refers to both the way in which speech is used (the intona-tion, volume, pitch, accent and so on) and the various visual cues of facial expression, eye-contact, posture, orientation, proximity, touch and general appearance. Both aspects of behaviour will be addressed in this chapter in relation to a number of skill areas.

As Brenner (1985b) notes, it is important for interviewers to be continuously monitoring whether their actions are effective in achieving their goals. If initial behaviour is ineffective the interviewer may then select alternative ways of responding. This chapter is designed to alert interviewers to a variety of ways of responding, which might enable them to be more flexible in dealing with pro-fessional situations. For example, most interviewers seem to believe that their main means of acquiring information is to ask questions. There are, however, many ways of responding in order to encourage the interviewee to give informa-tion such as responding approvingly to what has been said, pausing briefly after the interviewee has spoken, paraphrasing the interviewee's comments or indeed giving an opinion of an issue and inviting a response. Each of these methods might be used in appropriate circumstances to provide a break from the 'interrogation' of constant questioning.

It is useful to be aware of when these skills might be appropriate and what effect their use might have on the interview process. Appropriateness will depend upon many factors, including the stage which the interview has reached. Skills will be discussed in relation to four processes in interviewing, namely: opening the interview, obtaining information, giving information and closing the interview.

The ideas presented represent a synopsis of the material available in the research literature on interpersonal communication in general and interviewing in the specific contexts of counselling, health professional/client communication, appraisal, selection and research interviewing. This represents, therefore, a sample of what is available in the relevant literature and the interested reader may then follow up these sources. A final section of the chapter will discuss interviewer training and possible ways in which interviewers might develop their skill in interviewing.

THE OPENING OF AN INTERVIEW

It is commonly known that 'first impressions last'. This would seem to be true of perceptions of both the participants in an encounter and the nature of the situation. For example, once individuals have formed an overall evaluation of another person, it is usually difficult to alter that impression (Wyer and Srull, 1986). Such impressions can have an impact upon how people behave in interviews and how they react to others. Often an interviewee or interviewer who perceives a situation as threatening will find it difficult to settle into the interview and hence the entire interview can be influenced by a nervous beginning. We frequently form images concerning the nature of the situation and what will be expected to follow during the first few moments of an encounter (Stewart and Cash, 1988). Therefore, the interviewer's aim at this stage in the interview process would be to form with the interviewee a constructive, realistic and agreed image of how the interview will unfold and how the participants are expected to behave.

Setting the scene

Interviewees may have formed impressions concerning how they imagine the interview will be conducted and how both participants will behave. These expectations will be based directly upon prior experience and indirectly gained knowledge such as that acquired from others who are experienced in the setting, from reading or from television. For example, an interviewee for an appraisal interview may perceive this as a threatening situation in which the interviewer will be judging his performance and trying to find faults with his work. He will consequently be rather reluctant to discuss aspects of work which he finds difficult. Such perceptions and actions are detrimental to the achievement of the aims of this interview which are to improve employee performance by discussing areas of strength and weakness (Lawson, 1989). Therefore, the interviewer would be wishing to influence the interviewee's mental image of this situation. As mentioned earlier the first few minutes of an interview are the most important since what the interviewer does and says at this juncture can set the tone for the interview. During the initial few minutes of an interview the client will be searching for cues or indicators which will either confirm or alter his expectations, and which will signal how to behave, how to relate to the interviewer, what to say and what not to say. The interviewer, therefore, will have some opportunity to help to create constructive and realistic expectations. However, the expectations which people hold tend to act as a filter for information gathered throughout an interview.

Perceptual scene setting

This involves the interviewer's attempts to manipulate the environment so that favourable and constructive first impressions are created. The interviewer in a counselling setting might elect to organise the environment in order to create an atmosphere of privacy and warmth. Hence, a quiet private room would be selected and the switchboard instructed to intercept incoming calls. Soft armchairs and a coffee table could replace the more usual office furniture of desks and upright seating. In this way the environment could be designed in order to facilitate discussion of sensitive issues. Similarly, there is scope for making some attempt to influence the interviewee's impressions of the interviewer by adapting style of dress, and by making the initial appearance friendly and welcoming, as opposed to greeting the client while talking on the phone or reading notes.

Social scene setting

The interviewee's social set, or perception of the relationship which is established between the participants, may also be influenced by interviewer behaviour during these opening stages. Hargie *et al.* (1987) highlight the importance of such factors as the way in which the client is greeted, the use of 'small talk' or comments which are not directly related to the task. Further strategies might include attempts to ensure that the client's physical needs are met. Thus the interviewer would check if the interviewee is too hot or cold, or might offer coffee or other refreshments. In employing such measures the interviewer provides feedback concerning the preferred style of relationship, the degree of friendliness or level of formality. Taking time to focus upon the social aspect of the interview would seem to be important for the achievement of professional goals. In the context of research, the interviewer is required to maintain some distance from the respondents in order to ensure the objective and unbiased collection of data. However, even in this setting, it has been argued that it is necessary to establish rapport with the respondent in order to obtain truthful and sensitive information (Oakley, 1981). An interviewee who has been warmly treated in the initial stages of the interview will be more relaxed and hence more willing to supply necessary information. This point is also underlined within the context of medical interviews by Shuy (1983, p.200) who suggests that:

> The medical interview can be cold and frightening to a patient. If the goal of the physician is to make the patient comfortable, a bit of personal but interested and relevant chitchat, whatever the cost in precious time, is advisable.

This stage of social opening further provides an opportunity for the interviewee to orientate herself to the interview situation. It provides a bridge between the outside world of conversation and nonprofessional relationships, and the world of the interview with its different roles and rules of behaviour.

Factual scene setting

A further factor which affects the smooth operation and achievement of interviewer goals is the client's understanding of the purpose and likely content of the interview. Stewart and Cash (1988) refer to this procedure as 'orientation' of the interviewee and suggest that, in addition to the purpose of the interview, the interviewer might also mention at this stage the likely structure, nature of the content and time available for the interview. However, there can be a mismatch between how the interviewer and interviewee construe the nature of the interview. Taking the appraisal interview as an example, Hewton (1988) notes there would seem to be two main underlying philosophies which might direct the course of this type of interview. One of the philosophies would stress professional development, identification of individual needs and be concerned with job satisfaction. The second philosophy would place greater emphasis upon accountability, on the identification of unsatisfactory employees, on checking and assessing work performance. The employee may regard the situation as a threatening attempt to identify weaknesses in his performance, with a view to disadvantaging him. The employer, on the other hand, may subscribe to the former philosophy of staff development. Clearly such differing understandings of the interview purpose will have detrimental effects upon the operation of the interview. Hence the interviewer may wish to influence the interviewee's understanding of the situation.

This might be achieved through a number of interviewer actions. For example, the interviewer could review previous information in order to place the interview in context. In a research interview the interviewer might make the following opening remarks, 'As you will remember, we wrote to you to thank you for agreeing to. take part in this research study and to arrange today's meeting to collect some information on attitude to diet.'

Similarly, the interviewer in an employment interview could remind the interviewee of the procedures adopted prior to this stage to select candidates for interview. Doctors will frequently remind patients of the preceding examinations or treatment before continuing with their consultation. Additionally, the interviewer may wish to ascertain the extent of an interviewee's knowledge. For example the interviewer might ask whether the interviewee is familiar with the company's procedure for interviewing job candidates. Such measures allow the interviewee to place the interview in context and to recall important information which may help in understanding the current proceedings.

A further strategy in determining how the client will understand the interview involves ascertaining the client's expectations. It is interviewees who will bring to the interview issues which they wish to have discussed or action which they wish to see executed. These issues need to be identified, so that unrealistic or in-appropriate expectations can be dealt with and legitimate concerns can be included on the agenda for the interview. Failure to identify the interviewee's expectations can have damaging consequences for the smooth operation of the interview. As Hargie *et al.* (1987, p.123) point out:

> If the expectations of individuals are not clearly ascertained initially, the conversation may proceed for some time before these become explicit. In some instances this can cause frustration, embarrassment or even anger, where people feel their time has been wasted. It can also result in the discussion proceeding at dual purposes, and even terminating, with both parties reading the situation along different lines.

This feature of the opening stage should be particularly appropriate in appraisal interviews where the interviewee would be encouraged to raise issues or draw attention to pertinent information to aid the assessment process (Lawson, 1989). In the research interview this technique may be less appropriate. The interviewer may or may not ascertain the interviewee's expectations since it is commonly understood by subjects that the research interview is for the benefit of researchers and therefore is geared to meet their needs. However, in researching particularly sensitive issues such as domestic violence it may be necessary to determine whether the interviewee wishes a summary of data collected and/or the oppor-tunity to have deleted from records any information regarded by the subject as too personal for inclusion in the study. Finally, the interviewer may wish to state explicitly the agreed goals of the interview.

Ensuring that both parties are aware of and in agreement with the aims and structure of the interview should promote the smooth operation of the interview and cooperative working towards the achievement of the set goals.

Although a number of possible interviewer actions have been outlined not all of these would be necessary in every interview and certain elements would assume greater importance in particular types of interview. For example, it would be inappropriate in the counselling context for the interviewer to outline the likely content of the interview since this is usually determined by the client's needs. In this situation the process of building a relationship with the client is likely to assume greater importance.

OBTAINING INFORMATION

As noted in chapter five, interviews invariably involve an attempt to obtain information from interviewees. This is not always a simple task. Interviewees may be unresponsive for a variety of reasons including a natural shyness in social situations, a reticence to give the information requested or lack of experience in interviews resulting in nervousness. This can cause problems in obtaining a sufficient volume of information from interviewees. A somewhat different problem occurs where the interviewee is overly talkative and there is a resultant problem of controlling the interaction, keeping to a discussion of relevant issues and preventing unnecessary rambling. A final problem involves ineffective listening by the interviewer to the information expressed by the interviewee. In such a situation the relevant information has been covered during the interview, but the interviewer has not listened and therefore will have missed useful information. Each of these problems will be examined in this chapter. The skill areas which will be outlined in connection with the goal of obtaining information are questioning, reinforcement, reflecting and listening.

Questioning

One of the most obvious ways to obtain information is to ask questions. However, as Benjamin (1981) points out, this can be a deceptively simple skill and is often used ineffectively. His description of our practice in interviewing will be particularly familiar to those working in interview training, when he suggests that:

> we ask too many questions, often meaningless ones. We ask questions that confuse the interviewee, that interrupt him. We ask questions the interviewee cannot possibly answer. We even ask questions we don't want the answers to, and, consequently, we do not hear the answers when forthcoming.
>
> (Benjamin, 1981, p.71)

Benjamin notes that there are various types of question which serve different functions in interviewing. It is therefore important for interviewers to be aware of these types and their role in different interview contexts. As noted earlier the interviewer faces a number of problems including how to prevent discussion of irrelevant information and how to provide sufficient freedom in the interview to allow the interviewee to give relevant but unpredicted information. In an attempt to restrict rambling the interviewer may fall into the trap of exerting too much control in the interview and hence preventing highly significant information from emerging. The interviewer's choice of question types will, in conjunction with other skilled responses, help to determine the degree of interviewer restriction of interviewee responses at any stage in the interview. The question types available range in degree of restriction of topic choice from leading questions, which attempt to determine both the choice of topic and the response made by the interviewee; through closed questions, which nominate the topic but have a limited range of possible responses; to open questions which place less restriction upon the topic and permit greater freedom in possible responses; and to a final question type, probing questions, which encourage further expansion of an interviewee response and therefore give interviewees most freedom to continue with their own selected topic.

Leading questions

Leading questions are phrased in such a way that the interviewer is suggesting implicitly or explicitly the expected or desired answer (Stewart and Cash, 1988). For example, a doctor might ask: 'Don't you think you should give up smoking?' The wording of the question suggests that agreement is desired. The use of such questions is beneficial at times. For example, they are frequently used when interviewers wish to exert control over the length of client responses. They may wish to do this for a variety of reasons. In an appraisal interview the interviewer may wish to pass quickly over certain unproblematic areas of an employee's work performance, in order to move on to more substantive issues such as areas to be highlighted for notable achievement or deficiency in practice. In such cases, the interviewer might ask leading questions such as: 'Well, we're both happy with your progress in maintaining current customer sales, aren't we John?' or 'Don't you agree that there is no need to discuss this area of your work?' Following a limited interviewee response, the interviewer can move on to enquire about the employee's progress in attracting new customers.

Likewise, leading questions may be usefully employed to restrict further discussion of a topic which the interviewer considers to have been explored fully. Hence in an employment interview, the interviewer can use leading questions in order to draw to a close discussion of the candidate's outside interests which has ceased to provide useful information on personality. They might ask: 'So your interests would be mainly in sport?' Such a question allows the interviewer to regain control of the interview and also enables the interviewer to check on the accuracy of information received.

There are, however, a number of disadvantages in using questions which tightly predict a particular response from the interviewee. As French (1983) points out, the use of leading questions can often lead to patients giving the expected rather than accurate answers to questions asked by practitioners. The use of such questions in the medical context where diagnosis depends upon accurate information is, therefore, actively discouraged. In research interviews, where again accuracy of information is of paramount importance, interviewers are strongly discouraged from using leading questions (Brenner, 1985a). Furthermore, the use of a number of leading questions which inaccurately predict the client's responses may lead to considerable frustration on the part of the interviewee, who must then, in effect, continually disagree with the interviewer in order to correct misperceptions (Hargie et al., 1987).

Closed questions

Closed questions are 'restrictive in nature and may supply possible answers' (Stewart and Cash, 1988, p.60). Because closed questions tend to restrict interviewee responses, they can be fruitfully employed in a number of circumstances where such restriction is desirable. For example, they can be very useful in research interviews where the information desired is frequently factual, where responses must be limited to facilitate rapid coding and analysis, and where time is limited. Questions would be formulated prior to the interview and designed to be closed and restricting in nature. Hargie *et al.* (1987) highlight three types of closed question which they label: yes/no, identification and selection questions. In a survey of the smoking habits of a workforce all three types of closed question might be used. Hence employees might be asked 'Do you smoke cigarettes while at work?' (yes/no question), 'What is your job title?' (identification question) and 'Do you smoke a high/medium/low tar brand of cigarettes?' (selection question). Closed questions are therefore useful in identifying factual information required by the interviewer, when time is limited or when the interviewer wishes to limit interviewee responses. In this way overly talkative interviewees can be controlled more tightly and large quantities of specifically requested information collected quickly. However, the interviewer would not always wish to control an interview so tightly. For example, in counselling the interviewer may find that they have actually prevented rather than facilitated exploration of a client's problem through the use of closed questioning (Nelson-Jones, 1983).

Open questions

As highlighted in the previous paragraph it is not always desirable to restrict clients' responses too tightly. In counselling this may lead to a lack of progress in exploring a client's problem from the client's perspective. Further disadvantages might be noted in selection interviews, where valuable information for assessing clients may remain untapped simply because the interviewer's use of closed questions prevented the interviewee from introducing relevant information. It is therefore beneficial for the interviewer to be aware of the need for open questions and to develop skill in formulating and posing such questions. Stewart and Cash, 1988, p.59) describe open questions as:

> broad, often specifying only a general topic, and they allow the respondent considerable freedom in determining the amount and kind of information to give.

Examples of open questions include 'What aspects of your work would you like to see developed?' (appraisal context), 'How have you been feeling lately?' (medical/counselling context), 'What qualities do you feel are necessary in this type of work?' (selection context). Each of these questions attempts to provide freedom for the respondent in answering and therefore is useful in providing information concerning the respondents' thoughts, attitudes or feelings.

Responses can then be used for assessment purposes or to allow interviewees to raise issues which are of concern to them. Careful planning of questions to enable topics to be expressed openly is recommended in the context of selection and appraisal interviews (Dillon, 1990). It would also seem to be important in medical and counselling contexts to develop the ability to ask questions in an open and unrestricting manner.

Probing questions

A final area of interest for interviewers in using questioning to obtain information is the ability to ask a respondent to give further information on a response which they have made. For example, in the selection context an interviewee might mention a feeling of dissatisfaction in relation to some aspect of her previous work experience. In such a case the interviewer may wish to follow up or probe further this response to identify relevant information concerning the candidate's suitability for the post. In this case the goal is to remain with the topic identified by the interviewee by asking a probing question. Hargie *et al.* (1987, pp.77–8) suggest that probing questions are:

> designed to encourage respondents to expand upon initial responses, and in this sense they are 'follow-up' questions.

Examples would include 'In what way were you dissatisfied?' (clarification probe) or 'Can you tell me more about your dissatisfaction?' (extension probe). Development of the ability to probe further the responses offered by interviewees is of importance for interviewers. Fowler and Mangione (1990) note that this is one of the most difficult tasks for interviewers and that it requires time in training to develop this ability. Novice interviewers often find that they have obtained a wealth of superficial information because they have failed to explore interviewee responses in any depth. In training interviewers, the authors have witnessed many trainees who fail to follow up interviewee responses, often accepting vague, indeterminate and superficial answers to questions. However, interviewers should be cautious in their use of probing questions and be prepared to 'back off' if the interviewee becomes upset or considers the questions inappropriate or too interrogative.

To summarise, the skill of questioning is often ineffectively used in interviewing. Benjamin (1981) presents some interesting guidelines concerning questioning for helping interviews which may be useful in all interview contexts. He suggests that interviewers should:

1. become aware of the fact that we are asking questions. (Interviewers often do not realise that they are overusing questions.)
2. challenge the questions we are about to ask and weigh carefully the desirability and necessity of asking them.
3. examine the various sorts of questions available to us and assess the appropriateness of the type of question used.
4. consider the applicability of alternative responses to questioning.

It may be that, in reflecting upon these guidelines before questioning, the interviewer might use this skill more judiciously and effectively. In the sections which follow, alternatives to the use of questioning are explored.

Reinforcement

The use of a number of 'social reinforcement' techniques represents an alternative to interviewer use of questioning to obtain information (Hargie *et al.*, 1987). Here, rather than leading interviewees to give information by questioning, they are either encouraged or discouraged to elaborate on their responses by the ways in which the interviewer reacts to their comments. Many verbal and nonverbal interviewer responses have been identified as having either a positive or negative effect upon interviewee responses, and an awareness of the effects of such behaviours will help interviewers to control contributions from the interviewee. It is recognised that the response must be appropriate to the particular client, so that, for example, in an appraisal interview while the use of phrases such as 'well done' or 'you're coming on well' might be appropriate for some interviewees, other more senior members of staff may regard them as patronising. However, while reinforcement should be specific to the context and person being interviewed, some general areas of behaviour are more likely to have positive or negative effects.

Certain nonverbal behaviours tend to encourage or discourage interviewee responses. Ivey (1983) uses the term 'attending behaviour' to incorporate elements such as maintaining eye contact with the speaker, a forward trunk lean, attentive facial display, mirroring the expression of the speaker and using facilitative, encouraging gestures. Verbal behaviour which encourages interviewee responses includes 'minimal encouragers' (Ivey, 1983) such as 'mm hmm'; 'yes'; 'I see'. These responses indicate that the interviewer is attending to the interviewee yet are sufficiently brief to avoid interrupting the interviewee and taking control of the talk. As Hargie *et al.* (1987) point out, these phrases form the minimum of encouragement necessary to indicate attention and they therefore list additional categories of response which are more potent reinforcers. These include statements which indicate praise, encouragement or support for the interviewee's statement or actions. Examples include 'That's a most interesting comment', 'You seem to have coped admirably with that crisis', 'A very good point'. In most interviewing circumstances reinforcement is very important. In appraisal interviews, where the interviewer wants to acknowledge the interviewee's achievements, giving praise is particularly pleasant (Hodgson, 1987). In other contexts, however, such signs of approval may be inappropriate. For example, in research interviews, Brenner (1985a), while recognising the importance of showing interest to ensure respondents' full participation, nevertheless warns interviewers against displaying signs of approval or disapproval which may bias the respondents' answers to questions.

The criticism has been made that interviewers overuse questioning so that interviews seem to resemble interrogations and interviewees have little freedom to give information within the tight structure of interviewer questions. Using social reinforcement rather than questioning allows the interviewer to have an alternative way of responding. If the interviewee is discussing relevant information then she can be further encouraged to do so through the use of interviewer reinforcement. However, if the interviewee is beginning to ramble or to monopolise the choice of topic then the interviewer might attempt subtly to discourage such behaviour. This could be achieved by withdrawing encouraging nonverbal behaviour, that is, breaking eye contact or refraining from head nodding or smiling. Withdrawal of verbal reinforcement may also be effective in diminishing irrelevant interviewee responses. In this case, the interviewer would be purposefully discouraging interviewee talk. However, there are times when interviewers inadvertently block interviewee talk by the way in which they respond. For example, one of the authors can recall a careers counselling interview, where a young interviewee volunteered, rather excitedly, that she owned her own horse and had won a number of jumping competitions. In response the interviewer said, 'That's very interesting. Is there anything else that you do in your spare time?' The interviewee was completely 'crest-fallen'.

Nelson-Jones (1983) highlighted a number of 'blocking behaviours' which have the effect of discouraging clients from responding in counselling, wherein the counsellor may play too dominant a role in deciding what is talked about thereby denying the client the opportunity to discuss his 'own' issues and concerns. Hence counsellors are discouraged from overusing questions or from setting tight or unnegotiated agendas for the interview. Further blocking behaviours mentioned by Nelson-Jones (1983) include, 'reassuring or humouring the client' (e.g. preventing exploration of anxiety by telling the client that they 'will be all right'); 'inappropriately talking about yourself' (e.g. interviewer answering his own questions); and 'putting on a professional facade' (trying to convey the impression of being an expert and thereby communicating in a defensive or inauthentic way). Interviewers in contexts other than counselling may benefit from an awareness of blocking responses, since their, often unconscious, use can be detrimental to achieving the aims of the interview. In an appraisal interview, an interviewer may prevent the interviewee from raising issues of concern, thus making the process a one-way activity and perhaps causing hostility or anxiety on the part of the appraisee (Rae, 1988). Likewise in medical interviews it is crucial for the patient to be able to express her thoughts, although research evidence shows that health professionals often block patients' responses, by, for example, giving false reassurance (Dickson et al., 1989).

Clearly, in attempting to obtain information the interviewer needs to be aware of the effect which his behaviour is having upon interviewee behaviour. Frequently, inexperienced interviewers influence their interviewees' performance without being conscious of doing so. Following the interview they will explain that the interviewee was impossibly quiet or uncontrollably talkative, and yet they will be totally unaware of the extent to which their own behaviour discouraged the 'quiet' interviewee from responding or encouraged the 'talkative' client to talk.

Reflecting

In the previous section the focus was on influencing the amount and nature of information obtained through the way in which the interviewer reacts to interviewee contributions. A further response option, which will now receive some attention, is the skill of reflecting. Ivey (1983) notes that reflecting involves mirroring back to the interviewee in the interviewer's own words the essence of what she has just communicated. The interviewer may reflect either the factual or emotional content of the interviewee's messages. The reflection of factual content has been labelled paraphrasing (e.g. 'You worked in industry for three years, then returned to education two years ago') and mirroring emotions has been labelled reflection of feeling (e.g. 'You seem to be quite frustrated in your current job'). As Hargie et al. (1987, p.95) highlight, the use of reflecting serves many functions which are helpful to the process of obtaining information, some of which will be outlined below. When an interviewer mirrors back interviewee responses, they suggest that he is:

(1) demonstrating an interest in and involvement with the interviewee;
(2) indicating close attention to what is being communicated;
(3) checking the interviewer's perceptions and ensuring that his understanding is correct;
(4) focusing attention upon particular aspects and encouraging further exploration;
(5) indicating that it is acceptable in this situation for the interviewee to have and express feelings and facilitating their ventilation; and
(6) helping the interviewee to 'own' his feelings.

In all interview contexts, the interviewee will be more willing to give information to an interviewer who demonstrates interest and close attention. This commitment is amply demonstrated in the interviewer's use of reflecting since accuracy in mirroring back interviewee communication requires considerable concentration on the part of the interviewer (Hewton, 1988). This skill is also important in ensuring the accuracy of the interviewer's understanding of interviewee responses. For this reason, interviewers in research interviews are often trained to reflect back respondents' answers, and thereby check out the accuracy of data being collected in response to research questions (Fowler and Mangione, 1990). Similarly in medical, selection and appraisal interviews interviewers may wish, at various stages, to check their interpretations of interviewees' statements using this skill.

The use of reflecting tends to prompt further exploration of the issue high-lighted and therefore interviewers may wish to develop their use of this skill as an alternative to questioning when wishing to probe interviewee responses. The final functions mentioned relate to interviewee feelings and under many circum-stances the interviewer may wish to focus on interviewee feelings rather than on the factual arena. Clearly in counselling, it is important to acknowledge and accept clients' feelings and the use of reflecting can draw attention to clients' feelings and allow a hesitant client to express this part of their experience openly. As the final function of reflecting indicates, mirroring back to an interviewee the feelings which she is expressing enables her to take responsibility for these feelings by either accepting or correcting the interviewer's interpretation. For example, in an appraisal interview the interviewee may react defensively to a discussion of areas of weakness in work performance and as a consequence may respond aggressively towards the interviewer. When the interviewer reflects these strong feelings ('You seem very unhappy about this evaluation of your abilities'), the interviewee must either take responsibility for these feelings and actions, correct the misperception or change her behaviour rather rapidly.

Listening

Crucial to the process of obtaining information is the ability to listen effectively. Listening is a complex and difficult task involving both the process of assimi-lating and understanding the other person's messages and also the active process of communicating attention and understanding to the speaker. In other words, the listener both receives and sends messages. In order to obtain information the interviewer must show that she is physically attending to the interviewee. Listen-ing involves verbal and nonverbal attending responses. In brief, Nelson-Jones (1983) describes the nonverbal cues of listening as having a relaxed posture, being physically open (avoiding closed gestures such as folding the arms), good eye contact, appropriate facial expressions (relaxed expression mirroring the emotional tone of the conversation) and using head nods (signifying interest and continued permission to talk). In the absence of such cues interviewees very quickly become discouraged from talking. A further aspect of the skill of listen-ing is the ability to convey understanding of the messages received and to check the accuracy of this understanding. As outlined previously, this may be achieved through the use of reflecting or through questioning to clarify the interviewer's comprehension.

Part of becoming a good listener involves developing an awareness of the many obstacles to effective listening. Egan (1986) highlights an inability to concentrate as one of the main reasons why interviewers fail to listen effectively. He outlines several possible reasons for such inattentiveness. For example, the interviewer's physical condition may affect his ability to concentrate since he may be tired or ill. Interviewers frequently schedule too many interviews within the one day in spite of the knowledge that listening effectively is an exhausting exercise. A further reason may be a physical attraction or repulsion for the interviewee. Physical distractions of a different order, such as a noisy environment or constant interruptions, may also detract from the interviewer's ability to listen. Many of these factors can be considered prior to interviewing and steps can be taken to avoid inattentiveness.

A further obstacle to effective listening can be described as a process of filtering which takes place. Although attention is always selective since it would not be possible to attend to all available cues in an interview situation, the interviewer should be alert to the danger of 'only hearing what he wants to hear'. For example, Smith (1986) notes that, in interviewing, the interviewer often listens only to those aspects of the interviewee's message which confirm the mental image created of him. In other words, we often tend to pick up cues which confirm our prejudices or stereotypes (see chapter four). In addition to selectively listening to messages which confirm existing impressions, the interviewer may actually imagine that certain information is given simply because it confirms the stereotype (Snyder and Uranowitz, 1978). This process has been termed 'distorted listening' and involves inventing information which has not actually been presented by the interviewee (Egan, 1986). This can also occur when the interviewer believes that she is encountering a familiar situation, problem or set of ideas. Since she has either personally experienced what is being presented or 'has heard it all before', the interviewer fails to listen effectively and interjects parts of her own experience, thus distorting the information being presented. An awareness of such tendencies can help the interviewer to listen more effectively. For example, in a counselling situation the interviewer may have had similar problems and therefore must be alert to the possibility of not listening objectively to the client's unique experience. Similarly a doctor would need to be cautious that he did not pre-diagnose the patient before listening open-mindedly to the patient's full account. Perrott (1982) suggests that to listen effectively the listener must think with the interviewee and resist the temptations to take control or to judge or anticipate what might transpire.

In other words the interviewer should not be prejudging or predicting the messages which he is receiving. Patience is indeed a virtue!

A final area which diminishes the interviewer's ability to listen effectively is 'self-consciousness'. Egan (1986) notes that novice counsellors often make the mistake of responding too quickly in an effort to begin to help. This over-eagerness and consciousness of one's own role leads to the counsellor interrupting the client and responding after hearing only part of the client's message. In addition, inexperienced interviewers are often nervous and may spend considerable time and energy in formulating their own responses and wondering what kind of impression they are making. Naturally this detracts from their ability to pay careful attention to the speaker. Self-consciousness also occurs when the interviewer is concerned or concentrating upon their own preoccupations such as an important meeting which follows the current interview. An awareness of such obstacles to effective listening should help the interviewer to guard against some of the common pitfalls in listening to interviewees.

INFORMATION GIVING

In addition to collecting information, interviews are frequently used as an opportunity to give information. This might involve quite a lengthy and formal stage of information giving such as during selection interviews where the interviewer delivers information concerning the job and the employing institution. In the medical interview, also, the emphasis may be upon information giving when perhaps the results of a test, the nature of an illness or the prescribed treatment need to be explained (Ley, 1983). On the other hand, interviewers frequently give less protracted and formal explanations of, for example, their role as a counsellor or a brief description of the nature of an appraisal interview. However, regardless of the nature of the explanation, an interviewer's performance of this function can be enhanced by an understanding of the skills of information giving. The processes involved in giving information have been extensively investigated within the context of teaching, and many of the processes and skills identified are pertinent to the interviewing context.

Planning

The importance of preparation when the interviewer is expected to give information cannot be overstated. Such planning may be a lengthy process involving researching the topic and assembling detailed notes or may simply take place during a wise momentary pause before answering an interviewee's question. Turney et al. (1983) suggest that four stages are involved in successfully planning an explanation. Progression through each of these stages may determine to some extent the effectiveness of explanations given in the course of an interview. The first stage involves the accurate identification of the issue which requires explanation. In the interview context this may involve attempting to ascertain clearly what is being asked by the interviewee or what precisely requires explanation in this situation. In an appraisal interview the interviewee may ask 'What is this interview about?' It would be important that the interviewer established exactly what the interviewee wished to know in order to avoid wasting time and causing frustration through unnecessary explanations. Thoughtful questioning would clarify the need and may ascertain the interviewee's current knowledge on the topic.

The second stage involves consideration of what information might be included in the explanation in order to give a satisfactory response. In other words the interviewer may begin to think of what she might say in response to the question asked. In our example, thoughts which enter the interviewer's mind might include the likely progression of the interview, outcomes of the process, who has access to information, the aim of appraisal, how information is recorded and so on. If the interviewer begins to give an explanation based on the first thing which comes to mind, then the explanation may become garbled as other possible responses come to mind. Instead, Turney *et al.* (1983) suggest a third stage which involves finding the relationship between each of the possible responses. Thus in our example the interviewer may pause momentarily to consider the variety of possible responses. She might decide that the interview aims, progression and outcome form a logical sequence and that how the interview information is recorded and who has access to this information represent a different issue of confidentiality.

The fourth and final stage would then involve structuring the explanation to meet the needs of this particular recipient. Therefore, while the most logical sequence might be to begin with a discussion of aims, the interviewer might recognise that, for this particular interviewee, the question of confidentiality would be the more pressing concern. By beginning with this issue the interviewer would help to allay the interviewee's fears and hence make it possible for her to assimilate other relevant information.

All of these stages may take place in a matter of seconds while the interviewer prepares to answer a question or may be organised prior to an interview where the interviewer knows in advance that he will be giving information. In this way it can be seen that interviewers' ability to give information clearly and effectively can be improved by taking time to identify what is actually being asked and by allowing a moment's consideration for preparation.

Presentation

Even under circumstances where the interviewer has carefully planned the explanation difficulties might arise at the delivery stage, resulting in a lack of understanding on the part of the interviewee. Hargie *et al.* (1987) emphasise a series of factors which may determine the clarity of an explanation, including the rate of speech adopted in the explanation, the language used and interviewer fluency. Thus in a research interview, the interviewer may talk too quickly during the opening stage of the interview when explaining the procedure for answering questions, resulting in the interviewee giving inappropriate responses. The language used in giving information may also cause confusion, when terms are unfamiliar to the respondent. Fowler and Mangione (1990) note that research interviews can fail in their goal of collecting valid information because the respondent does not understand the terms used by researchers. Hodgson (1987) suggests that interviewers in all contexts should be prepared to translate jargon terms into language which the interviewee can understand. Finally, clarity is affected by the degree of fluency in the interviewer's presentation. Explanations punctuated with abundant 'um's, 'er's and half-finished sentences do little for interviewee comprehension. Hargie *et al.* (1987) suggest that time taken to plan the explanation greatly improves fluency.

A further important feature of effective explanations is the interviewer's ability to highlight the most important aspects of the explanation. This is particularly useful for longer explanations, where the interviewee may have difficulty in identifying the key points to be remembered from the information presented. Several verbal and nonverbal markers may be used as a means of providing emphasis for important points (Perrott, 1982). These include nonverbal signals such as the conscious use of eye contact, leaning towards the interviewee or using hand gestures to mark the key elements of the explanation. Such behaviours have been found to correlate with greater understanding on the part of the listener (Brown and Armstrong, 1984). Verbal markers of important points or focusing statements include repeating the key phrases, or verbally cueing the important points with phrases such as 'it is important to note...', or 'one of the main features...'. In this way the interviewee is alerted to the key aspects of the information conveyed by the interviewer.

A final aspect of presentation relates to skill in maintaining and promoting interest during the presentation of information. This may be achieved through what has been described as 'stimulus variation', that is, through the purposeful changing of the stimulus presented to the listener (Turney et al., 1983). Everyone has had the experience of listening to a monotonous speaker delivering a lengthy explanation during which the listener very quickly loses concentration. Perrott (1982) outlines a number of possibilities for promoting interest and helping the listener to maintain concentration. These include some consideration and evaluation of the interviewer's own style of presentation. Variety may be incorporated into the interviewer's speech patterns through changes in intonation, volume and rate of speech. There can also be variety in the interviewer's nonverbal behaviour. Likewise, the content of the presentation can also be varied to include complex and simple levels of explanation, examples, focusing statements and, where appropriate, humour. Finally, the medium by which information is transmitted can be varied to incorporate a combination of interviewer speech and visual material (diagrams, photographs and so on). Through planned use of variety in the presentation of information, the interviewer can promote greater attention, understanding and interest.

When the interviewer has presented the desired information, he may take some time to close his explanation effectively. The skill of closure will be discussed in detail later in this chapter. However, in relation to information giving, this phase of presentation may involve two elements, namely, summarising the information presented and obtaining feedback concerning the listener's understanding. Hodgson (1987) emphasises the importance of drawing information together for the interviewee, in the form of a summary of the essential information covered in the presentation. Evaluation of the effectiveness of the explanation may take many forms including the search for nonverbal evidence of comprehension, inviting interviewee questions on areas of the explanation which have not been understood, or, perhaps more unusually, inviting the listener to summarise her understanding of the information presented.

When attempting to gain feedback from listeners the responsibility for any lack of understanding should be borne by the interviewer, since interviewees may be rather reluctant to admit to any confusion. Thus, interviewers may wish to preface feedback questions by saying something like 'I'm not sure whether I explained that very well...'.

CLOSURE OF THE INTERVIEW

Many interviewers seem to find that closing an interview satisfactorily can be difficult. Interviews which both parties would agree were proceeding smoothly and effectively can often end badly. In the context of counselling, for example, the interviewee might be exploring issues which are sensitive and the interviewer might be responding effectively and warmly in helping this exploration. At a late stage in the interview the interviewer then realises that he must close the discussion and rather hurriedly advises the client that the interview must be concluded. The client agrees and tells the interviewer how helpful it has been to talk this problem through. Outside the office door the client cringes on recalling all that he has told this person. He leaves with the impression that the interviewer was not interested, that he was being a nuisance, that it was inappropriate to have opened up to this person.

Following a research interview, the interviewer thanks the respondent for taking part and, following a brief chat about the weather, they pleasantly part having both enjoyed the experience. Later that day, the interviewer recalls that he has forgotten to explain that the respondent will be contacted for a follow-up study. The respondent is also worrying about the interview and trying to recall who exactly the interviewer said would have access to the information collected. The participants are left with an uneasy feeling about the success of the interview. The saying 'all's well that ends well' would seem to be most true for interviewing. When there are problems with the final stages of an interview, this colours the participant's views of what occurred. Closure would then seem to be a most important point in the interview. However, this has not been reflected in the attention this area has received in the literature. Saunders (1986, p.175) notes that:

> despite both the importance and universality of openings and closings, systematic investigations of how people begin and end their human transactions have largely been neglected.

Saunders explores a number of possible responses for closing interviews effectively. Each of these areas will be outlined and their relevance in differing contexts will be discussed. The type of closure used will differ across contexts so that in counselling interviews, for example, the desire for closure needs to be sensitively signalled and carefully negotiated. In appraisal interviews, on the other hand, factual closure is of great importance since the agreements made following appraisal form the basis for the employee's future directions in work and assessment.

Closure signals

One of the ways in which the success of an interview can be either enhanced or diminished is through the feeling of participants that they are ready for and expecting the interview to end. As noted earlier, interviews can often come to a rather abrupt and unnegotiated end with resulting negative consequences. It is therefore desirable that participants are in agreement that the closure process should begin. Saunders (1986) suggests that this agreement can be facilitated by the introduction of closure signals or cues which make clear in an unhurried manner that the interviewer wishes to draw the interview to a close.

This can be achieved by a variety of nonverbal and verbal 'markers'. Non-verbal markers would include momentarily breaking eye contact, shifting position or altering posture, frequent head nodding. Each of these examples involves introducing slight changes in nonverbal behaviour in order to alert the interviewee to possible changes in the interview process. Less subtle cues such as looking at a watch or clock, shifting position dramatically from sitting to standing, clearing the desk of all paperwork pertaining to the interview, might be reserved for the less observant interviewees. Nonverbal cues frequently accompany a variety of verbal markers. Verbal cues which alert the interviewee of the intention to close the interview similarly seem to vary in their degree of explicitness. Thus the interviewer might simply state that 'we'll need to draw things to a close shortly' or might request closure through questions such as 'can we begin to draw things together?' More subtle markers include the interviewer beginning his next response with 'right, then', 'so' or 'well'. This again signals to the interviewee that there is going to be a change in topic or structure of the interview. The interviewee should then be alerted to the interviewer's wishes and this should facilitate a negotiation of closure.

Factual closure

Having signalled to the interviewee the desire to begin closure, the interviewer must then commence to draw the interview to a close by creating some coherent sense of the interview. Saunders (1986) points out that this might involve providing a summary of what has been discussed or agreed upon during the interview. This would allow the participants the opportunity to check out their understanding of what had occurred. A further stage of factual closure involves initiating or inviting questions. Stewart and Cash (1988) suggest that the interviewer should offer to answer any interviewee questions. They stress that such an offer should be sincere rather than simply a formality and highlight the need to provide adequate time for interviewees to consider possible queries. They further recommend the use of 'clearing-house' questions which may facilitate the discovery of unanswered questions, information or areas of concern which have not been discussed adequately. Examples include 'Is there anything which we have missed?', 'Anything else before we finish?'

Finally, the interviewer may wish to focus upon what happens after the interview (Saunders, 1986). Further meetings may need to be arranged or future action decided upon. In this way, the factual closure stage states the progress made during the interview, clears up unfinished business and plans for the future. The formality and extent of this phase will depend upon such factors as the time available and the nature of the interview. However, given the importance of effective closure, it is clearly beneficial to make sufficient time for an adequate factual closure.

Social closure

When the 'business' element of the closure has been completed, the interviewer may turn her attention to the social aspect of the encounter. The main function of social closure according to Saunders (1986, p.195) is:

> to establish a conducive relationship so that participants look forward with pleasure and enthusiasm to a future encounter.

This stage may include an expression of appreciation or satisfaction with the meeting where the interviewer thanks the interviewee for her time and contribution, and may indicate that the interview has gone well or that much has been achieved. Finally, the interviewer may make 'non-task-related statements' (Saunders, 1986). In other words the interviewer refers to matters other than the interview, such as statements related to the weather or personal enquiries. Providing such statements are genuine they make a pleasant way to end the interview.

TRAINING IN INTERVIEW SKILLS

The need for training in interview skills in order to improve interviewer effectiveness is recognised in most interview contexts. Fowler and Mangione (1990) strongly advocate the use of training to improve research interviewers' skill in interviewing. In an evaluation study, they conclude that training can have beneficial effects on interviewer level of skill. In counsellor education, training in the skills of interviewing is considered to be essential for effective practice (Egan, 1986). Indeed training programmes in counselling skills have long been established (Ivey, 1971). More recently, developments in medical training now incorporate training in communication skills (Carroll and Munroe, 1979), since research in this area is bringing to light the deficit in interview skill often displayed by the medical profession (Dickson et al., 1989). Again, evaluations of training for health professionals show improvement in skill following training (Crute et al., 1989; Maguire, 1981).

Goodale (1989) is most critical of the poor record for training in interview skills given to interviewers involved in the selection process. He makes the point that there is now a sharp contrast between what he terms the 'professional' applicant and the untrained interviewer. Recognising the growth in interviewee training for job interviews, he claims that interviewers are often poorly prepared to deal with the increasingly sophisticated applicants they face. He describes the experience of many practising managers in the following way:

> Literally thousands of managers have said that they learned to interview through trial and error, with no instruction or coaching. Some individuals have had the opportunity to observe a more senior colleague in action, and are then turned loose on their own. Others receive even less guidance; many are simply told that they have staffing responsibilities and will need to interview applicants. (Goodale, 1989, p.309)

If these managers are to be able to deal with applicants who may be trained in impression management techniques (Baron, 1989) they require professional training in interview skills. Lawson (1989) argues that, for similar reasons, interviewer training is essential for effective appraisal interviews.

Egan (1986) suggests that skill development has four phases: the development of a cognitive or conceptual understanding of the skills involved in interviewing; development of a behaviourally-based understanding, where interviewers can recognise the observable elements of the skill; initial mastery, where the skills are consciously practised and performance feedback provided; and further mastery, where the interviewer's command of the skills improves and there is greater flexibility in use. The training techniques used to achieve these levels of development vary but tend to include certain basic training elements. One well-researched and systematic training method, which illustrates these training techniques, is the microtraining approach (Hargie and Saunders, 1983). This approach facilitates skill acquisition by progressing through the following stages: skill analysis, skill discrimination, practice and focused feedback. Hargie and Saunders (1983, p.156) suggest that the skill analysis stage involves the provision of:

> a theoretical rationale for each skill, a summary of relevant research findings pertaining to the use of the skill, and finally, descriptions of the behavioural components included in each skill.

This may be provided in a lecture format or through written material, and it facilitates the development of conceptual understanding of the skills. Skill discrimination involves training novice interviewers to identify the behavioural components of each skill from 'model' video- or audio-tapes which have been produced to illustrate the use of the skill in a relevant professional setting. At this stage, trainees attempt to discriminate between effective and ineffective skill performance, thereby developing a behaviour-based understanding. Following evaluation of other professionals' skill use on the model tapes, trainees have the opportunity to develop initial mastery through practice coupled with immediate feedback on their own interview performance. This takes place during practical sessions where students practise in a role play or simulated interview situation with other trainees playing the part of interviewees. The interviews are usually video-recorded and the recording is available for subsequent detailed analysis. Feedback is provided based upon the replay of each trainee's video-recording, and tutor and peers comment upon the trainee's use of the particular skill under consideration. This progress is used to develop each of the skill areas outlined in this chapter.

The time devoted to training and the nature of the training methods suggested vary both within and between interview contexts. For example, Fowler and Mangione (1990) summarise details of the average length of training in academic and governmental survey organisations as basic interviewer training lasting from two to five days, with telephone interviewers generally being trained for a shorter period of time than face-to-face interviewers. It can be seen, therefore, that the focus on training varies depending upon the nature of the research task and various other factors such as cost. The methods used in training include lectures, demonstrations, supervised practice and monitoring performance with evaluation and feedback. Fowler and Mangione report that trainees' level of skill increased in relation to the time in training. Those interviewers who had less than one day of training were generally inadequate in the way they carried out the interview. They were rated significantly worse than those trainees with two or more days' training on measures of, for example, 'non-biasing interpersonal behaviour' and the ability to 'ask probing questions'. Indeed Bayne (1977) cites better training as one means of improving selection interviewing.

SUMMARY

As the preceding discussion indicates, a variety of skills are necessary for effective interviewing. The appropriateness of the interviewer's responses is determined by the effectiveness of the response in achieving the interview goals. Interviewers need to develop the ability to assess the effectiveness of their behaviour and to respond flexibly when their approach is ineffective with a particular interviewee or interview context. For example, while most interviewees would consider eye contact to be essential in demonstrating attentiveness, some interviewees may be intimidated by such actions and hence the interviewer must monitor the effects of his behaviour and adapt his style according to feedback received. In this chapter an attempt has been made to outline a number of skill areas which are of relevance in most interview contexts, and which make up a range of possible ways of responding. To this end skills in opening an interview, obtaining information, giving information and closure have been discussed.

Chapter 8

The interviewee's perspective

As noted in chapter one, certain roles are adopted in interviews, namely those of interviewer and interviewee. These roles carry with them related expectations concerning how each individual should behave. The interviewer is expected to direct the interview selecting relevant content mainly through the deployment of appropriate questions. The interviewee, on the other hand, is expected to play a responsive role mainly involving providing information as requested. The previous chapters have focused on the interviewer and discussed the influence which this role can have on the interview process. In the selection interview, for example, the interviewer will determine the general structure of the interview, the degree of formality, topic for discussion and often, through verbal and nonverbal cues, the nature and length of interviewee responses. The interviewers' controlling influence is acknowledged and accepted in interviewing, although they may vary their style in order to be more or less dominant in their approach (see chapter six).

Although the interviewer may often have more direct control in the interview, it would be a mistake to assume that the interviewee is a totally passive participant in the process. The interview involves both parties, and each person will influence the nature and outcomes of the encounter. This influence can be direct through interviewees' active attempts to influence the situation. Thus, in a medical interview, the interviewee may take control of the situation by requesting a full and frank discussion of her illness and the prescribed treatments. Less explicit, though nonetheless conscious, efforts may be made by the interviewee to influence interview outcomes by self-presentation techniques. It can be seen therefore that the nature of the interview is influenced by both participants.

The extent of this influence is determined by such characteristics as the context and purpose of the interview; the extent to which interviewees share the goals of the interviewer; how much they value the interview; and personal characteristics of the interviewee. In the counselling or helping context the counsellor's goals are often formulated to enhance the probability of the client achieving his goals for the situation (Cormier and Cormier, 1985). The client's perceptions are, therefore, of paramount importance and will often implicitly determine the choice of topic and nature of the interview. Likewise, in appraisal interviews, Nemeroff and Wexley (1979) stress the importance of interviewee perceptions, and their role in setting goals and actively participating in the interview. On the other hand, interviewee goals and perceptions may play a much less central role in the research interview.

It is important in any interview to have an understanding of the processes occurring in the interviewee, how these processes can affect the interview and how the interviewer might respond accordingly. Previous chapters have addressed the principal processes in the social interaction model mainly in relation to the interviewer. This chapter will focus on the same processes as they relate to the interviewee with the focus falling on the development of an understanding of the interviewing process from the interviewee's perspective. It should be clear from this discussion that, while the role of interviewee has certain general characteristics across all interview settings, the particular nature of the interviewee role differs in various contexts. For example, although the initiation of the interview is generally the interviewer's prerogative, in some contexts, such as medical and counselling settings, the interviewee will instigate the interview process. Termination of interviews is also more likely to be the responsibility of the interviewer, although again, in certain specific contexts, the interviewee may undertake this role. This may be carried out with the cooperation of the interviewer, such as in counselling, or simply through interviewee initiative. For example, Stewart and Cash (1988) note that the interviewee in research interviews may terminate the interview at any stage by simply walking away or hanging up the telephone. However, even in this context interviewees would tend not to behave in this manner. Once the interviewee has agreed to take part in the interview, he has to some extent agreed to follow the dictates of the interviewer. Thus, as these examples illustrate, the role of the interviewee will vary from one interview context to another.

INTERVIEWEE PERCEPTIONS

An array of information is available to the interviewee during an interview. This information includes feedback from her own responses during the interview and also cues from both the interviewer and the environment. The interviewee uses both this current information and her prior knowledge and experience to form impressions of her own performance, impressions of the interviewer and of the situation. The main processes affecting our social perceptions are discussed in detail in chapter four. However, these processes will now be recalled and explored from the interviewee's perspective, focusing upon interviewee self-perception and perceptions of the interviewer.

Self-perception

How interviewees perceive themselves may affect the interview process in a number of ways. For example, once we form self-perceptions these structures can strongly influence the ways in which we process new information (see chapter four). Thus, the interviewee in an appraisal interview may have difficulty in accepting negative feedback concerning his work performance if he formerly had the impression that this was an area of personal strength rather than weakness. Likewise, in medical interviews, patients who are told that they are seriously ill when they in fact perceive themselves to be 'fit and well', will be likely to reject this contradictory and threatening information.

A further characteristic of self-perception, which may be important from the interviewee's perspective, is the tendency to be aware of personal features which are unusual in the situation encountered. Thus, it may be that interviewees would be highly self-conscious of the ways in which they differ from the interviewer. This may result in a female interviewee being less comfortable with a male interviewer, and indeed in counselling many clients seem to prefer a counsellor of the same sex or ethnic origin (Shertzer and Stone, 1980).

An awareness of one's own behaviour in interviews can have both positive and negative effects. For example, many nervous interviewees can become so aware and critical of their own responses that they perform badly in interviews. In such cases, the interviewee may spend too much time and energy in responding to negative thinking ('I am not doing very well', 'This interviewer must think I'm stupid'), rather than concentrating on the task of responding to the interviewer's questions. However, self-awareness does not always have such negative effects but can, in fact, lead to improvements in performance. When the interviewee is able to analyse her behaviour, evaluate different strategies and learn to adapt her behaviour positively, this can lead to improved responding during the interview and in subsequent interviews.

Finally, interviewees' self-perceptions may affect how they are evaluated in interviews. The question of how interviewees perceive themselves and the effect of such perceptions on interview outcomes has received little attention in research. There is some evidence that clients in counselling who see themselves as 'unhelpable' do indeed benefit less from counselling and tend to terminate the process prematurely (Paradise and Wilder, 1979). In the selection interview context, it would seem likely that an interviewee who perceived herself to be a poor candidate for the post would be less likely to be successful in an interview than a candidate who had a more positive self-image. King and Manaster (1977) examined the relationship between interviewee self-esteem and their own and others' ratings of interview performance. Interestingly, they found that interviewees with high self-esteem tended to overestimate their own performance, and that interviewers' ratings of performance were unrelated to interviewees' self-perception. Keenan (1978) investigated the relationship between pre-interview motivation to succeed and interview outcomes and found that interviewees who were highly motivated were also more confident of success at the end of the interview. Interviewers' ratings, however, were most favourable when the level of interviewee motivation was intermediate. It would seem therefore that the highly positive interviewees may have been overestimating their performance, and that moderate levels of self-esteem and confidence may result in better interview performance. Commenting on these studies, Arvey and Campion (1984) suggest that interviewees with highly positive self-images may tend to 'aggrandise' their actual performance, and that this may detract from their interview performance (see chapter four for discussion of the 'too much of a good thing' effect).

Perception of the interviewer

In the same way that the interviewer is making judgements concerning the interviewee, the interviewee also assesses and forms impressions of the interviewer. The impressions which are formed can significantly influence interviewees' behaviour, motivation and commitment to the interview. In this way an interviewee who likes an interviewer will be more willing to accept a job offer (Keenan, 1978), while a patient who perceives his doctor to be approachable and understanding will be more likely to discuss emotional problems. Conversely, in an appraisal interview, an open and frank discussion of problematic work practices is unlikely to develop if the interviewee perceives the interviewer to be untrustworthy or punitive. It is clear that the perceptions which interviewees hold of the interviewer may strongly influence the nature and outcome of the interview, and in some cases may even determine whether or not the interview actually takes place at all. The impressions formed of the interviewer are based upon a variety of factors including interviewer characteristics, and characteristics of the interviewee as perceiver.

Characteristics of the person observed, in this instance the interviewer, are influential in forming perceptions. Thus, as noted previously, interviewees often prefer to be interviewed by someone of the same sex or ethnic background (Shertzer and Stone, 1980). Interviewer behaviour can also have a strong effect upon interviewees' perceptions. In the context of selection interviews, interviewer behaviour has been found to be an influential factor in interviewees' perceptions, with interviewees preferring interviewers who display nonverbal approval (Arvey and Campion, 1984).

The impact of an interviewee's perception of the interviewer as 'expert, attractive and trustworthy' was discussed in detail in chapter three. In brief, the interviewer has greater influence over the interviewee when the former is perceived as possessing these characteristics. Gorden (1987) claims that the information-gathering process in interviews is more effectively achieved when the interviewer is perceived as having 'power and prestige'. This can be particularly noticeable in the medical context, where consultants are perceived by patients as having extensive expert power. Such perceptions enable the consultants to have considerable influence over their patients' actions and decisions (Bernstein and Bernstein, 1985). (See chapter three for a full discussion of perceived interviewer characteristics and social influence in the interview process.)

   Person perception is influenced not only by characteristics of the person observed, but also by factors relating to the observer. Hence, the interviewee's perception of the interviewer will be influenced by factors such as implicit personality theories, stereotyping and feelings or attitude towards the interviewer (see chapter four for details). For example, if an interviewee is approached by a research interviewer and asked if he will take part in a survey interview, his response will to some extent depend upon his perception of the interviewer. Everyone has a set of beliefs about what people are like. These beliefs may be organised in a variety of ways which allow rapid, although at times inaccurate, assessments of complex characteristics of the person observed. The interviewee may have beliefs concerning a variety of character traits which he considers 'go together'. Thus, if he judges the research interviewer to be 'polite', he may construe from this observation that she is also trustworthy, respectful and considerate following his 'implicit personality theories'. Such judgements may lead to his agreement to take part in an interview. He may, on the other hand, be influenced in his perceptions by the stereotypes which he holds of certain groups of people. On hearing, for example, that the research interviewer is a student at university, the interviewee might assume that this person will be self-opinionated or lacking in respect for the views of others. He may consequently refuse to take part in the interview on the grounds of this stereotype.
   The observers' feelings can also affect their perceptions of others. Hence, if the interviewee has a fearful or negative attitude towards the interview, this may influence his perceptions of the interviewer. For example, patients attending medical interviews can be rather frightened, particularly when the process might involve a physical examination or other medical intervention. In some appraisal situations, the interviewee can be most reluctant to take part in what she perceives as an assessment situation, and she may view the appraiser with great suspicion. Similarly, selection interviews can be most stressful for interviewees and they often approach such events and the participants involved with considerable dread. Under such circumstances, the interviewer may wish to facilitate the forming of a more positive image of the process by attempting to influence the interviewees' feelings.
   Forgas (1985) notes that positive feelings, which can be induced through being in relaxed and pleasant surroundings, can lead the observer to perceive others in a more positive light. It is therefore important for interviewers to attempt to conduct interviews in pleasant and comfortable surroundings and to make efforts to help interviewees to relax. This may encourage the development of a positive attitude towards both the interviewer and the interview process. Such efforts to induce a more positive response to the interview and interviewer are vital since negative interviewee attitudes strongly affect the success of the interview. For example, as Arvey and Campion (1984) highlight, the interviewee's perception of the interviewer can have an impact on job applicants' choices of whether or not they take up job offers. Also, in the counselling context,

Egan (1986) notes that 'reluctant' clients, that is those individuals who are not self-referred, come to the interviews with negative attitudes and feelings and consequently can often 'sabotage' the counselling process. This issue of interviewee tactics and possible interviewer responses are discussed later. A positive perception of the interview situation can, on the other hand, lead to the co-operative pursuit of interview goals.

INTERVIEWEE GOALS

One definition of interviewing included in chapter one suggested that an interview has been construed as a conversation with a purpose. However, the purpose lies not only with the interviewer but also with the interviewee who comes to the interview with her own goals. As chapter five indicated, goals tend to be hierarchically organised and therefore the interviewee may find that some of her goals are conflicting. Indeed, such conflicts may lead to uncoordinated or contradictory interviewee behaviour in the interview. Interviewees may further find that their goals are in conflict with those of the interviewer and that consequently little progress is made in the interview. This section will explore the nature and importance of interviewee goals, and the implications of such goals for interviewer practice.

Nature of interviewee goals

As pointed out in chapter five, both participants in the interview process come to the situation with a variety of goals or aims which they hope to achieve through dialogue. These goals tend to be hierarchical in nature, in that there may be long-term or higher-order goals and short-term, lower-order goals. Long-term goals are achieved through the attainment of more immediate short-term goals, in the same way that a general aim is achieved by the attainment of more specific objectives, each taking the actor nearer to the ultimate higher-order goal. Thus the interviewer in a selection interview may have the long-term goal of developing new areas of expertise within a firm by appointing members of staff with appropriate knowledge and experience. This long-term goal can be achieved by more specific objectives in the interview such as questioning the candidate on the possible relevance of their qualifications to the company. Again at a lower order level, the latter goal may be achieved through a number of subgoals such as encouraging interviewee exploration of their past experience. This subgoal could be achieved by responding positively to the interviewees' initial responses and showing interest and enthusiasm in the interviewees' ideas. The interviewee will likewise have a hierarchy of goals in any interview situation. In the employment interview, for example, the interviewee would have the goal of being hired by a company, in order to achieve the longer-term aim of having a satisfying and financially secure lifestyle. He would attempt to achieve this goal of being hired through the subgoal of performing well in the interview. The strategy of 'impression management' might therefore be adopted to achieve this subgoal; this will be discussed later in the chapter. In other interview situations, the interviewee would similarly have a variety of goals; some lower- and higher-order, and some short- and long-term goals.

At times these goals may conflict. For example, in the medical context, the ultimate goal of attending the medical consultation will be to return, once again, to a healthy condition. This might involve the subgoal of cooperating with the doctor's instructions during the interview and ensuring his continued support by not being in any way critical of the doctor's performance. However, the patient may find that achieving this subgoal involves the violation of other goals such as maintaining personal integrity. If the patient complains that the doctor is not explaining the procedures adequately, she risks losing the doctor's support. If, on the other hand, the patient fails to express serious dissatisfaction, she does not achieve the goal of maintaining integrity. MacLean and Gould (1988) give a further example of conflicting client goals in the counselling context. They point out that often in the counselling situation, clients will wish to make progress in understanding their lives and feelings in order to be able to cope more effectively with life. Frequently, however, they have the conflicting goal of avoiding painful explorations of their past experiences. These conflicting goals can lead to a stalemate in counselling where little progress is made. The interviewee must resolve these conflicts by prioritising goal attainment before the interview can be beneficial.

Importance of interviewee goals

Some studies have examined the influence of interviewee goal attainment on their satisfaction with the interview. In the context of vocational counselling, Cherry (1974) found that when clients' goals were achieved in the interview, they were more likely to rate the sessions as 'helpful' than when their goals were not met. She further emphasised the importance of interviewees' goals being realistic in determining the success of the counselling process. She noted, for example, that some interviewees come to counselling wanting to have a decision made for them and are disappointed when this does not happen. Consequently, she suggests that the interviewee's goals should be the starting point for vocational counselling interviews and that interviewers should attempt to establish some realism in client goal setting. These thoughts and recommendations are echoed in a more recent study of pupils' perceptions of careers counselling (Cherry and Gear, 1987). In more general counselling contexts, these views are also supported. Shertzer and Stone (1980, p.76) note that clients often have the goal of being 'directed or told how and what to do to obtain whatever it was that led them to seek counseling'. This, they argue, does not represent a realistic understanding of what counselling involves, and because of this discrepancy between client expectations and reality, the counselling process is less effective. The importance of ascertaining interviewee goals and of attempting, where realistic, to see that these goals are satisfied is fundamental to success in any interview context. The interview involves both participants and where the goals of the interviewee are ignored, the outcomes of the process can only be partly met.

Interviewee involvement in setting interview goals

The interviewee may at times have radically different goals from the interviewer. For example, in an appraisal interview, the interviewer may wish to identify areas of weakness in the appraisee's work performance whereas the interviewee may have the conflicting goal of concealing all areas of weakness, particularly if appraisal is linked to financial reward or promotion. Alternatively the interviewee may wish to use the time available in discussing the shortcomings and limitations created by the work environment. In either case, such discrepancies in goals can lead to neither person's goals being achieved and as a consequence to a long and fruitless interview (Lawson, 1989). It is important to involve both parties in goal setting, thereby allowing the agenda for the interview to be negotiated (Wicks, 1982). This would then lay the foundation for the cooperative attainment of goals.

Indeed, recent studies of counselling interviews have shown that counselling sessions are more valuable when the goals for therapy have been agreed by both interviewer and interviewee (Foon, 1986; Benbenishty and Schul, 1987). Stewart and Cash (1988) emphasise the importance of negotiating the goals of interviews with the interviewee in terms of subsequent commitment to the interview process and motivation to have the interview succeed in achieving its objectives. Interviewees tend to feel less responsible for the success of interviews when they have not been involved in formulating the aims of the exercise.

The role of the interviewer in interviewee goal setting

As discussed in chapter five, our goals in social encounters are not always consciously in our thoughts as we converse with others. It is, however, likely that the participants in a formal structured interview will be more aware of what they are trying to achieve than would be the case in an ordinary conversation. This holds true for interviewer and interviewee since for both participants the interview is conducted for specific purposes. Nevertheless, although the interviewee may be aware of a general goal in taking part in the interview it would not always be the case that more specific goals would be recognised. For example, in counselling interviews the client is often only aware of a general or vague goal of wanting to take action to alleviate his problems (Egan, 1986). In the absence of more specific goals, the interviewee may have difficulty in evaluating any progress made during counselling. Additionally, interviewees' goals may often be unrealistic due to a lack of experience in interviewing and given the limited time involved. Interviewees, therefore, at times need assistance in formulating specific and realistic goals for interview sessions. The process of goal setting was discussed in chapter five.

INTERVIEWEE TACTICS

In chapter one it was noted that the interviewer would generally be in a position of control or dominance in the interview. Interviewers are therefore in a better position to achieve their goals by being able to implement certain strategies or tactics. Some approaches were outlined in chapter six and included the interviewer's ability to direct the topic for discussion. However, although the interviewer does have more control in the interview it would be erroneous to believe that the interviewee has no recourse to tactics with which to influence the nature of the interview. These tactics may be fully or partially conscious strategies used by the interviewee to influence the interview process, such as 'impression management' in the selection interview. Other strategies may be largely subconscious although regularly employed, such as 'defence mechanisms' in a counselling or appraisal interview. In this section some of the tactics used by interviewees will be outlined and implications for interviewer responses will be discussed.

Impression management or strategic self-presentation

In all interview contexts the interviewee will be able to exert a certain amount of influence over the messages which he is presenting to the interviewer. Thus, to some degree, the interviewee can select his responses to interviewer questions and decide how much information to reveal and how much will be concealed. To a lesser degree interviewees can also control negative and adopt positive body language in order to present desired impressions. This process of controlling verbal and nonverbal messages so that positive or desired images are created is known as 'impression management' (Schlenker, 1980) or 'strategic self-presentation' (Jones and Pittman, 1982). Such tactics are particularly notable in the context of selection interviews. As Baron (1989, p.204) notes:

> Because many applicants recognise the importance of this initial contact, they engage in strenuous efforts to ensure that it yields a positive outcome. In short, they use every skill and tactic at their disposal to induce positive reactions among interviewers, and so 'tip the balance' in their favour.

Verbal messages

Interviewees can to some extent manage the impressions that are formed of themselves by having some say in what information is presented in the interview. In this way, the interviewee can select topics which give a positive impression and neglect topics which portray him in a negative light. Interview contexts differ in the extent to which interviewees are able, or are facilitated by the interviewer, to have an influence over the nature of topics discussed. This has been described in chapter six as the degree of directiveness in interviewer approach. Thus a survey interview would tend to be highly directive with preset topics and questions which tightly control the interviewees' response alternatives (Fowler and

Mangione, 1990). This allows little opportunity for interviewee influence over what will be discussed. Some determined or socially unaware interviewees will tend to talk about whatever they like regardless of the tight structure, often to the research interviewer's horror! However, when interviewees are concerned to give a positive impression, they generally cooperate with the interviewer's directives. Other interviews may be less directive and hence give interviewees greater scope to influence the information which they are presenting to the interviewer. Thus, in counselling interviews, the interviewee is given more freedom, and is actively encouraged to decide or determine what will be discussed. The survey and counselling interviews could be described as representing either end of the interview control dimension. It is, however, recognised that not all research interviews are directive (qualitative research interviews employ nondirective strategies) and not all counselling interviews are nondirective (particularly a number of cognitive approaches).

Medical interviews tend to be rather tightly controlled so that interviewees often have difficulty in presenting self-selected information. Many studies have shown that health professionals generally tend to restrict patient response (Dickson *et al.*, 1989), although even in this context the patient may choose to withhold certain information.

Selection interviews would fall somewhere between these extremes, where interviewees would have a certain amount of freedom in determining their responses to interviewer questions. Hence interviewees can draw upon appropriate and positive aspects of their experience to present in the interview. They can further choose to restrict elaboration on negative areas of their experience, although this freedom is determined by the interviewer's choice of follow-up questions. A similar approach might be adopted by the interviewee in an appraisal interview.

Nonverbal messages

A further aspect of interviewee behaviour which is used as a tactic in creating positive impressions is in the area of nonverbal behaviour. Interviewees will engage in positive nonverbal cues such as smiling, making eye contact, head nodding in agreement with interviewer statements and demonstrating interest through posture and orientation. Such cues have been shown to be associated with positive ratings by interviewers (Imada and Hakel, 1977; Rasmussen, 1984). This aspect of interviewee behaviour together with the influence of general appearance is discussed in greater detail later.

It has been noted, however, that interviewees must use caution in adopting overly positive nonverbal tactics, since there is some evidence that overuse of such tactics can have a negative effect on interviewers' perceptions. Baron (1989) argues that the interviewer may be aware of, and expect, the interviewee to adopt tactics of impression management. Beyond a certain level, he suggests, such tactics may be considered excessive and result in a negative evaluation. In other words, tactics which, when used singly, produce a positive effect may, when used in concert, produce negative reactions. Some evidence supporting the contention that interviewees can 'go too far' with impression management has been reported (Baron, 1981; Baron, 1989).

Lack of cooperation/resistance

A further interviewee tactic which interviewers encounter in certain contexts is a lack of cooperation or disruption of the interview by the interviewee. There may be many reasons for this lack of involvement or disruption of the interview. For example, in a research interview the interviewee may have agreed to participate without realising the extent of the commitment in terms of time, and may consequently regret giving permission for the interview or indeed may be somewhat irritated that the length of time necessary was not fully made clear at the outset, leading to a consequent lack of cooperation. In the counselling context, interviewers would also, at times, encounter 'unwilling' or reluctant clients who might demonstrate resistance in the interview. Egan (1986) defines reluctant clients as those who do not want to come to counselling in the first place, in other words, clients who are not self-referred. He cites the examples of marriage counselling, where one of the parties may attend for counselling only following pressure from the other partner, or where employees or students have been 'strongly advised' to seek counselling following deterioration in work performance. Such clients are often directly or indirectly uncooperative. A lack of cooperation may also result from a fear and misunderstanding of the nature and purpose of counselling or appraisal interviews. This lack of cooperation may take a variety of forms including nonparticipation through the use of silence, non-attentive body language or minimal responses to interviewers' invitations to talk, to active attempts to terminate the interview. Examples of disruption of the interview might include avoidance or refusal to discuss issues raised by the interviewer, the use of humour, distractions or aggressions (Manthei and Matthews, 1989).

Defence mechanisms

At times interviewees may unconsciously or habitually use defence strategies in order to protect themselves in some way from unpleasant or painful experiences in the interview. For example in counselling or appraisal interviews, interviewees may receive feedback which they find threatening and therefore defence mechanisms would be mobilised. The interviewee may not even be aware such tactics are being used or may become aware of this only once they have begun to respond defensively. Nelson-Jones (1990) summarises some examples of responses which can be applied to interviews. The following defence strategies might be used by interviewees in an appraisal interview when the interviewer has raised the question of certain areas of weakness in work performance.

Denial – refusal to acknowledge or accept evidence of weaknesses in work performance. They may claim that this aspect of their work is effective.

Projection – disguising personal reactions, thoughts or actions by ascribing them to someone else. For example, becoming aggressive in the interview yet claiming that the interviewer has become aggressive.

Rationalisation – attempting to explain behaviour so as to conceal the true responsibility. Thus, an interviewee might suggest that he is unable to fulfil his duties due to organisational constraints, rather than his own dislike and neglect of this area of work.

Defensive lying – distorting reality to the point of believing the distortions. This differs from deliberate lying in that the interviewee actually believes the story. The interviewee may, of course, be deliberately evasive or deceptive.

Attack or aggression – putting pressures on the interviewer to give only positive feedback through the use of overt or subtle threats. (Adapted from Nelson-Jones, 1990, p.240)

Such defensive reactions tend to sabotage all attempts to gain anything constructive from the interview. The interviewee is perceived as 'difficult to deal with' or unhelpfully sensitive and the interview makes very little or slow progress.

INTERVIEWEE SKILLS

Many of the skill areas discussed in chapter seven have relevance for both interviewer and interviewee. Some of the necessary skills for interviewees include presenting information, listening, nonverbal behaviour and questioning.

Presenting information

Since the main role of the interviewee in most contexts is to provide information, skill in presenting information effectively is of fundamental importance. The importance of planning and preparation for information presentation was emphasised in chapter seven and this applies equally to interviewer and interviewee. Hodgson (1987) suggests that interviewees attending all forms of interview should draw up notes concerning the information, issues and queries which they wish to present. This, he argues, applies equally to selection interviews, appraisals and 'a visit to the doctor'. In research interviews, the respondent often is given little or no notice of the interview and is therefore not in a position to plan beforehand the information which is requested. However, even in this context, interviewees are advised to insist upon time to consider their responses to questions (Stewart and Cash, 1988).

The steps involved in effective planning for giving information are detailed in chapter seven, and will be reiterated briefly at this point in relation to interviewee preparation. As Turney et al. (1983) point out, the first stage in planning involves clearly identifying the issue that requires explanation. Thus, for a selection interview, the interviewee may consider what questions they are likely to be asked during the interview. The information required for an appraisal interview tends to have a more standardised form with questions relating to areas of strength and weakness in work performance, and directions for development (Breakwell, 1990).

The second stage involves identifying relevant elements which might be included in response to interviewer questions. Thus, the appraisee might consider all aspects of her work performance in which she had experienced some success. The third stage involves assessing the relationship between these elements. Again taking the appraisal example, some of the elements may be the ability to work well with colleagues, while other areas of success may be linked with personal ambitions and aptitudes which could be developed. The final stage in planning would involve organising and structuring the information to meet the needs and interests of the interviewer. In this connection, the interviewee needs to be aware of the dangers of giving too much information or being too brief and leaving out something important (Hodgson, 1987). Systematic preparation is therefore most important so that interviewees have sufficient time to consider all possible responses and to identify and structure succinctly the most crucial options.

Interviewees' responses must be clearly presented. The factors relating to clarity and how to provide emphasis are discussed in chapter seven. In summary, the following factors influence clarity: rate of speech, fluency and language used. The interviewee needs to pay attention to his speech rate, which may increase due to nervousness. Fluency of presentation affects both the clarity of presentation and also interviewer perceptions, since the interviewer may regard excessive hesitation and garbled sentences as evidence of incompetence. As Hargie *et al.* (1987) indicate, fluency can be improved greatly by taking some time to plan responses. Finally, the interviewee must ensure that the language used in presenting information is familiar to the interviewer. For example, in describing relevant knowledge for a job, students may use language which is customary in educational settings but totally unfamiliar in industry. Thus, the statement 'I have completed a module in social perception' may mean considerably less to an interviewer than if the interviewee had said 'I have studied the ways in which our impressions of people can be biased'.

In conclusion, since the interviewee must often be brief in his responses to interviewer questions, the ability to summarise information and to indicate the most important elements in responses is of great importance. As Hodgson (1987, p.84) graphically points out:

> if you have a way with words, make it a short way rather than the bells and whistles version. The interviewer can always ask for more detail, but will be irritated if it is necessary to ask for less.

Important points within the information presented can be highlighted non-verbally through gestures or establishing eye contact at key stages, or verbally by explicitly identifying the main points (e.g. 'the most important aspect of my previous job was...').

Listening

A further area which is important in the role of interviewee is the skill of listening. In order to be able to participate fully and constructively in an interview, the interviewee must listen effectively to the various instructions and requests made by the interviewer. This is particularly important in interviews where information is being given. In all contexts interviewees need to be able to listen effectively to gain an accurate understanding of the goals and structure of the interview and the specific role they are being asked to play. Stewart and Cash (1988, p.121) suggest that in survey interviews the interviewee must listen carefully to opening explanations of:

> who the interviewer represents, why the interview is being conducted, how answers will be used and how the interviewee was chosen.

Through effective listening the interviewee can then make an informed choice as to whether or not he wishes to participate. Listening effectively to the interviewer's opening explanations is also most important in selection and appraisal interviews where the interviewee has much to lose by behaving inappropriately.

In addition to the importance of understanding the nature of the interview and how to behave during this process, the ability to demonstrate that he is listening attentively has also been shown to create favourable impressions with the interviewer. Hargie *et al.* (1987) note that verbal and nonverbal cues of attention reward the speaker. Hence by demonstrating that he is listening, the interviewee will be making the interview a more pleasant activity for both parties. The interviewer also requires feedback concerning the interviewee's level of understanding and interest in her explanations. For example, in the context of selection interviews the interviewer may give a lengthy and informative response to an interviewee question at the end of an interview. The interviewer will need feedback concerning the interviewee's understanding of, and opinion about, the information presented. Following an explanation that it was a company's policy to relocate trainee managers every six months, the interviewer would be likely to want some comment from the interviewee demonstrating understanding and acceptance of this message. In such contexts, the skill of reflecting may be of relevance to the interviewee.

Chapter seven outlined a number of obstacles to effective listening which may be experienced by the interviewer. Some of these processes can also interfere with the interviewee's ability to listen effectively. For example, one of the main obstacles to effective listening is the tendency to try to respond before fully hearing what the speaker has to say (Egan, 1986). This problem would be of considerable importance in effectively answering interviewer questions. In the research context, Fowler and Mangione (1990) draw attention to the need to allow the questioner to finish before attempting to answer the question. At times, they suggest, interviewees try to guess what the question is going to be and therefore answer on the basis of their predictions rather than the actual question asked. This can also occur in the context of selection or appraisal interviews where the nervousness experienced by the interviewee leads to ineffective listening and answering questions prematurely. Smith (1986) notes that it is 'crucial' to be patient in attempting to listen accurately. Fatigue may be another factor in limiting the interviewee's ability to listen carefully to interviewer questions. Hence, late night preparation or lack of sleep due to excessive worrying may damage interviewee performance.

Nonverbal behaviour

Interviewee nonverbal behaviour can have considerable impact in an interview situation. In counselling, for example, the interviewee may reveal significant emotional information through such cues and counsellors are advised to pay careful attention to this aspect of interviewee behaviour (Ivey, 1983). However, information is also transmitted intentionally and skilfully through nonverbal behaviour and therefore interviewees may use this skill to achieve their goals in interviews. Many studies have indicated that an interviewer's reactions to an interviewee are strongly influenced by the applicant's appearance. Interviewees have considerable scope in manipulating facets of appearance in order to create more favourable impressions. They may dress in the appropriate manner for an interview and improve physical attractiveness through efficient personal grooming or through artificial aids such as cosmetics. Investigations have shown that interviewees whose appearance is attractive, or who are appropriately groomed and attired, receive higher ratings than candidates judged to be unattractive (Cash, 1985; Forsythe et al., 1985).

Interviewees may also use nonverbal skill in indicating their general attention and interest in interview situations. Hence, interviewees may adopt an open posture, use frequent eye contact, appropriate facial expressions and head nods to demonstrate their attention to the interviewer (Nelson-Jones, 1983). Regarding body language and speech, Stewart and Cash (1988, p.156) summarise their advice in the following way:

> Dynamism or energy level is communicated through the way you shake hands, sit, walk, stand, and move your body. Try to appear calm, relaxed, and in control by avoiding nervous gestures and movements. Speak in a normal conversational tone with vocal variety that exhibits confidence and interpersonal skill.

SUMMARY

The interviewee's role is primarily concerned with providing the information requested by the interviewer. However, as anyone experienced in interviewing will know, eliciting information from an interviewee can be much less straightforward than this assertion would imply. For example, in an appraisal interview the interviewee can perceive the situation as most threatening and hostile and therefore may attempt to sabotage the process by actively withholding information. This will have a considerable effect on how successful the interview turns out to be. It is important that interviewers try to understand the role of the interviewee and the influence which they bring to bear on the interview process. This chapter has attempted to outline some of the more pertinent characteristics of interviewees' perceptions, goals, strategies and skills.

The goals and perceptions of interviewees can have a major impact on the success of interviews. For example, when the goals of interviewer and interviewee are in conflict this can lead to a fruitless or even destructive interview outcome. Interviewers, therefore, need to ascertain and take account of interviewee perceptions and goals and, where possible, involve interviewees in goal setting.

Interviewees may also use a variety of strategies to influence the process and outcomes of the interview. Such strategies include adopting impression management techniques, such as providing only positive information and using nonverbal behaviours such as smiling, attentive posture and appropriate dress to influence interview outcomes. Strategies may also include less sophisticated options such as not cooperating with the interviewer by evading or refusing to answer questions. The interviewee may engage in a variety of defensive strategies when feeling threatened. Finally, several skill areas for interviewees were discussed in this chapter including presentation tactics, listening and nonverbal behaviours.

Chapter 9

The professional context of interviewing

Readers will recall that throughout the preceding chapters a number of brief references were made to issues which often exercise the minds of professional practitioners. For example, there were issues which pertained to the influence of a range of interviewer errors (chapters three and four), to the selection of appropriate interview goals including the non-violation of interviewee values (chapter five) and to the ascertainment of relevant, reliable and valid interview tactics (chapter six). It is the purpose of this chapter to focus explicitly on a number of factors pertinent to interviewers who are striving to offer a responsible, ethical and competent service to their respective clients.

Given the complexity of the issues, it is not intended, here, to offer neat and tidy solutions for interviewers to follow – interviewers rarely operate in a simple 'black and white' world characterised by dichotomies, but rather function in multicoloured contexts where intricate shades of meaning typify the numerous unique situations encountered. Any attempt slavishly to adopt mechanistic rules will, more likely than not, be a hindrance rather than a help. The very situation of being faced with choices with respect to a range of contextual elements which comprise the interview process emphasises the pivotal role played by the professional interviewer. This chapter seeks to introduce some thoughts on a number of these key contextual issues by presenting material around those components which comprise the main aspects of professional codes of practice.

PROFESSIONAL CODES OF PRACTICE

There are a number of professions in existence today where interviewing constitutes one of their major methods of intervention. One important criterion of professional legitimation is the presence of a professional association which can, through the adoption of a formal code of practice, impose sanctions on any members who are adjudged to be in contravention of this formal code. So, for example, interviewers working in the fields of counselling, medicine, social work, psychology and personnel management all have professional associations, many of which have drafted formal codes of both ethics and practice fully endorsed by all members. Lewis and Murgatroyd (1976) suggest that the professionalisation process refers to the role, which, as a consequence, carries with it expectations of specified professional behaviours; role incumbents are obliged to display these behaviours. It is these obligations that are explicitly set out in the codes prepared by each of the professional associations, the main function of which is to ensure the protection of those who come into contact with the professional worker by setting down adequate standards mainly relating to issues of responsibility and to issues of competence (BAC, 1984; ICO, 1987). With respect to counsellors, Blackham (1982, p.295) suggests that their ethical code indicates that they are responsible for:

> professional competence, the counselling relationship confidentiality, exert-ing and refraining from direction, certain values and assumptions, equity amongst clients, intra-professional relations.

It should be noted that these standards relate to all tasks undertaken by such professionals and therefore will include any functions carried out by means of one-to-one interviews. Those interviewers who are cognizant of, and act upon, ethical principles will as a consequence tend to practise as responsibly and competently as they consciously can. That is, they will earn their professional label.

Issues of responsibility

According to Fairbairn (1987, p.253) a responsible person 'is one we can trust to act sensibly, perhaps one we can trust to carry out duties to the best of her ability'. From the client's perspective, strong expectations are held that these well-trained, responsible professionals will have the specialised expertise necessary to help with problem resolution whether the problem be obtaining a job, over-coming a personal trauma, seeking medical treatment or going for a promotion. This gulf in 'know-how' between the professional and the interviewee suggested to McKechnie (1987) that considerable power and authority are bestowed on the professional. Under these circumstances McKechnie (1987) cautions against the possibility of counsellors exploiting their clients, materially, physically or psychologically.

However, this power relationship is not an inevitable outcome even though it might be embodied in initial client expectations. What seems to be important and constitutes a significant part of the interviewer's responsibility is to clarify with all interviewees just what their expectations might be for their forthcoming encounter. At the outset, therefore, it is the responsibility of the interviewer to ensure that each interviewee is fully aware of what can be expected from the interviewer and what cannot. Clarifications of process and outcome possibilities should precede decisions about whether to continue or whether to discontinue the professional association. Whatever agreement is reached is often contained in a formal contract which commits both parties to the agreement. Writing about counselling, Blackham (1982, p.295) notes that there is:

an implied contract, certain expectations on the one hand, a certain undertaking on the other, which carries with it a standard of conduct to be observed and upheld.

Responsibilities for and of interviewees

Of all aspects of professional practice enshrined in the various ethical codes those relating to the place of the interviewee are conspicuously included. For example, the code of practice for careers officers issued by the Institute of Careers Officers (1987, 3.1) states that they will:

Respect clients as individuals and seek to ensure that their dignity, individuality, rights and responsibilities are safeguarded.

Similarly the British Association of Counselling (1984, 2.3) asserts that:

Counsellors respect the dignity and worth of every human being and their ultimate right to self-determination, whilst having due regard for the interests of others.

and furthermore (2.5):

Counsellors respect clients as human beings working towards autonomy, able to make their decisions and changes in the light of their own beliefs and values.

Munro *et al.* (1983) include values such as concern for others, recognition of the worth of each individual, trustworthiness, goodwill and caring, as important for successful counselling. Cormier and Cormier (1985) reproduce a number of 'codes' issued by various American associations all of which assert similar professional responsibilities for psychologists and social workers. The showing of respect for interviewees is an unequivocal responsibility of all interviewers particularly within the helping contexts of guidance, counselling, medicine and appraisal (Fairbairn, 1987).

It is generally accepted that to take responsibility for one's own life is to be an adult human being. Indeed, those who do not are often referred to as childish and those who cannot as in some way handicapped. Professional helpers, by adherence to their respective codes of practice, are committed to facilitating growth towards adulthood rather than towards the irresponsibility of childhood or the dependence of handicap or illness. The former value reflects a degree of respect for the person whereas the latter outcomes, by not maximising the interviewee's capacity to take on personal responsibility, are more disrespectful (Fairbairn, 1987). We are, however, not suggesting that all individuals are necessarily capable of assuming equal degrees of personal responsibility – there are clearly individual differences with respect to such characteristics but we would endorse Fairbairn (1987, p.276) when he asserts that:

Although an individual may not be able to take much responsibility, respect for him as a person demands that he be enabled and encouraged to take whatever responsibility he can.

The implications of such respectful value positions will exert significant influences on the process of goal setting (outlined in chapter five) and will serve to reduce the chances of assuming too little of the interviewee and to break out of the vicious circle of self-fulfilling prophecies.

The idea of accepting and going along with the wishes of the interviewee may run a smooth course, especially if a degree of congruence exists between interviewee and interviewer values. Varying degrees of discrepancy are not uncommonly found between two individuals, each of whom has every right to hold his or her respective values. The important point is to be aware that such values belong to the interviewer or the interviewee and that neither of them is of greater absolute importance or worth than the other. Interviewers cannot pretend that they do not hold any values for this would be disrespectful to themselves, rendering them somewhat less human. What interviewers do not have the right to do is to attempt to impose their values on their clients (Benjamin, 1981; Egan, 1982; Munro *et al.*, 1983) as if they somehow know that their perspectives are 'better', more worthwhile or more acceptable than those expressed by their interviewees. The occurrence of this potential conflict in interviews led Benjamin (1981, pp.36–7) to recommend that interviewers ask themselves:

to what extent we have a need to control his life, to tell him what to do and how to do it; to what extent can we tolerate his disagreeing with us; to what extent can we encourage him to find his own way, not ours, and become self-functioning, independent of us, as soon as possible.

The extent to which the resulting interaction will be directive–nondirective will be greatly influenced by the range of answers obtained to Benjamin's questions. Within this context the judgemental, paternalistic, 'I know best' attitude raises major ethical problems. However, what we are not saying is that interviewers must accept or condone interviewee values. Situations where systems conflict encourage both participants to explore, justify, defend or change their values – they can no longer be taken for granted or assumed to be the only possible 'correct' alternative (Benjamin, 1981). At the end of the day, however, both interview participants have the right to self-determination and self-government.

Adherence to this principle can, however, create some difficulties for interviewers. It is difficult to enable an individual to pursue her wishes which appear to the interviewer to be self-defeating or harmful to the individual. These may be circumstances where the interviewer, out of concern, may choose to intervene more directively in the interviewee's affairs. This possibility is advocated by Fairbairn (1987, p.249) when he says:

Although I think that respecting another as a person will most often involve respecting her wishes, there are circumstances in which I think one can override them without qualms.

The inherently uncomfortable experiences encountered by a doctor who is asked to assist a patient to sustain a lifestyle that is patently unhealthy or the counsellor helping a client to work out a plan for committing suicide are self-evident and collusive. The choice of whether such goals can form the basis of a contract for helping is of considerable ethical importance. Under such circumstances a helper may not be willing to continue to participate in a process that seems to be so ethically irresponsible. Indeed, Cormier and Cormier (1985) conclude that whether to continue or not or whether to modify the direction in which the interviewee is helped (to enable the interview to continue) are significant questions. Unless attempts to 're-evaluate' the client's goals are undertaken openly, honestly and explicitly, there is the distinct possibility of the helper imposing more appropriate goals on to the client covertly. In terms of respecting the person, attempts to redirect the client should, therefore, be undertaken only with the informed consent of the interviewee who, being fully in the picture, is in a position to choose whether to engage in the process of re-evaluation or whether to retain the right to adhere to their original goals.

A second area where conflict may occur concerns personal versus institutional value systems. The code of practice for counsellors (BAC, 1984, 1.4) includes:

Counsellors who become aware of a conflict between their obligation to a client and their obligation to an agency or organisation employing them will make explicit the nature of the loyalties and responsibilities involved.

Individual needs may become subordinated to those of the institution for whom the interviewer works. This may serve to impose severe restrictions on the range of potential outcomes or acceptable goals. For example, the grammar school pupil who seeks help in exploring his options may find such help more forthcoming with respect to the university option rather than for one which entails leaving school after A-levels. Alternatively, in the context of falling school rolls the pressure on a guidance teacher to persuade potential school leavers to continue their education at their current school can be great. Furthermore, interviewers should resist the temptation to jump automatically to the defence of their institution or their colleagues, and, in so resisting, recognise the injustices which interviewees can suffer (Munro et al., 1983). The interviewer's role is not one of judge and jury, assigning guilty or innocent verdicts, but to explore and understand situations in as objective a manner as possible.

The final aspect in this section stems essentially from the realisation that not only do interviewees need interviewers but that the converse is also highly likely and potentially intrusive (Benjamin, 1981). Such is the importance attributed to this potential danger that it is commonly included in codes of practice. For instance, BAC (1984, 2.6) states that:

Counsellors are responsible for ensuring that the satisfaction of their own emotional needs is not dependent upon relationships with their clients.

Cormier and Cormier (1985, p.598) include within the social worker's ethical responsibility to clients:

The social worker should not exploit relationships with clients for personal advantage.

The extent to which interviewers can function in the absence of any self-interest is arguable but, from the health perspective, Bernstein and Bernstein (1985, p.2) suggest it 'ought to be at a minimum'. Professional interviewers should, therefore, strive to ensure that clients receive the assistance required to meet *their* needs. When this objective has been met then clients should not be encouraged to return nor should they be encouraged to develop dependency upon the interviewer (Benjamin, 1981). The development of disrespectful associations primarily for the gratification of the interviewer's egocentric needs, to win their clients' undying gratitude (Bernstein and Bernstein, 1985) or to demonstrate their superior wisdom, expertise or splendid personal qualities (Benjamin, 1981) has been described by Heron (1976) as manipulative. Heron (1976, p.260) defines a manipulative intervention as one in which the practitioner:

intervenes exclusively to meet his own needs and interests regardless of, or to the actual detriment of, the needs and interests of the client.

Motivations for engaging in interviews, if not solely related to meeting the identified needs of interviewees, are likely to be unethical, disrespectful and irresponsible. It is crucial that interviewers interview for genuine reasons rather than for ulterior motives. Furthermore, Dorn (1984, p.47) notes that trustworthiness will be enhanced when:

the client notices the counselor's open and sincere manner and realizes that there is a lack of desire and motivation on the counselor's part to attain any personal gain through the relationship.

The important element relates to the interviewee 'noticing', perceiving or experiencing interviewer sincerity, genuineness or trustworthiness – interviewer intention itself is insufficient.

Issues of competence

All professional practitioners operate from a sound theoretical foundation derived from evidence available from relevant cognate discipline areas. Professionals are required to ensure that their practice remains informed as additional evidence becomes available. This implies that professionals should engage in formal training (often validated by their appropriate professional association) and thereafter seek further training at appropriate intervals. This tenet is well represented in the code of practice issued by the Institute of Careers Officers (1987, 2.4) where one of their seven principles states:

Careers Guidance is based upon a body of theoretical knowledge and the use of continually developing skills, practice and techniques. Careers Officers have an obligation to increase and update their professional knowledge and to contribute to the total body of knowledge within the profession, through constant evaluation of research and methods in the light of changing needs.

Interviewees enter the interview carrying with them expectations that the professional interviewer will possess a high degree of professional competence in terms of both tactics and techniques. They expect the interviewer to know what he or she is doing, to know where he or she is going and they expect to take this journey without coming to any physical or psychological harm. This outcome is made more likely where the interviewer possesses competence and operates responsibly. Awareness of levels of competence defines both what can be handled in terms of client concerns and also identifies the limits of such competence, which, if exceeded, would reflect unethical and irresponsible professionalism (Cormier and Cormier, 1985; Lewis and Murgatroyd, 1976; Munro et al., 1983).

The onus is very much on the interviewer to select from her armoury of tactics, techniques and styles in an attempt to adapt to the unique needs of each individual interviewee. In this sense there is no single way to operationalise interviewing but many equally appropriate and effective approaches to intervention (Rae, 1988; Stewart and Cash, 1988). It is a matter of choice concerning which type of help is offered, which personal style of interviewing is adopted by, for example, a doctor working with a young patient, or what particular technique of selection interviewing is employed by a personnel manager. According to Banaka (1971, p.14):

The challenge is not to get the [interviewee] to change his mode of communicating to fit the style you prefer. The goal of effective interviewing is for you to learn to adapt to his preferred mode of communicating, to allow him to feel comfortable with it.

Writing from within the research interviewing context Gorden (1987, pp.22–3), using his experience, concludes that:

no single approach, style or technique of interviewing is adequate except within narrow limits. The interviewer should strive to use an increasingly wide range of techniques and should have the ability to adapt flexibly to the purposes of the interview and the requirements of the specific situation.

It should be added that any such flexibility should, nonetheless, emanate from within the interviewer's range of competence. Interviewees who seek assistance that requires techniques which are beyond the acquired competences of the interviewer will have unethical restrictions placed upon them. In such instances,

Cormier and Cormier (1985) suggest that the helper has an obligation to consider the possibility of referral.

However, interviewers should endeavour to develop a range of strategies from which they can select a way of working with a specific interviewee. In the helping field there are a number of different strategies which, when employed appropriately, can be extremely helpful (e.g. giving information, teaching skills, giving advice or offering counselling). The notion of having alternatives is a strongly emphasised feature of effective professionals (Cormier and Cormier, 1985; Heron, 1976; Stewart and Cash, 1988). In commenting upon the 'truly skilful practitioner', Heron (1976, p.145) offers a relatively comprehensive summary of typical characteristics when he says that:

> (a) he is equally proficient in each of the six types of intervention, (b) he can move elegantly and cleanly from one type of intervention to any other as the developing situation and the purposes of the interaction require, and (c) he is aware at any given time of what type of intervention he is using and why.

This concept of being familiar with alternative ways of working with people and with 'multiple ways to work with particular problems' (Cormier and Cormier, 1985, p.227) is central to professional competence.

Heron's third point, quoted above, invokes the principle of accountability which implies a type of moral responsibility (Blackham, 1982). Fairbairn (1987) regards this notion as referring to a requirement of practitioners to be able to justify their methodology, to account for the way in which they attempt to intervene in an individual's life. Evidence from research on careers guidance, for instance, suggests that careers officers are surprisingly unable to articulate a theoretical explanation of their interventions (Reddy and Brannigan, 1982). In keeping with the spirit of codes of practice this type of moral responsibility is of substantial importance because the person of whom accountability is demanded is the interviewer himself – it is a form of self-regulation, self-reflection and a major contributor to self-determined growth.

As indicated earlier, part of this self-awareness includes the developing sense of personal limitations, of drawing boundaries. Ethical and unethical practice lie on either side of a line which does not necessarily remain cast in cement, fixed for all time. Heron (1976) has previously indicated that 'truly skilful practitioners' will strive to redraw such boundaries, increasing the range of alternative intervention strategies at their disposal. However, the establishment of professional boundaries does assume some importance where a number of people are working with a single client each making use of his specific competences while recognising the contributions of others. For example, the senior author recalls contacting a doctor to obtain some medical information (with the client's consent) when helping with career planning only to be told, 'You tell me what job the person wants to do and I'll tell you whether it is possible or not'. So, boundaries are not always mutually observed or specific expertise always recognised.

In the light of the trends towards more holistic images of persons where apparently discernible personal areas are seen as less separable, the blurring of boundaries within an interview seems more and more likely. Doctors have been urged to view patients as integrated thinking, feeling and acting human beings rather than medical cases (DiMatteo and DiNicola, 1982a, 1982b) and recent theories in the careers guidance field have similarly emphasised the relatedness between 'worker' roles and other major life roles such as spouse, parent, leisurite or citizen (Super, 1980). These theories, it is claimed, more adequately reflect the complexities of real life decisions and real life problems. Crucial life decisions cannot as a consequence be taken in the absence of a full understanding of the richness of an individual's circumstances and their individuality – it is this depth of understanding that is the goal of interviewers. Given that, ethically, professionals should recognise the limits of their own particular expertise, it becomes essential to consider the possible and particular contributions of fellow professionals. This situation logically leads on to the process of referral.

REFERRAL

On the basis of the preceding discussion, it seems reasonable to suggest that practitioners should accept and work with only those individuals with whom they are in a position to interact competently because of their particularly appropriate knowledge, skills and experience. For example, psychodynamic psychotherapists assess the suitability of potential clients in terms of the type of therapy/treatment available and may decline to take on a client who is felt to be unsuitable (that is, has a poor prognosis). Of course the client may also feel that the personal cost of this type of treatment is too great and may decide to withdraw from 'selection'.

The important point to be noted concerning referral is that it is not something 'done to' the client in his or her best interests but it is rather an explicit item on the agenda of the interview. It is a process that requires managing by the interviewer openly and honestly and not slipping it in by the back door (Cormier and Cormier, 1985). Referral considered openly allows the interviewee to explore the possibility and offers them the opportunity to assume a major part of the responsibility for following through with the outcome.

Whatever the outcome of the process the interviewer will need to earmark time in the interview to contemplate seriously the reasons for, and the costs and benefits of, a referral. The point is that managing a referral takes time. Part of the time-consuming nature of effecting a referral may derive from the array of personal feelings experienced by both participants. The interviewer may experience feelings of having failed, of being incompetent or of abandoning the interviewee. Correspondingly, the interviewee may also experience feelings of having been abandoned, dumped, rejected and of not wanting to leave the security of the relationship which has been established with this interviewer only to have to 'start again' with a new person. (After all, it was hard enough with this one!) These feelings need to be recognised, accepted and worked through before the referral is implemented. Therefore, most writers appear to agree that if a referral seems to be in the best interests of the interviewee it may be considered but only with the consent and full agreement of the interviewee (Cormier and Cormier, 1985; Munro *et al.*, 1983; Murgatroyd, 1985).

For interviewers contemplating making a referral a couple of important points should be considered at the outset. First, when an interviewer takes on an interviewee then he or she assumes the responsibility for the outcome of the interviewing process which may include the careful managing of a referral (Cormier and Cormier, 1985). In this sense referring an interviewee does not constitute an abdication of responsibility, a dumping exercise, but a decision made out of respect and concern for the interviewee and a personal recognition of limited competence. The feeling of being abandoned can be further diminished by ensuring that the interviewee's progress is followed up periodically by the referring interviewer. Indeed, just as changes in the nature of the difficulties experienced by the interviewee led to the initial referral, subsequent development under the auspices of the receiving interviewer may necessitate a referral back to the initial interviewer who can now competently and responsibly assist the interviewee once again. This is frequently experienced by patients seeking medical treatment when their symptoms cannot be fully comprehended by the doctor who refers the patient to a more specialised expert from whence the patient returns to their 'own' doctor who continues the treatment. The reason for the referral is usually clear and is accepted albeit with some trepidation. Where the reason is not clear, being passed from pillar to post usually generates considerable irritation, anger and occasionally a more violent reaction.

When a legitimate referral is not considered by an interviewer then ethical issues are raised. For example, Cormier and Cormier (1985, p.22), writing about counselling, caution that:

> Too often, either knowingly or unwittingly, counselors may lead a client toward a goal they are personally comfortable with or feel more competent to treat.

A somewhat comparable situation can be identified with respect to medical interviewers. Patients who present themselves with ostensibly psychological problems which are technically outside the scope of experience of many doctors are treated as if they actually have a physical condition treatable by methods within the doctor's range of expertise, e.g. pills. The ethics of this professional response are arguable (in the same way that the doctor cited earlier who regarded himself as an expert in vocational guidance could be called to account).

For the interviewer and interviewee considering making a referral a further element requires attention and raises a major issue pertaining to the practice of interviewing – the confidentiality of information.

CONFIDENTIALITY

Woods and McNamara (1980, p.714) employ, as a definition of confidentiality, the following:

> Confidentiality is a moral promise that a therapist gives a client that disclosures will be protected from unauthorized revelation (except in unusual circumstances) without the informed consent of the patient.

The generalisability of this definition would seem to be appropriate whatever type of interview context is being considered. It is not unusual for interviewers to ignore or not make explicit what Wicks (1982, p.317) calls the 'public relations aspects of interviewing'. In the absence of any explicit statement by the interviewer regarding issues of confidentiality the interviewee is left with his or her expectations or assumptions about the nature of the service being sought. In the absence of any explicit statement pertaining to confidentiality interviewees may, not unreasonably, assume that personal information disclosed will be regarded as strictly confidential and would not be revealed for any purposes deemed to be detrimental to themselves (Marchant, 1982). Interviewees often find it hard to talk about themselves and will be even more reticent if they do not feel that their disclosures are private. Indeed, Benjamin (1981) argues that to encourage revelations about the private self without being in a position to guarantee confidentiality is immoral. In the short term interviewees may divulge more about themselves than they otherwise would but eventually the growth of distrust will attest to the counterproductivity of such deceitful practices. Again, Marchant (1982, p.305) suggests that:

> to make the contract open and explicit (even at the risk of a loss of information in the early stages) seems...to be more useful in the long run to user, worker, agency and to society, than to cope with the growing distrust between all parties which follows.

Since we cannot usually guarantee complete confidentiality (Munro *et al.*, 1983; Woods and McNamara, 1980) the interviewee has the right to know where he or she stands with respect to what can be kept totally confidential, what might be and what almost certainly cannot (Benjamin, 1981; Munro *et al.*, 1983). There is a need, therefore, in the opening phase of interviews to state explicitly and precisely what the term 'in confidence' actually denotes, leaving nothing to the imagination of the interviewee. Based on their analogue study, Woods and McNamara (1980) reported that assurances of confidentiality exerted powerful effects on the depth of interviewee disclosures. Under their somewhat extreme conditions of confidentiality/non-confidentiality, Woods and McNamara (1980) also point out the very detrimental effects of statements of (total) non-confidentiality on the levels of self-disclosure by interviewees. However, the extent to which such extreme situations exist in real life counselling are uncertain and, therefore, the generalisability of the findings remains uncertain.

Of course, interviewers, when considering the extent to which they, as employees, can offer users of their agency the security of confidentiality, must take into account the ethics which prevail in the institution. The potential for conflict may be high. These dilemmas may be complex and have been depicted by Marchant (1982, p.301) as a:

> collision of contracts; contracts between the counsellor and the person being counselled, between the counsellor and the agency he represents, the counsellor and his professional colleagues, and between the counsellor and the society of which he is a member.

While this image is supported by Blackham (1982), he asserts that the interviewer's primary responsibility is to his client. It follows, therefore, that prior to the disclosure of 'confidential' material the release must be discussed with the interviewee who as a result may give consent or may request that certain aspects remain confidential. Such requests should, in principle, be respected by the interviewer (Benjamin, 1981). However, respecting such confidences in practice has placed interviewers in major dilemmas of conscience where demands for information by their agency conflict with their loyalties to their interviewees. Professionals are accountable, not only to their clients and themselves but also to their employers and hence operate under an institutional code of ethics/practice. The extent to which individual professionals can endorse their institution's codes will vary and in extreme cases, where a drastic conflict occurs, Benjamin (1981) advocates that professionals should in the first instance attempt to change their institutional code and, where failing to do so, they should resign their position and seek another in a more congruent organisation. Whatever the code, the practitioner should take it into account when explaining the limits to which confidentiality can be assured (Marchant, 1982).

Similarly, some institutions may require that information disclosed during individual interviews should be available on request to all or selected members of that institution (e.g. schools, work organisations). In settings such as schools, young interviewees would listen with some incredulity to assurances of total confidentiality – indeed a more open and honest conversation which more accurately reflects the limits within which disclosures may be made will serve to protect both interview participants. The cost to the interviewer of this type of contract may be the disclosure of a very selective, safe picture which leaves the interviewee feeling unthreatened, investing little of their egos in the process. However, the relationship is permitted to form on an honest and agreed basis of complete confidence within clearly accepted boundaries (Marchant, 1982). The rules of the game are clearly set out, and, although maybe not entirely satisfactory to both 'players', are the agreed basis for the game to commence. Once the players become comfortable with and begin to trust each other more, they may agree to modify the rules slightly, and play a more risky game (Dorn, 1984).

A somewhat similar scenario may pertain to employees in organisations that operate appraisal systems, or that employ their own counsellor or doctor. While

genuine guarantees of total confidentiality would certainly increase the likelihood of more honest interactions it is unlikely that such guarantees would carry
much credibility in the eyes of the interviewees whose experience may lead them
to treat such claims with a certain suspicion.

In situations where the interviewer feels that interviewee confidentiality, if
observed, would create more difficulties for the interviewee it may be per-
missible to break confidentiality. One of Munro *et al.*'s (1983, p.110) suggested
guidelines recommends that:

> Where confidentiality has to be broken because of the law or because of
> danger to the client's life, she should be informed as soon as possible.

The principle of non-disclosure obtains except in life-threatening situations
(either the client's or someone else's life) or when compelled to disclose under
legal directives. It will be evident then that there are very few situations where a
practitioner has the right to act 'unilaterally' on behalf of an interviewee on the
grounds of 'knowing best' (Marchant, 1982).

INVASION OF PRIVACY

The issue of invasion potentially applies to all assessment or data collection
situations ranging from observation, through interviewing to the use of more
sophisticated psychological tests. The right to privacy has been characterised as
essential to ensure personal dignity and freedom to be self-determined. Anastasi
(1982, p.50) defines this as:

> the right of an individual to decide for himself how much he will share with
> others his thoughts, his feelings and the facts of his personal life.

An individual, therefore, has the right to keep confidential from the interviewer
any information he or she chooses. However, where an individual volunteers to
disclose personal information in order to pursue a personal goal of, say, seeking
help with a problem or securing a job or obtaining an increase in salary via a
positive appraisal, invasions of privacy do not pose a threat. Whatever an interviewee is asked to reveal by an interviewer must at least be perceived as relevant
to the purpose – the interviewee should be able to see why the interviewer has
asked the particular question. The important point here is that what the interviewee discloses is in response to the interviewer's questions; the extent to which
this is perceived as a choice will be highly dependent upon the climate of the
interview, the style of the interviewer and the attitude displayed towards the
interviewee by the interviewer.

Whether information is relevant or not, the sensitivity of the material may also
influence the feelings of the interviewer. Although evidence is equivocal,
hypotheses have been proposed by Fowler and Mangione (1990, p.79) suggesting
that:

interviewer expectation about whether a question would be troublesome or sensitive to respondents was related to the likelihood that they would get an adequate answer to the question. Interviewers who thought a question would be sensitive to respondents were less likely to get an answer at all.

However, Fowler and Mangione (1990) failed to confirm this finding in their own research. Interestingly, when one notes the areas least likely to be covered in vocational guidance interviews then these turn out to be areas concerned with health and home circumstances. Although both have been shown to be highly related to career development, questions do surround the relevance of and the right to probe into these areas of the interviewee's private life. The senior author is reminded of a student interviewer interviewing a sixth form girl about her career plans, who started off with a long rambling monologue, followed by much stammering and stuttering accompanied by averted eye contact, ending up with an apology for having to ask such a personal question (to a young lady!) of, well here goes (the interviewee at this point is absolutely terrified of what is to come), 'Hm ... How ... old are you?' The relief felt all round was unbelievable! Of course interviewers can never be absolutely sure of just what might come up in an interview and in this sense should be ready for anything, in whatever context they might be working. If, however, as a result of their asking certain questions, the interviewee becomes upset or distressed, then it seems to us imperative that the interviewer assumes his or her responsibility for contributing to this situation and should at least consider apologising (and not taking the opportunity to escape to make the magical cup of tea). Therefore, in order to delve into an individual's more private life, relevance should be demonstrated and the individual should be able to consent or decline consent to such explorations. Whatever emerges as a result of such explorations is material that the interviewer shares responsibility for, however distressing it might turn out to be.

DOCUMENTATION

Note-taking

Note-taking is an integral part of the interviewing process (Benjamin, 1981; Bernstein and Bernstein, 1985) and, indeed, Benjamin (1981) suggests that an absence of taking notes may form the basis for an interviewee inference of negligence or a lack of interest on the part of the interviewer. Furthermore, interviewees may expect interviewers to take notes during the interview to ensure that the details are accurately documented (Hetherington, 1970). We need notes to reduce our reliance on memory, to serve as a record of agreed action plans or to form the basis of a cumulative case history (Benjamin, 1981). An over-reliance on memory can lead, not simply to serious omissions, but also to distortions, selectivity, and to varying amounts of fabrication (Breakwell, 1990; Hetherington, 1970).

The general consensus appears to suggest that human memory is just too fallible to be relied upon to recall with sufficient accuracy the contents of a completed interview. Indeed, when several interviews are scheduled one after the other the interviewee is in grave danger of becoming an amalgamation of others interviewed in the same session.

Therefore, if note-taking is considered necessary it is essential to discuss this with each interviewee during the opening phase of the interview. Interviewees should be offered reasons for note-taking and should be reassured that any notes taken are available for inspection.

In the event of interviewers' note-taking behaviour disrupting the interview it is highly likely that deficits in the calibre of the relationship will contribute to a reduction in the flow of information. It is therefore important that the inclusion of note-taking does not jeopardise the very interview itself. A number of pre-cautionary measures have been proposed to minimise the potential dangers to the effectiveness and satisfactoriness of the interview of taking notes.

First, as implied above, it is not usually helpful to be secretive about taking notes. Interviewees will be somewhat curious at best or possibly anxious at worst about what is being recorded about them – the piece of paper may in fact become the focus of the whole interview, the *raison d' être* for the interview taking place.

Second, Benjamin (1981) warns against note-taking turning the interview into an interrogation, rather like an orally administered questionnaire. In time-limited interviews where copious note-taking is undertaken there may be little else the interviewer can do but to fire question after question and hurriedly record the interviewee's responses. The first two points noted hardly attest to the worth of the individual or to a very respectful attitude on the part of the interviewer.

Third, and possibly the most important consideration, is to ensure that the flow of effective communication is preserved. Bernstein and Bernstein (1985, p.27) believe that:

> attentiveness to the patient is lessened if one is also concerned with one's notes...it would be difficult to observe and respond to nonverbal behavior while note taking.

A valuable source of data is unavailable mainly due to the frequent breaks in eye contact necessary in order to focus attention on writing things down. The senior author witnessed a careers interview where the careers officer asked the interviewee what careers she had thought of. As the interviewee began to disclose a number of ideas the careers officer repeated them syllable by syllable as he wrote them down. On witnessing this, the interviewee stopped to let him catch up; all eyes were on the piece of paper. On reaching the last career idea, and without re-establishing eye contact, the careers officer said, 'Continue!' This was a regrettable incident and had a significant influence on the climate of the interview. Interviewees who speak fluently and rapidly pose a particular problem for interviewers who attempt to take copious notes. It is rarely possible to take down verbatim records without a significant loss of attention ensuing (Stewart and Cash, 1988).

Under circumstances where extensive notes are required, interviewers are normally advised to increase the amount of eye contact by both developing a personalised method of abbreviating what is taken down and being selective in what they choose to record (Hetherington, 1970; Stewart and Cash, 1988). Additionally, methods which focus attention on key words and related phrases or on 'patterned notetaking' (Rae, 1988) have been commended. In the latter approach key ideas are noted down as they occur and can subsequently be linked together and expanded diagrammatically. The outcome is a patterned whole contained on just a single piece of paper. The use of such techniques will serve to reduce the potentially obtrusive nature of note-taking.

However, this selectivity may lead to a further problem in that interviewees may be inadvertently conditioned to discuss only those areas that they see the interviewer noting down (Bernstein and Bernstein, 1985). In an attempt to avoid communicating such a message Stewart and Cash (1988, p.89) suggest:

> not taking notes frantically during an answer but waiting until the interviewee is answering another question. Or develop the habit of taking notes throughout.

Great care and sensitivity should be exercised by interviewers regarding what is written down and when. Interviewees discussing a very sensitive personal matter charged with emotion can hardly be reassured by an interviewer scribbling the details down on his record form on which his gaze is focused. Again this is unlikely to communicate a respectful and caring attitude. 'Whose needs are being met?' would be a reasonable question to pose to this interviewer.

Fourth, there is the danger of using note-taking as a sort of prop, a means of surviving the interview. Beginning interviewers are especially vulnerable and tend to seek solace in pieces of paper from which great inspiration can be found. Mutterings such as 'Let me see what I've missed here' are indicative of what Benjamin (1981) termed 'hiding or escaping into note taking'. Unfortunately, the message communicated to interviewees implies that the task of compiling 'good and complete' records is the objective of the exercise rather than any genuine interest in them as unique worthy individuals.

Fifth, interviewees should be fully aware of how the information that they disclose will be used, which, of course, revisits the issue of confidentiality discussed earlier. Any information recorded that is intended for the interviewer's use only (e.g. evaluations, conclusions, decisions or assessments) should not be written down in the presence of the interviewee, for, if it is, then the interviewee has the right to see it (Benjamin, 1981). However, care should be taken to ensure that the interviewee and interviewer are the only individuals who will have access to the notes and subsequent records. This entails taking considerable care not to leave confidential documents lying around on a desk where unauthorised personnel could happen upon them (Benjamin, 1981). Ideally, any confidential materials should be kept in lockable cabinets, accessible only to specified individuals, and should be destroyed when the interviewing contract is terminated or after some agreed length of time (Munro *et al.*, 1983).

The principles of maintaining confidentiality previously discussed apply with increased force whenever material is committed to paper whether in note form or in more complete summaries and/or record forms.

Stewart and Cash (1988, p.89) summarise the debate concerning whether to take notes or not thus:

> Some interviewers say you should never take notes; others warn against too few or selective notes....The best advice is to select the means best suited to your objectives, the situation, the interviewee and the interview schedule.

Interview records

The taking of notes within the interview usually serves as a means of compiling a more complete record of the interview (for the agency) and/or a more succinct summary for both agency and interviewee. Once again there are differences of opinion as to whether such records should be completed during or after the interview. The potentially disruptive effects of note-taking would seem to be somewhat less than the interference likely when records are completed during the actual interaction. In situations where relatively short periods of time are available for face to face interviews the utilisation of large proportions of this time for the purpose of record completion appears to be a gross waste of the interviewee's time. We have never witnessed an interview where record completion has not severely and detrimentally affected the climate of the interview. It is as if this practice brings into question the actual purpose of the interview from the interviewee's perspective. With the exception, possibly, of the research interview, the main purpose of the interview should never be to complete a neat and final written record (Benjamin, 1981).

Within the research context, the job of the interviewer, according to Fowler and Mangione (1990, p.46) is:

> to write down the answer the respondent gives...with no interviewer judgement, no interviewer summaries, no interviewer effects on what is written down.

In this highly standardised context the intrusion of interviewer summaries and paraphrases simply introduces interviewer errors due to personal prejudices and perceptual biases. Requiring research interviewers to write down verbatim the exact words employed by each respondent removes the need to distil out what the interviewer perceives to be the essence of the interviewee's response. The attractiveness of using audio recordings will be obvious, providing that this does not serve to distort interviewee responses.

In a number of other contexts completion of records from notes immediately after the interview seems to find favour (Rae, 1988), provided that the management of successive interviews allows appropriate spaces for this task. These spaces should allow for the record to be completed plus some additional time prior to the next interviewee attending. The management of human resources (i.e. interviewers) is an important responsibility of both the individual and his agency since an interviewer whose resilience and personal resources are depleted cannot maintain his ability to deliver an ethical and competent service. The senior author recalls being told by an experienced interviewer, 'When you get as good as I am you can easily handle 26 interviews per day!' Fortunately, for our interviewees and ourselves, none of the authors ever did become quite as good as this!

A final point concerning interview records relates to the extent to which the system of recording is systematic and formalised. In situations where a number of interviewers may be involved, as in many selection procedures, it will be essential for individual interviewers to record data in similar ways and to be able to pool this information readily to aid effective decision making (Breakwell, 1990). Record forms have a higher utility where they derive from the structure employed for conducting the interview whether this is a simple guide (i.e. topic headings) or a more structured schedule.

Audio records

Opinions concerning the use of audio recordings of interviews are wide ranging. Hetherington (1970, p.169) claims that audio recordings are 'clearly the best' because they preserve nonverbal as well as verbal information, whereas Benjamin (1981) questions the utility of audio recordings as a credible alternative to written accounts.

Once again, the appropriateness of using audio recordings as opposed to written records depends primarily on the purpose for which the record is being made. For example, the main purposes suggested for taping sessions are to enable interviewers to reconstruct interview content (Bernstein and Bernstein, 1985), to provide a means of reviewing missed cues/interviewee responses (Stewart and Cash, 1988), to provide an undeniable record of what was actually said (Fowler and Mangione, 1990; Stewart and Cash, 1988) or to assist in interviewer learning/ training and research (Benjamin, 1981; Fowler and Mangione, 1990). However, Kline (1975, p.159) suggests that:

> unless we want a detailed record, notes seem preferable to a tape recording which really only throws the problems of a record one step back.

If exact records are required as in some research contexts, the tape recorder can be an immense asset provided that interviewees are not adversely affected by its presence. Research undertaken by Fowler and Mangione (1990, p.130) led them to conclude that:

> The extent to which respondents rated questions as too personal, or whether they had difficulty answering questions completely accurately because the

answers were embarrassing, was not related at all to whether the interviews were tape recorded or not.

However, although the majority of respondents (10 per cent declined to be tape recorded) were relatively unaffected by the presence of the tape recorder, interviewers who were being taped were rated by interviewees as being significantly less relaxed than those not being tape recorded. In some cases it clearly makes a difference, more so to interviewer behaviours than to interviewee responses (Fowler and Mangione, 1990).

As with taking notes during the interview, interviewees have the right to consider whether they are prepared to allow the interviewer to record the interview. While many interviewees will be quite willing for notes to be taken many will be much less enthusiastic about being recorded. There are a number of inclusions that may help to reduce the fears and suspicions which may contribute to an interviewee objecting to the recorder. These include providing a full explanation of why tape recording the interview will be advantageous to both participants (e.g. it will help increase understanding and suggest future directions), locating the tape recorder in an inconspicuous position, offering to turn it off whenever requested by the interviewee and reassuring the interviewee about what the recording will be used for, including the limits of confidentiality which can be enforced (Bernstein and Bernstein, 1985; Stewart and Cash, 1988). Furthermore, any interviewee who asks to listen to the tape has the right to do so (Banaka, 1971).

In our experience a great deal of apprehension surrounds the use of tape recorders by interviewers but if the points suggested above are discussed openly without any attempt to conceal the issue interviewees usually feel able to 'see how it goes'. If the relationship is a sound one we would support Benjamin's (1981, p.66) observation when he says:

> I am fairly convinced that after the first few minutes he will not react to it at all for he will no longer take notice of it.

THE LEGAL PERSPECTIVE

While it is beyond the scope of this final section to present an extensive account of all pertinent legislation it was felt to be important to include reference to some of the more pertinent legal issues for professionals who tend to employ the interview as their main method of intervention. In addition to protecting the rights of individuals by recommending that practitioners operate according to published codes of ethics and practice, legislation has also evolved to bolster individual rights, sometimes, however, at the expense of the rights of others and sometimes in conflict with the wishes of agencies. With respect to confidentiality, there are no professionals who are protected by the law (except for lawyers) regarding the holding of privileged information on individuals. Therefore, confessions made to a doctor, a priest or a counsellor are not regarded in law as privileged and, if requested, must be disclosed in a court of law (but not in response to police questioning). Lewis and Murgatroyd (1976, p.10) observe that despite 'the Hippocratic Oath (which dates from the 5th century BC)...doctors may still be *required* to breach such confidence at the direction of the judge'.

It should be noted that such directions to disclose information collected 'in confidence' relate both to the verbal exchange between interviewer and interviewee and to any personal records maintained by the interviewer. Personal records can be defined as (BAC, 1989):

> those acquired in the course of a trade, business or profession and held in confidence. They are documents or records that make it possible to identify an individual and which relate to their physical or mental health; or spiritual counselling; or help given for the purpose of the individual's personal welfare by a voluntary agency or by an individual who has responsibility for a person's personal welfare.

Access to such records, even for the police, requires that an application for a search warrant is formally made. The Data Protection Act (1984) concerning information held on computer gives individuals the right of access to their own personal files and disclosure may also be demanded by a court of law.

One further point needs to be made which concerns information disclosed 'in confidence' which suggests that the interviewee may be intending to cause harm to another individual. Although codes of ethics have always allowed such disclosures (by doctors, social workers and counsellors) in these special circumstances, Lewis and Murgatroyd (1976) cite a ruling in the State of California by the Supreme Court where it:

> determined that a doctor or psychotherapist or counsellor who has reason to believe that a person may harm someone must notify the potential victim, his friends or relatives or the authorities.

In Lewis and Murgatroyd's (1976, p.13) words, 'the protective privilege ends where public peril begins'.

The second major context in which legal issues have been more prevalent is in selection interviewing. Campion and Arvey (1989) suggest that there are a number of problematic areas with respect to employment interviewing which relate to deterrent recruitment practices, the poor selection and training of interviewers in appropriate behaviours and subjectivity in evaluation. Many of the shortcomings of selection interviewing also apply to performance appraisal situations and Campion and Arvey (1989) suggest a number of ways that the legal defensibility of the interview can be enhanced.

First, interviewers should ensure that the content of selection interviews is job related and relevant and derived from a thorough job analysis (Feild and Gatewood, 1989). Interviews derived from job analyses are more likely to be able to justify their content, their questioning strategies and their evaluation standards (Campion and Arvey, 1989; Latham, 1989; Runnymede/BPS, 1980). As was suggested in chapter six, interviewing strategies which adopt a degree of structure tend to reduce the opportunities for interviewer biases to intrude into the process (Runnymede/BPS, 1980) and therefore reduce the operation of a 'ready mechanism for illegal discrimination' (Campion and Arvey, 1989). Current legislation enshrined in the Fair Employment (NI) Act (1989) now compels employers to review their recruitment, training and promotion practices at least once every three years. Direct discrimination, outlawed since 1976, has been joined by the outlawing of (more widespread) indirect discrimination.

Second, Campion and Arvey (1989, p.63) cite what they call 'Taboo Interviewer Behaviors' as a major source of error when they state that:

> The courts have also raised doubts about the appropriateness of certain interviewer behaviours, especially when interviewer questioning varies across groups of applicants.

The potential for legal proceedings is more likely if applicants perceive that different people are asked different questions or if their answers to the same questions are evaluated differently (Latham, 1989). This is particularly pertinent to indirect discrimination based on sex, age or race criteria. It should be noted, however, that simply ensuring that the same questions are posed to all candidates, in itself, may not automatically eradicate discrimination. It is plausible to propose that certain questions could systematically discriminate either against or in favour of specific human groups. Presumably asking all interviewees if they would be prepared to have their hair cut (as an entry requirement) would systematically discriminate against certain religious groups. Under current legislation this rather more subtle, indirect discrimination contravenes the law. It is therefore important that interviewers are well trained with respect to legally defensible questioning techniques.

The final point refers to the importance of keeping records which document the basis of selection decisions, particularly those which involve a reject decision (Runnymede/BPS, 1980). Adequate defence against lawsuits would be greatly enhanced by the keeping of accurate records of the evidence underlying selection decisions previously made. A lack of such records has been a serious problem for some organisations (Campion and Arvey, 1989). A similar line of reasoning has been proffered for the use of written summaries of guidance within the careers guidance field. A similar rationale would be equally appropriate for those engaged in appraisal interviewing where cumulative records are an essential component of this developmental process.

In summary Campion and Arvey (1989, p.72) assert that:

> Errors by interviewers can leave the company open to costly and time consuming charges of unfair discrimination. Thus, employers and interviewers must be sensitive to the subtleties of discrimination against females, minorities, the aged, the handicapped and other protected classes.

Of course the benefits which might accrue to the employer are not just a reduction in potential lawsuits and legal fees but, more importantly, will result in the recruitment, training and promotion of more suitable and more effective employees.

SUMMARY

This chapter has presented some thoughts on a range of professional issues which have an important bearing on the practice of interviewing as employed by a range of personal services. Reference was made to the provision of codes of ethics and codes of practice issued by the appropriate professional associations which attempt to protect and safeguard the rights of the individual users of the various services. As the main method of service delivery is by personal interviewing, the ethical and legal issues relating to professional practice are highly pertinent. Hopefully, this chapter will serve to raise these complex matters in the minds of professional interviewers and as a result will increase their sensitivities to the rights of those individuals with whom they interact. In order to effect these safeguards professional interviewers strive to develop the range and depth of their competences and further seek to be mindful of issues pertaining to respect for and the rights of their interviewees.

Chapter 10

Concluding comments

This book has been concerned with the study of interviewing. The interview is a ubiquitous activity. Everyone will have had the experience of being interviewed at one time or another, and an increasing number of people are required to play the role of interviewer in a professional capacity. For this latter group, a knowledge of the nature of interviewing can make an important contribution to effective practice, and it is for this target audience that the present text has been designed.

However, the task of producing a generic text on interviewing has not been an easy one. The literature on this subject is voluminous (as a quick scan of the reference section of this book will verify). For example, one book on research interviewing published some years ago (Sudman and Bradburn, 1974) lists nearly one thousand studies in its bibliography. Likewise, the literature in other interviewing fields is also vast. As a result, it would be impossible to write a 'definitive' text on interviewing, since it is necessary to be selective in terms of what should be included. Furthermore, as we have illustrated in this book, interviews are carried out in a wide range of locations and for a variety of purposes. In this sense, interviewing is clearly a context-related activity and so it was necessary to link our analysis to specific interviewing situations. We selected five main categories of interview upon which to base our examples, namely counselling, selection, research, medical and appraisal, since these have been the main focus of research and evaluation within the literature. At the same time, our definition of interviewing as presented in chapter one recognises the core themes of all interviews as being primarily face-to-face, dyadic, role-related, requested by one of the participants, purposeful and engaged in voluntarily by both parties.

The overall approach which we adopted was to base our analysis of the interview firmly upon a model of interpersonal interaction which is theoretically embedded in the discipline area of social psychology. This model, as outlined in chapter two, highlighted seven main facets of interviewing. These were the *goals* of the interviewer and interviewee, the influence of *mediating factors* such as cognitions and emotions upon the actual *responses* of both participants, the *feedback* available during interviews and the ability of both people to *perceive* accurately all the available information, *personal aspects* including the age and gender of those involved and, finally, *situational factors* such as the location and physical lay-out of the interview. This analysis of the central processes involved in interviewing was then widened to encompass social psychological perspectives including attribution theory and social influence processes (chapter three).

The remaining chapters explored these dimensions, and their applications to interviewing, in more depth. Thus, chapter four was concerned with the area of perception, chapter five focused upon the nature of goals, chapter six examined interview stages and strategies while in chapter seven the core interpersonal skills necessary for effective interviewing were analysed. Chapter eight was then devoted to the study of the client's perspectives within the interview process and chapter nine presented a number of issues pertaining to the professional practice of interviewing such as confidentiality, record keeping and referral.

Although we have selected five main interviewing contexts upon which to base examples, the information contained throughout this book will be of relevance to those involved in all types of interviewing. At the same time, it is recognised that our selection of material is by no means exhaustive, since it would have been possible to include more detailed coverage of specific psychological topics or to extend our range of specialised interviewing situations. However, given the constraints of space and our objective of producing a generic interviewing book, we believe that the information presented does represent the core elements of professional interviewing.

It has not been our intention to offer a cook-book approach to the study of interviewing. There is no set recipe for 'The Effective Interview' since there is no predestined right or wrong way to interview. Rather, there is a range of alternative skills and strategies which can be employed in different ways depending upon the context and the nature of the interviewee, and it is the job of the interviewer to select those she considers to be most appropriate. Such decision-making, however, demands an awareness of the nature of interviewing as an interpersonal process, together with a knowledge of those factors which influence success or failure in interviews. It is at this level that the present book has been geared. A knowledge of the theory, research and practical applications covered herein will enable the reader to increase his understanding of the many facets of interviewing. At the very least it provides a language which can be used to study, interpret and evaluate the practice of interviewing.

In the final analysis, however, improvements in interviewing performance necessitate practice. Thus, we would encourage all interviewers to make a commitment to develop, refine and extend their existing approach to interviewing. By so doing, the individual becomes a more effective professional with the ability to adapt and adjust to varying interview situations.

In conclusion, therefore, this book has been concerned with a comprehensive analysis and evaluation of professional interviewing in terms of: offering a meaningful applied theoretical model upon which to base the study of the interview; providing an insight into many of the nuances of this activity; examining the behaviour of interviewers and the ways in which this can influence interviewees; interpreting and making sense of the responses of interviewees; and generally attempting to contribute to an increased social awareness and professional competence on the part of interviewers. As such, this book should be a valuable reference text, both for professionals undergoing interview training and for experienced interviewers.

References

Anastasi, A. (1982) *Psychological Testing* (5th edition), New York: Macmillan.

Anderson, N. and Shackleton, V. (1990) Decision making in the graduate selection interview: a field study. *Journal of Occupational Psychology*, 63, 63–76.

Argyle, M. (1988) *Bodily Communication* (2nd edition). London: Methuen.

Argyle, M., Furnham, A. and Graham, J. (1981) *Social Situations*. Cambridge: Cambridge University Press.

Arvey, R. and Campion, J. (1984) Person perception in the employment interview. In M. Cook (ed) *Issues in Person Perception*. London: Methuen.

Asch, S.E. (1946) Forming impressions of personality. *Journal of Abnormal and Social Psychology*, 41, 258–90.

Authier, J. (1986) Showing warmth and empathy. In O. Hargie (ed) *A Handbook of Communication Skills*. London: Routledge.

Averill, J. (1975) A semantic atlas of emotional concepts. *JSAS Catalogue of Selected Documents in Psychology*, 5, 330.

Balthazar, E.E. (1973) *Balthazar Scales of Adaptive Behavior II. Scales of Social Adaptation*. Palo Alto, California: Consulting Psychologists Press.

Banaka, W.H. (1971) *Training in Depth Interviewing*. New York: Harper & Row.

Baron, R.A. (1981) The role of olfaction in human social behavior: effects of a pleasant scent and attraction on social perception. *Personality and Social Psychology Bulletin*, 7, 611–17.

Baron, R.A. (1989) Impression management by applicants during employment interviews: the 'too much of a good thing' effect. In R.W. Eder and G.R. Ferris (eds) *The Employment Interview: Theory, Research and Practice*. California: Sage.

Baron, R.A. and Byrne, D. (1984) *Social Psychology. Understanding Human Interaction* (4th edition). Boston: Allyn & Bacon.

Bayne, R. (1977) Can selection interviewing be improved? *Journal of Occupational Psychology*, 50, 161–8.

Bedford, T. (1982) *Vocational Guidance Interviews Explored: A Model and Some Training Implications*. London: Careers Service Branch, Department of Employment.

Beggs, R.M., MacFarlane, A. and Sloman, W. (1970) *Interviewing in the Clinical Situation*. English Speaking Board.

Benbenishty, R. and Schul, Y. (1987) Client–therapist congruence of expectations over the course of therapy. *British Journal of Clinical Psychology*, 26, 17–24.

Benjamin, A. (1981) *The Helping Interview* (3rd edition), New York: Houghton-Mifflin.

Bernstein, L. and Bernstein, R.S. (1980) *Interviewing: A Guide for Health Professionals* (3rd edition), New York: Appleton-Century-Crofts.

Bernstein, L. and Bernstein, R.S. (1985) *Interviewing. A Guide for Health Professionals* (4th edition). Norwalk, Conn.: Appleton-Century-Crofts.

Bernstein, L. and Dana, R.H. (1970) *Interviewing and the Health Professions*. New York: Appleton-Century-Crofts.

Beveridge, W.E. (1975) *The Interview in Staff Appraisal*. London: Allen & Unwin.

Bilodeau, E. and Bilodeau, I. (1961) Motor-skills learning. *Annual Review of Psychology*, 12, 243–80.

Blackham, H.J. (1982) Responsibility of the counsellor. In A.W. Bolger (ed) *Counselling in Britain. A Reader*. London: Batsford.

Bower, G.H. (1983) *Affect and Cognition*. London: Philosophical Transactions of the Royal Society.

Bradac, J.J. and Wisegarver, R. (1984) Ascribed status, lexical diversity and accent: Determinants of perceived status, solidarity and control of speech style. *Journal of Language and Social Psychology*, 3, 239–55.

Bradburn, N. and Sudman, S. (1980) *Improving Interview Method and Questionnaire Design: Response Effects to Threatening Questions in Survey Research*. Chicago: Aldine.

Breakwell, G. (1986) *Coping with Threatened Identities*. London: Methuen.

Breakwell, G.M. (1990) *Interviewing*. London: Routledge.

Brenner, M. (1981) Skills in the research interview. In M. Argyle (ed) *Social Skills and Work*. London: Methuen.

Brenner, M. (1985a) Survey interviewing. In M. Brenner, J. Brown and D. Canter (eds) *The Research Interview. Uses and Approaches*. London: Academic Press.

Brenner, M. (1985b) Intensive interviewing. In M. Brenner, J. Brown and D. Canter (eds) *The Research Interview. Uses and Approaches*. London: Academic Press.

Brenner, M., Brown, J. and Canter, D. (eds) (1985) *The Research Interview. Uses and Approaches*. London: Academic Press.

British Association for Counselling (1979) *Proposed Definitions of Counselling*. BAC Standards and Ethics Committee. London: BAC.

British Association for Counselling (1984) *Code of Ethics and Code of Practice for Counsellors*. London: BAC.

Brown, G.A. and Armstrong, S. (1984) On explaining. In E.C. Wragg (ed) *Classroom Teaching Skills*. London: Croom Helm.

Byrne, P. and Long, B. (1976) *Doctors Talking to Patients*. London: HMSO.

Campion, J.E. and Arvey, R.D. (1989) Unfair discrimination in the employment interview. In R.W. Eder and G.R. Ferris (eds) *The Employment Interview: Theory, Research and Practice*. Newbury Park, Ca.: Sage.

Cannell, C.F. and Kahn, R.F. (1968) Interviewing. In G. Lindzey and E. Aronson (eds) *The Handbook of Social Psychology*, Volume 2. Reading, Mass.: Addison-Wesley.

Cantor, N. and Mischel, W. (1979) Prototypes in person perception. In L. Berkowitz (ed) *Advances in Experimental Social Psychology*, Volume 12. New York: Academic Press.

Carlson, R. (1984) *The Nurse's Guide to Better Communication*. Glenview, Ill.: Scott, Forseman & Co.

Carlson, R.E., Thayer, P.W., Mayfield, E.C. and Peterson, D.A. (1971) Research on the selection interview. *Personnel Journal*, 50, 268–75.

Carroll, J. (1980) Analysing decision behaviour: the magician's audience. In T. Wallsten (ed) *Cognitive Processes in Choice and Decision Behavior*. Hillsdale, NJ: Lawrence Erlbaum.

Carroll, J.G. and Munroe, J. (1979) Teaching medical interviewing: a critique of educational research and practice. *Journal of Medical Education*, 54, 478–500.

Cash, T.F. (1985) The impact of grooming style on the evaluation of women in management. In M. Solomon (ed) *The Psychology of Fashion*. New York: Lexington Press.

Cherry, N. (1974) Clients' experience of vocational guidance. *Journal of Vocational Behavior*, 4, 67–76.

Cherry, N.M. and Gear, R. (1987) Young people's perceptions of their vocational guidance needs: 1. priorities and preoccupations. *British Journal of Guidance and Counselling*, 15, 59–71.

Claiborn, C.D. (1979) Counselor verbal intervention, nonverbal behavior, and social power, *Journal of Counseling Psychology*, 26, 378–83.

Clark, M., Milberg, S. and Erber, R. (1984) Effects of arousal on judgements of others' emotions. *Journal of Personality and Social Psychology*, 46, 551–60.

Cohen, A.A. (1987) *The Television News Interview*. Newbury Park, Ca.: Sage.

Cohen, C.E. (1981) Person categories and social perception: testing some boundaries of the processing effects of prior knowledge. *Journal of Personality and Social Psychology*, 40, 441–52.

Cohen, L. and Mannion, L. (1980) *Research Methods in Education*, Beckenham, Kent: Croom Helm.

Cook, M. (1984) *Issues in Person Perception*. London: Methuen.

Cormier, W.H. and Cormier, L.S. (1985) *Interviewing Strategies for Helpers* (2nd edition). Monterey, Ca.: Brooks/Cole.

Corrigan, J.D. (1978) Salient attributes of two types of helpers: friends and mental health professionals. *Journal of Counseling Psychology*, 25, 588–90.

Corrigan, J.D., Dell, D.M., Lewis, K.N. and Schmidt, L.D. (1980) Counseling as a social influence process: a review. *Journal of Counseling Psychology*, 27, 395–441.

Crute, V.C., Hargie, O.D.W. and Ellis, R.A.F. (1989) An evaluation of a communication skills course for health visitor students. *Journal of Advanced Nursing*, 14, 546–52.

Devries, D., Morrison, A., Shullman, S. and Gerlach, M. (1981) *Performance Appraisal on the Line*. New York: Wiley.

Dickson, D. (1986) Reflecting. In O. Hargie (ed) *A Handbook of Communication Skills*. London: Routledge.

Dickson, D., Hargie, O. and Morrow, N. (1989) *Communication Skills Training for Health Professionals: An Instructor's Handbook*. London: Chapman & Hall.

Dijkstra, W., Van Der Veen, L. and Van Der Zouwen, J. (1985) A field experiment in interviewer–respondent interaction. In M. Brenner, J. Brown and D. Canter (eds) *The Research Interview. Uses and Approaches*. London: Academic Press.

Dillon, J. (1990) *The Practice of Questioning*. London: Routledge.

DiMatteo, M.R. and DiNicola, D.D. (1982a) *Achieving Patient Compliance. The Psychology of the Medical Practitioner's Role*. New York: Pergamon.

DiMatteo, M.R. and DiNicola, D.D. (1982b) Social science and the art of medicine. In H.S. Friedman and M.R. DiMatteo (eds) *Interpersonal Issues in Health Care*. London: Academic Press.

Dipboye, R.L. (1989) Incremental validity of interviewer judgements. In R.W. Eder and G.R. Ferris (eds) *The Employment Interview: Theory, Research and Practice*. Newbury Park, Ca.: Sage.

Dorn, F.J. (1984) *Counseling as Applied Social Psychology. An Introduction to the Social Influence Model*. Springfield, Ill.: Charles C. Thomas.

Dougherty, T.W., Ebert, R.J. and Callender, J.C. (1986) Policy capturing in the employment interview. *Journal of Applied Psychology*, 71, 9–15.

Downs, C., Smeyak, G. and Martin, E. (1980) *Professional Interviewing*. New York: Harper & Row.

Dryden, W. (1987) *Counselling Individuals: The Rational-Emotive Approach*. London: Taylor & Francis.

Echterling, L.G., Hartsough, D.. and Zarle, T.H. (1980) Testing a model for the process of telephone crisis intervention. *American Journal of Community Psychology*, 8, 715–25.

Eder, R.W. and Ferris, G.R. (eds) (1989) *The Employment Interview: Theory, Research and Practice.* Newbury Park, Ca.: Sage.

Eder, R.W., Kacmar, K.M. and Ferris, G.R. (1989) Employment interview research: history and synthesis. In R.W. Eder and G.R. Ferris (eds) *The Employment Interview: Theory, Research and Practice.* Newbury Park, Ca.: Sage.

Egan, G. (1982) *The Skilled Helper* (2nd edition). Monterey, Ca.: Brooks/Cole.

Egan, G. (1986) *The Skilled Helper* (3rd edition). Monterey, Ca.: Brooks/Cole.

Einhorn, L.J., Bradley, P.H. and Baird, J.E. (1982) *Effective Employment Interviewing: Unlocking Human Potential.* London: Scott, Forseman, Little & Brown.

Elliot, J. (1980) Introduction. In L. Bernstein and R. Bernstein (eds) *Interviewing: A Guide for Health Professionals.* New York: Appleton-Century-Crofts.

Ellis, A. (1962) *Reason and Emotion in Psychotherapy.* New York: Lyle Stuart.

Ellis, A. Rational-emotive therapy. In E.L. Shostrum (producer) *Three Approaches to Psychotherapy–Gloria* (video). Ipswich: Concord Video and Film Council.

Ellis, A. and Beattie, G. (1986) *The Psychology of Language and Communication.* Hillsdale, NJ: Lawrence Erlbaum Associates.

Ellis, R. and Whittington, D. (1981) *A Guide to Social Skills Training.* Beckenham, Kent: Croom Helm.

Ellis, R. and Whittington, D. (eds) (1983) *New Directions in Social Skills Training.* Beckenham, Kent: Croom Helm.

Fairbairn, G. (1987) Responsibility, respect for persons and psychological change. In S. Fairbairn and G. Fairbairn (eds) *Psychology, Ethics and Change.* London: Routledge & Kegan Paul.

Farr, J.L. and York, C.M. (1975) Amount of information and primacy–recency effects in recruitment decisions. *Personnel Psychology,* 28, 233–8.

Farr, R. (1982) Interviewing: the social psychology of the interview. In A.J. Chapman and A. Gale (eds) *Psychology and People.* London: BPS/Macmillan.

Feild, H.S. and Gatewood, R.D. (1989) Development of a selection interview: a job content strategy. In R.W. Eder and G.R. Ferris (eds) *The Employment Interview: Theory, Research and Practice.* Newbury Park, Ca.: Sage.

Festinger, L. (1957) *A Theory of Cognitive Dissonance.* Stanford, Ca.: Stanford University Press.

Fitts, P. and Posner, M. (1973) *Human Performance.* London: Prentice-Hall.

Fletcher, C. and Williams, R. (1976) The influence of performance feedback in appraisal interviews. *Journal of Occupational Psychology,* 49, 75–83.

Fletcher, C. and Williams, R. (1985) *Performance Appraisal and Career Development.* London: Hutchinson.

Fletcher, J. (1988) *Effective Interviewing* (3rd edition). London: Kogan Page.

Fong, M.L. and Cox, B.G. (1983) Trust as an underlying dynamic in the counseling process: how clients test trust. *Personnel and Guidance Journal,* 66, 163–6.

Foon, A.E. (1986) Locus of control and clients' expectations of psychotherapeutic outcome. *British Journal of Clinical Psychology,* 25, 161–71.

Forbes, R.J. and Jackson, P.R. (1980) Non-verbal behaviour and the outcome of selection interviews. *Journal of Occupational Psychology,* 53, 65–72.

Forgas, J. (1983) What is social about social cognition? *British Journal of Social Psychology,* 22, 129–44.

Forgas, J. (1985) *Interpersonal Behaviour,* Oxford: Pergamon.

Forgas, J.P., Bower, G.H. and Krantz, S.E. (1984) The influence of mood on perceptions of social interactions. *Journal of Experimental Social Psychology,* 20, 497–513.

Forgas, J.P., O'Connor, K. and Morris, S. (1983) Smile and punishment: the effects of facial expression on responsibility attribution by groups and individuals. *Personality and Social Psychology Bulletin,* 9, 587–96.

Forsythe, S., Drake, M.F. and Cox, C.E. (1985) Influence of applicants' dress on interviewer's selection decisions. *Journal of Applied Psychology*, 70, 374–8.

Fowler, F.J. and Mangione, T.W. (1990) *Standardized Survey Interviewing. Minimizing Interviewer-Related Error*. Applied Social Research Methods Series Volume 18. Newbury Park, Ca.: Sage.

French, P. (1983) *Social Skills for Nursing Practice*. Beckenham, Kent: Croom Helm.

Frijda, N.H. (1986) *The Emotions*. Cambridge: Cambridge University Press.

Gage, N.L. and Cronbach, L.J. (1955) Conceptual and methodological problems in interpersonal perception. *Psychological Review*, 62, 411–22.

Gallagher, M.S. (1987) The microskills approach to counsellor training: a study of counsellor personality, attitudes and skills. Unpublished D.Phil. Thesis, University of Ulster, Jordanstown, Northern Ireland.

Gamsu, D.S. and Bradley, C. (1987) Clinical staff's attributions about diabetes: scale developments and staff vs patient comparisons. *Current Psychological Research and Reviews*, 6, 69–78.

Gill, C. (1973) Types of interview in general practice: the flash. In E. Balint and J. Norell (eds) *Six Minutes For The Patient: Interactions in General Practice Consultations*. London: Tavistock.

Gill, D. (1977) *Appraising Performance: Present Trends and the Next Decade*. London: Institute of Personnel Management.

Gillespie, C.R. and Bradley, C. (1988) Causal attributions of doctor and patients in a diabetes clinic. *British Journal of Clinical Psychology*, 27, 67–76.

Glassman, W.E. (1979) The cognitive approach. In J. Medcof and J. Roth (eds) *Approaches to Psychology*. Milton Keynes: Open University Press.

Goldstein, A.P. (1962) *Therapist–Patient Expectancies in Psychotherapy*. Oxford: Pergamon Press.

Goodale, J.G. (1989) Effective employment interviewing. In R.W. Eder and G.R. Ferris (eds) *The Employment Interview: Theory, Research and Practice*. Newbury Park, Ca.: Sage.

Goodworth, G.T. (1979) *Effective Interviewing for Employment Selection*. London: Business Books.

Gorden, R.L. (1975) *Interviewing: Strategies, Techniques and Tactics* (2nd edition). Homewood, Ill.: Dorsey Press.

Gorden, R.L. (1987) *Interviewing: Strategies, Techniques and Tactics* (4th edition). Homewood, Ill.: Dorsey Press.

Gothard, W.P. (1985) *Vocational Guidance Theory and Practice*. Beckenham, Kent: Croom Helm.

Graves, L.M. and Powell, G.N. (1988) An investigation of sex discrimination in recruiters' evaluation of actual applicants. *Journal of Applied Psychology*, 73, 20–9.

Greenwald, M. (1981) The effects of physical attractiveness, experience and social performance on employee decision-making in job interviews. *Behavioral Counseling Quarterly*, 1, 275–88.

Hamilton, D.L. and Rose, T.L. (1980) Illusory correlation and the maintenance of stereotypic beliefs. *Journal of Personality and Social Psychology*, 139, 832–45.

Hamilton, D.L. and Zanna, M.P. (1972) Differential weighting of favourable and unfavourable attributes in impressions of personality. *Journal of Experimental Research in Personality*, 6, 204–12.

Hargie, O. (ed) (1986) *A Handbook of Communication Skills*. London: Routledge.

Hargie, O.D.W. and Marshall, P. (1986) Interpersonal communication: a theoretical framework. In O.D.W. Hargie (ed) *A Handbook of Communication Skills*. London: Routledge.

Hargie, O.D.W. and Saunders, C. (1983) Training professional skills. In P. Dowrick and S. Biggs (eds) *Using Video*. London: Wiley.

Hargie, O., Saunders, C. and Dickson, D. (1987) *Social Skills in Interpersonal Communication* (2nd edition). Beckenham, Kent: Croom Helm.

Harn, T.J. and Thornton, G.C., III (1985) Recruiter counselling behaviours and applicant impressions. *Journal of Occupational Psychology*, 58, 57–66.

Harvey, J.H. and Weary, G. (1981) *Perspectives on Attributional Process*. Dubuque, Iowa: Wm. C. Brown.

Havighurst, R.J. (1972) *Developmental Tasks and Education* (3rd edition). New York: David McKay.

Hawkins, R.P. and Daly, J. (1988) Cognition and communication. In R.P. Hawkins, J.M. Wiemann and S. Pingree (eds) *Advancing Communication Science: Merging Mass and Interpersonal Processes*. Beverly Hills, Ca.: Sage.

Heath, C. (1986) *Body Movement and Speech in Medical Interaction*. Cambridge: Cambridge University Press.

Heider, F. (1958) *The Psychology of Interpersonal Relations*. New York: Wiley.

Heilman, M.E. (1980) The impact of situational factors on personal decisions concerning women: varying the sex composition of the applicant pool. *Organizational Behavior and Human Performance*, 26, 386–96.

Heilman, M.E. and Saruwatari, L.E. (1979) When beauty is beastly: the effects of appearance and sex on evaluations of job applicants for managerial and nonmanagerial jobs. *Organizational Behavior and Human Performance*, 23, 360–72.

Heppner, P.P. and Heesacker, M. (1982) The interpersonal influence process in real life counseling: investigating client perceptions, counselor experience level, and counselor power over time. *Journal of Counseling Psychology*, 29, 215–23.

Heppner, P.P. and Pew, S. (1977) Effects of diplomas, awards and counselor sex on perceived expertise. *Journal of Counseling Psychology*, 24, 147–9.

Heritage, J.C. (1985) Analysing news interviews: aspects of the production of talk for an overhearing audience. In T.A. Van Dijk (ed) *Handbook of Discourse Analysis*, Volume 3, *Discourse and Dialogue*. London: Academic Press.

Herman, C.P., Zanna, M.P. and Higgins, E.T. (1986) *Physical Appearance, Stigma and Social Behavior*. Hillsdale, NJ: Lawrence Erlbaum Associates.

Heron, J. (1976) A six category intervention analysis. *British Journal of Guidance and Counselling*, 4, 143–55.

Herriot, P. (1981) Towards an attributional model of the selection interview. *Journal of Occupational Psychology*, 54, 165–73.

Herriot, P. (1985) Give and take in graduate selection. *Personnel Management*, May, 33–5.

Herriot, P. (1989) Attribution theory and interview decisions. In R.W. Eder and G.R. Ferris (eds) *The Employment Interview: Theory, Research and Practice*. Newbury Park, Ca.: Sage.

Hetherington, R.R. (1970) The clinical interview. In P. Mittler (ed) *The Psychological Assessment of Mental and Physical Handicaps*. London: Tavistock.

Hewton, E. (1988) *The Appraisal Interview*. Milton Keynes: Open University Press.

Hodgson, P. (1987) *A Practical Guide to Successful Interviewing*. Maidenhead: McGraw-Hill.

Hollandsworth, J.G. Jr., Kazelskis, A., Stevens, J. and Dressel, M.E. (1979) Relative contributions of verbal, articulative, and nonverbal communication to employment decisions in the job interview setting. *Personnel Psychology*, 32, 359–67.

Hopson, B. (1981) Counselling and helping. In D. Griffiths (ed) *Psychology and Medicine*. London: Macmillan.

Hopson, B. (1982) Counselling and helping. In A.J. Chapman and A. Gale (eds) *Psychology and People. A Tutorial Text*. London: BPS/Macmillan.

Hopson, B. and Scally, M. (1981) *Lifeskills Teaching*. London: McGraw-Hill.

Hui, C.H. and Yam, Y-M. (1987) Effects of language proficiency and physical attractiveness on person perception. *British Journal of Social Psychology*, 26, 257–61.

Hunt, G.T. and Eadie, W.F. (1987) *Interviewing: A Communication Approach*. New York: Holt, Rinehart & Winston.

Imada, A.S. and Hakel, M.D. (1977) Influence of nonverbal communication and rater proximity on impressions and decisions in simulated employment interviews. *Journal of Applied Psychology*, 62, 295–300.

Institute of Careers Officers (1987) *A Code of Practice for Careers Guidance*. Stourbridge: Institute of Careers Officers.

Ivey, A.E. (1971) *MicroCounseling: Innovations in Interview Training*. Springfield, Ill.: Charles Thomas.

Ivey, A.E. (1983) *Intentional Interviewing and Counseling*. Monterey, Ca.: Brooks/Cole.

Ivey, A., Ivey, M. and Simek-Dowling, L. (1987) *Counseling and Psychotherapy: Integrating Skills, Theory and Practice*. Englewood Cliffs, NJ: Prentice-Hall.

Izard, C.E. (1977) *Human Emotions*. New York: Plenum Press.

Jackson, D.N. (1972) A model for inferential accuracy. *Canadian Psychologist*, 13, 185–95.

Jackson, D.N., Peacock, A.C. and Holden, R.R. (1982) Professional interviewers' trait inferential structures for diverse occupational groups. *Organizational Behavior and Human Performance*, 29, 1–20.

Jackson, D.N., Peacock, A.C. and Smith, J.P. (1980) Impressions of personality in the employment interview. *Journal of Personality and Social Psychology*, 39, 294–307.

Janz, T. (1989) The patterned behavior description interview: the best prophet of the future is the past. In R.W. Eder and G.R. Ferris (eds) *The Employment Interview: Theory, Research and Practice*. Newbury Park, Ca.: Sage.

Jones, E.E. and Berglas, S. (1978) Control of attributions about the self through self-handicapping strategies: the appeal of alcohol and the role of underachievement. *Personality and Social Psychology Bulletin*, 4, 200–6.

Jones, E.E. and Davis, K.E. (1965) From acts to dispositions: the attribution process in person perception. In L. Berkowitz (ed) *Advances in Experimental Social Psychology*, Volume 2. New York: Academic Press.

Jones, E.E. and Harris, V.A. (1967) The attribution of attitudes. *Journal of Experimental Social Psychology*, 3, 1–24.

Jones, E.E. and McGillis, D. (1976) Correspondent inferences and the attribution cube: a comparative reappraisal. In J.H. Harvey, J.W. Ickes and R.F. Kidd (eds) *New Directions in Attribution Research*, Volume 1. Hillsdale, NJ: Lawrence Erlbaum.

Jones, E.E. and Nisbett, R.E.(1972) The actor and the observer: divergent perceptions of the causes of behavior. In E.E. Jones, D.E. Kanouse, H.H. Kelley, R.E. Nisbett, S. Valins and B. Weiner (eds) *Attribution: Perceiving the Causes of Behavior*. Morristown, NJ: General Learning Press.

Jones, E.E. and Pittman, T.S. (1982) Towards a general theory of strategic self-presentation. In J. Suls (ed) *Social Psychological Perspectives on the Self*. Hillsdale, NJ: Lawrence Erlbaum.

Jones, R.A. (1982) Expectations and illness. In H.S. Friedman and M.R. DiMatteo (eds) *Interpersonal Issues in Health Care*. London: Academic Press.

Jones, R.A. (1986) Perceiving other people: stereotyping as a process of social cognition. In J. Stewart (ed) *Bridges Not Walls: A Book About Interpersonal Communication*. New York: Random House.

Kaul, T.J. and Schmidt, L.D. (1971) Dimensions of interviewer trustworthiness. *Journal of Counseling Psychology*, 18, 542–8.

Keenan, A. (1977) Some relationships between interviewers' personal feelings about candidates and their general evaluation of them. *Journal of Occupational Psychology*, 50, 275–83.

Keenan, A. (1978) The selection interview: candidates' reactions and interviewers' judgements. *British Journal of Social and Clinical Psychology*, 17, 201–9.

Keenan, A. and Wedderburn, A.A.I. (1980) Putting the boot on the other foot: candidates' descriptions of interviewers. *Journal of Occupational Psychology*, 53, 81–9.

Kelley, H.H. (1972) Causal schemata and the attribution process. In E.E. Jones, D.E. Kanouse, H.H. Kelley, R.E. Nisbett, S. Valins and B. Weiner (eds) *Attribution: Perceiving the Causes of Behavior*. Morristown, NJ: General Learning Press.

Kelley, H.H. (1967) Attribution theory in social psychology. In D. Levine (ed.) *Nebraska Symposium on Motivation*. Lincoln, Nebr.: University of Nebraska Press.

Kelley, H.H. (1973) The processes of causal attribution. *American Psychologist*, 28, 107–28.

Kelley, H.H. and Michela, J.L. (1980) Attribution theory and research. *Annual Review of Psychology*, 31, 457–501.

Kelly, G. (1955) *The Psychology of Personal Constructs*. New York: W.W. Norton.

Kenny, D.A. and Albright, L. (1987) Accuracy in interpersonal perception: a social relations analysis. *Psychological Bulletin*, 102, 390–402.

Kerr, B.A. and Dell, D.M. (1976) Perceived interviewer expertness and attractiveness: effects of interviewer behavior and attire and interview setting. *Journal of Counseling Psychology*, 23, 553–6.

King, M.R. and Manaster, G.J. (1977) Bossy image, self-esteem, expectations, self-assessments, and actual success in a simulated job interview. *Journal of Applied Psychology*, 62, 589–94.

Klayman, J. and Ha, Y-W. (1987) Confirmation, disconfirmation and information in hypothesis testing. *Psychological Review*, 94, 211–28.

Kleinke, C. (1986) *Meeting and Understanding People*. New York: Freeman.

Kline, P. (1975) *The Psychology of Vocational Guidance*. London: Batsford.

Klinzing, D. and Klinzing, D. (1985) *Communication for Allied Health Professionals*. Dubuque, Iowa: W.C. Brown.

Kruglanski, A.W. and Ajzen, I. (1983) Bias and error in human judgement. *European Journal of Social Psychology*, 13, 1–44.

LaFromboise, T.D. and Dixon, D.N. (1981) American Indian perception of trustworthiness in a counseling interview. *Journal of Counseling Psychology*, 28, 135–9.

Latham, G.P. (1989) The reliability, validity, and practicality of the situational interview. In R.W. Eder and G.R. Ferris (eds) *The Employment Interview: Theory, Research and Practice*. Nebury Park, Ca.: Sage.

Lawson, I. (1989) *Appraisal and Appraisal Interviewing* (3rd edition). London: The Industrial Society.

Leeper, R. (1935) The role of motivation in learning: a study of the phenomenon of different motivation control of the utilisation of habits. *Journal of Genetic Psychology*, 46, 3–40.

Levine, M.W. and Schefner, J.M. (1981) *Fundamentals of Sensation and Perception*. London: Addison-Wesley.

Lewis, D.G. and Murgatroyd, S.J. (1976) The professionalisation of counselling in education and its legal implications. *British Journal of Guidance and Counselling*, 4, 2–15.

Ley, P. (1983) Patients' understanding and recall in clinical communication failure. In D. Pendleton and J. Hasler (eds) *Doctor–Patient Communication*. London: Academic Press.

Ley, P. (1988) *Communicating with Patients*. London: Chapman & Hall.
Lingle, J.H., Geva, N., Ostrom, T.M., Lieppe, M.R. and Baumgardener, M.H. (1979) Thematic effects of person judgements on impression organization. *Journal of Personality and Social Psychology*, 37, 674–87.
Livesey, P. (1986) *Partners in Care: The Consultation in General Practice*. London: Heinemann.
Locke, E.A. and Latham, G.P. (1984) *Goal Setting: A Motivational Technique That Works!* Englewood Cliffs, NJ: Prentice-Hall.
Lopez, F.M. (1975) *Personnel Interviewing: Theory and Practice* (2nd edition), New York: McGraw-Hill.
McArthur, L.Z. and Baron, R.M. (1983) Towards an ecological theory of social perception. *Psychological Review*, 90, 215–38.
McCroskey, J. (1984) Communication competence: the elusive construct. In R. Bostrom (ed) *Competence in Communication*. Beverly Hills, Ca.: Sage.
McGovern, T.V., Jones, B.W. and Morris, S.E. (1979) Comparison of professional versus student ratings of job interviewee behavior. *Journal of Counseling Psychology*, 26, 176–9.
McGovern, T.V. and Tinsley, H.E. (1978) Interviewer evaluations of interviewee nonverbal behavior. *Journal of Vocational Behavior*, 13, 163–71.
McGuire, W.J., McGuire, C.V., Child, P. and Fujioka, T. (1978) Salience of ethnicity in the spontaneous self-concept as a function of one's ethnic distinctiveness in the social environment. *Journal of Personality and Social Psychology*, 36, 511–20.
McGuire, W.J., McGuire, C.V. and Winton, W. (1979) Effects of household sex composition on the salience of one's gender in the spontaneous self-concept. *Journal of Experimental Social Psychology*, 15, 77–90.
McHenry, R. (1981) The selection interview. In M. Argyle (ed) *Social Skills and Work*. London: Methuen.
McKechnie, R. (1987) The moral context of therapy. In S. Fairbairn and G. Fairbairn (eds) *Psychology, Ethics, and Change*. London: Routledge & Kegan Paul.
McKitrick, D.S. and Gelso, C.J. (1978) Initial client expectancies in time-limited counseling. *Journal of Counseling Psychology*, 25, 246–9.
Maclean, D. and Gould, S. (1988) *The Helping Process: An Introduction*. London: Croom Helm.
Maguire, P. (1981) Doctor–patient skills. In M. Argyle (ed) *Social Skills and Health*, London: Methuen.
Maier, N.R.F. (1958) *The Appraisal Interview. Objectives, Methods, and Skills*. New York: Wiley.
Makin, P., Cooper, C. and Cox, C. (1989) *Managing People at Work*. London: Routledge/BPS.
Manthei, R.J. and Matthews, D.A. (1989) Helping the reluctant client to engage in counselling. In W. Dryden (ed) *Key Issues for Counselling in Action*. London: Sage.
Marchant, H. (1982) Confidentiality and the counselling relationship. In A.W. Bolger (ed) *Counselling in Britain. A Reader*. London: Batsford.
Markus, H. and Sentis, K. (1982) The self in social information processing. In J. Suls (ed) *Social Psychological Perspectives on the Self*. Hillsdale, NJ: Erlbaum.
Maslow, A. (1954) *Motivation and Personality*. New York: Harper & Row.
Mayo, C. and Henley, N. (eds) (1981) *Gender and Nonverbal Behavior*. New York: Springer-Verlag.
Millar, R. (1979) Give the VGI a break! *Careers Quarterly*, 30, 27–32.
Miller, G. and Steinberg, M. (1975) *Between People: A New Analysis of Interpersonal Communication*. Chicago: Science Research Associates.

Mishler, E.G. (1986) *Research Interviewing. Context and Narrative.* Cambridge, Mass.: Harvard University Press.

Morrow, N.C. and Hargie, O.D.W. (1989) A new focus for CST: pharmacy practice as a helping relationship. *Pharmaceutical Journal,* 243, E16–E19.

Munro, E.A., Manthei, R.J. and Small, J.J. (1983) *Counselling. A Skills Approach* (revised edition). New Zealand: Methuen.

Munro Fraser, J. (1971) *Psychology. General/Industrial/Social.* (3rd edition). London: Pitman.

Murgatroyd, S.J. (1985) *Counselling and Helping.* London: BPS/Methuen.

National Development Group (1977) *Day Services for Mentally Handicapped Adults.* Pamphlet Number 5, July.

Neisser, U. (1967) *Cognitive Psychology.* New York: Appleton-Century-Crofts.

Nelson-Jones, R. (1982) *The Theory and Practice of Counselling Psychology.* London: Holt, Rinehart & Winston.

Nelson-Jones, R. (1983) *Practical Counselling Skills.* London: Holt, Rinehart & Winston.

Nelson-Jones, R. (1990) *Human Relationship Skills* (2nd edition). London: Cassell Educational Limited.

Nemeroff, W.F. and Wexley, K.N. (1979) An exploration of the relationships between performance feedback interview characteristics and interview outcomes as perceived by managers and subordinates. *Journal of Occupational Psychology,* 52, 25–34.

Nisbett, R. and Ross, L. (1980) *Human Inference: Strategies and Shortcomings of Social Judgement.* Englewood Cliffs, NJ: Prentice-Hall.

Oakley, A. (1981) Interviewing women: a contradiction in terms. In H. Roberts (ed) *Doing Feminist Research.* Boston: Routledge & Kegan Paul.

Paradise, L.V. and Wilder, D.H. (1979) The relationship between client reluctance and counseling effectiveness. *Counselor Education and Supervision,* 19, 35–41.

Perrott, E. (1982) *Effective Teaching.* London and New York: Longman.

Phillips, A. and Dipboye, R.L. (1989) Correlational tests of predictions from a process model of the interview. *Journal of Applied Psychology,* 74, 41–52.

Pillsbury, W.B. and Meader, C.L. (1928) *The Psychology of Language,* New York: D. Appleton.

Powell, G.N. (1986) Effects of expectancy confirmation processes and applicants' qualifications on recruiters' evaluations. *Psychological Reports,* 58, 1003–10.

Pratt, K.J. (1985) *Effective Staff Appraisal.* Wokingham, Berkshire: Van Nostrand Reinhold.

Rae, L. (1988) *The Skills of Interviewing.* Aldershot: Gower.

Rand, T.M. and Wexley, K.N. (1975) Demonstrations of the effect 'similar to me' in simulated employment interviews. *Psychological Reports,* 36, 535–44.

Rasmussen, K.G. (1984) Nonverbal behavior, verbal behavior, resume credentials and selection interview outcomes. *Journal of Applied Psychology,* 72, 569–603.

Rawling, K. (1985) *The Seven Point Plan: New Perspectives Fifty Years On.* Windsor: NFER-Nelson.

Reddy, H. and Brannigan, C. (1980) What do careers officers talk about? *Careers Journal,* 1, 25–33.

Reddy, H.A. and Brannigan, C.H. (1982) *Interview Handling by Careers Officers. A Summary of LGTB Research Project R34.* Luton: LGTB.

Ribeaux, P. and Poppleton, S.E. (1978) *Psychology and Work. An Introduction.* London: Macmillan.

Richardson, S.D., Dohrenwood, B.S. and Klein, D. (1965) *Interviewing: Its Forms and Functions.* New York: Basic Books.

Rodger, A. (1970) *The Seven Point Plan* (3rd edition). London: National Institute of Industrial Psychology.

Rogers, C.R. (1951) *Client-Centered Therapy*. London: Constable.

Roger, C.R. (1966) Client-centred therapy. In E.L. Shostrum (producer) *Three Approaches to Psychotherapy – Gloria* (video). Ipswich: Concord Video and Film Council.

Rogers, T.B., Kuiper, N.A. and Kirker, W.S. (1977) Self-relevance and the encoding of personal information. *Journal of Personality and Social Psychology*, 35, 677–88.

Roloff, M. and Berger, C. (eds) (1982) *Social Cognition and Communication*. Beverly Hills, Ca.: Sage.

Roloff, M. and Kellerman, K. (1984) Judgements of interpersonal competence. In R. Bostrom (ed) *Competence in Communication*. Beverly Hills, Ca.: Sage.

Ross, L. (1977) The intuitive psychologist and his shortcomings: distortions in the attribution process. In L. Berkowitz (ed) *Advances in Experimental Social Psychology*, Volume 10. New York: Academic Press.

Rothstein, M. and Jackson, D.N. (1980) Decision making in the employment interview: an experimental approach. *Journal of Applied Psychology*, 65, 271–83.

Rothstein, M. and Jackson, D.N. (1984) Implicit personality theory and the employment interview. In M. Cook (ed) *Issues in Person Perception*. London and New York: Methuen.

Rowe, P.M. (1989) Unfavorable information and interview decisions. In R.W. Eder and G.R. Ferris (eds) *The Employment Interview: Theory, Research and Practice*. Newbury Park, Ca.: Sage.

Rubin, J., Provenzano, F. and Luria, Z. (1974) The eye of the beholder: parents' views on the sex of newborns. *American Journal of Orthopsychiatry*, 44, 512–19.

Runnymede Trust/BPS Joint Working Party (1980) *Discriminating Fairly. A Guide to Fair Selection*. BPS/Runnymede Trust.

Saunders, C. (1986) Opening and closing. In O. Hargie (ed) *A Handbook of Communication Skills*. London and New York: Croom Helm.

Schiffenbauer, A. (1974) Effect of observer's emotional state on judgements of the emotional state of others. *Journal of Personality and Social Psychology*, 30, 31–5.

Schlenker, B.R. (1980) *Impression Management: The Self-Concept, Social Identity and Interpersonal Relations*. Monterey, Ca.: Brooks/Cole.

Schmidt, L.D. and Strong, S.R. (1970) 'Expert' and 'inexpert' counselors. *Journal of Counseling Psychology*, 17, 115–18.

Schmidt, L.D. and Strong, S.R. (1971) Attractiveness and influence in counseling. *Journal of Counseling Psychology*, 18, 348–51.

Schuh, A.J. (1978) Effects of an early interruption and note taking on listening accuracy and decision making in the interview. *Bulletin of the Psychonomic Society*, 12, 333–8.

Schuler, H. and Funke, U. (1989) The employment interview as a multimodal procedure. In R.W. Eder and G.R. Ferris (eds) *The Employment Interview: Theory, Research and Practice*. Newbury Park, Ca.: Sage.

Schwarz, N. (1984) Mood and information processing. Paper presented at the Congress of the European Association of Social Psychologists, Tilbury, Holland.

Schweinitz, E. and Schweinitz, K. (1962) *Interviewing in the Social Services*. National Institute for Social Work Training Series. National Council of Social Service, Bedford Square Press.

Shackleton, V.J. and Spurgeon, P.C. (1982) The relative importance of potential outcomes of occupational guidance: an assessment by occupational guidance officers. *Journal of Occupational Psychology*, 55, 191–6.

Shaver, K.G. (1983) *An Introduction to Attribution Processes*. Hillsdale, NJ: Lawrence Erlbaum Associates.

Sheppe, W. and Stevenson, I. (1963) Techniques of interviewing. In H. Lief, F. Lief and N. Lief (eds) *The Psychological Basis of Medical Practice*. New York: Hoeber.

Shertzer, B. and Stone, S.C. (1980) *Fundamentals of Counseling* (3rd edition). Boston: Houghton Mifflin.

Shouksmith, G. (1968) *Assessment Through Interviewing*. Oxford: Pergamon Press.

Shouksmith, G. (1978) *Assessment Through Interviewing* (2nd edition). Oxford: Pergamon Press.

Shuy, R.W. (1983) Three types of interference to an effective exchange of information in the medical interview. In S. Fisher and A.D. Todd (eds) *Social Organization of Doctor–Patient Communication*. Centre for Applied Linguistics, Washington, DC.

Skopec, E. (1986) *Situational Interviewing*. New York: Harper & Row.

Smith, V. (1986) Listening. In O. Hargie (ed) *A Handbook of Communication Skills*. London: Routledge.

Snyder, M. (1987) *Public Appearances, Private Realities*. New York: Freeman.

Snyder, M. and Uranowitz, S.W. (1978) Reconstructing the past: some cognitive consequences of person perception. *Journal of Personality and Social Psychology*, 36, 941–50.

Sommer, R. and Sommer, B.A. (1980) *A Practical Guide to Behavioral Research*. Oxford and New York: Oxford University Press.

Stafford, L. and Daly, J. (1984) Conversational memory: the effects of time, recall mode, and memory expectancies on remembrances of natural conversations. *Human Communication Research*, 10, 379–402.

Stewart, C.J. and Cash, W.B. (1985) *Interviewing: Principles and Practices*. Dubuque, Iowa: W.C. Brown.

Stewart, C.J. and Cash, W.B. (1988) *Interviewing: Principles and Practices* (5th edition). Dubuque, Iowa: W.C. Brown.

Stewart, L. and Ting-Toomey, S. (eds) (1987) *Communication, Gender and Sex Roles in Diverse Interaction Contexts*. Hove, Sussex: Guilford Press.

Stewart, R., Powell, G. and Chetwynd, S. (1979) *Person Perception and Stereotyping*. Farnborough: Saxon House.

Stone, C.I. and Sawatski, B. (1980) Hiring bias and the disabled interview: effects of manipulating work history and disability information of the disabled job applicant. *Journal of Vocational Behavior*, 16, 96–104.

Strong, S.R. (1968) Counseling: an interpersonal influence process. *Journal of Counseling Psychology*, 15, 215–24.

Strong, S.R. and Dixon, D.N. (1971) Expertness, attractiveness, and influence in counseling. *Journal of Counseling Psychology*, 18, 562–70.

Strong, S.R. and Matross, R. (1973) Change processes in counseling and psychotherapy. *Journal of Counseling Psychology*, 20, 25–37.

Sudman, S. and Bradburn, N. (1974) *Response Effects in Surveys: A Review and Synthesis*. Chicago: Aldine.

Sudman, S. and Bradburn, N.M. (1982) *Asking Questions*. San Francisco: Jossey-Bass.

Super, D.E. (1980) A life-span, life-space approach to career development. *Journal of Vocational Behavior*, 16, 282–98.

Swann, W.B. Jr and Read, S.J. (1981) Acquiring self-knowledge: the search for feedback that fits. *Journal of Personality and Social Psychology*, 41, 1119–28.

Sypher, B.D. (1984) The importance of social cognitive abilities. In R. Bostrum (ed) *Competence in Communication*. Beverly Hills, Ca.: Sage.

Tagg, S.K. (1985) Life story interviews and their interpretation. In M. Brenner, J. Brown and D. Canter (eds) *The Research Interview. Uses and Approaches*. London: Academic Press.

Taylor, M.S. and Sniezek, J.A. (1984) The college recruitment interview: topical content and applicant reactions. *Journal of Occupational Psychology*, 57, 157–68.

Taylor, S.E. (1979) Hospital patient behaviour: reactance, helplessness or control? *Journal of Social Issues*, 35, 156–84.

Trower, P., Bryant, B. and Argyle, M. (1978) *Social Skills and Mental Health*. London: Methuen.

Turney, C., Eltis, K.J., Hatton, N., Owens, L.C., Towler, J. and Wright, R. (1983) *Sydney Micro Skills Redeveloped: Series 1 Handbook*. Sydney, Australia: Sydney University Press.

Von Cranach, M., Kalbermatten, V., Indermuhle, K. and Gugler, B. (1982) *Goal-Directed Action. European Monographs in Social Psychology, 30*. London: Academic Press.

Warr, P. and Knapper, C. (1968) *The Perception of People and Events*. London: Wiley.

Watson, K. and Barker, L. (1984) Listening behavior: definition and measurement. In R. Bostrum and B. Westley (eds) *Communication Yearbook '8'*. Beverly Hills, Ca.: Sage.

Weiner, B. (1985) An attributional theory of achievement motivation and emotion. *Psychological Review*. 92, 548–73.

Weiner, B. (1988) Attribution theory and attribution therapy: some theoretical observations and suggestions. *British Journal of Clinical Psychology*, 27, 99–104.

Weiner, B., Frieze, I.H., Kukla, A., Reed, I., Rest, S. and Rosenbaum, R.M. (1972) Perceiving the causes of success and failure. In E.E. Jones, D.E. Kanouse, H.H. Kelley, R.E. Nisbett, S. Valins and B. Weiner. *Attribution: Perceiving the Causes of Behavior*. Morristown. NJ: General Learning Press.

Wessler, R. (1984) Cognitive-social psychological theories and social skills: a review. In P. Trower (eds) *Radical Approaches to Social Skills Training*. Beckenham, Kent: Croom Helm.

Wible, D.S. and Hui, C.H. (1985) Perceived language proficiency and person perception. *Journal of Cross-Cultural Psychology*, 16, 206–22.

Wicks, R. (1982) Interviewing: practical aspects. In A.J. Chapman and A. Gale (eds) *Psychology and People. A Tutorial Text*. London: BPS/Macmillan.

Wiesner, W.H. and Cronshaw, S.F. (1988) A meta-analytic investigation of the impact of interview format and degree of structure on the validity of the employment interview. *Journal of Occupational Psychology*, 61, 275–90.

Williams, M.R. (1972) *Performance Appraisal and Management*. London: Heinemann.

Woods, K.M. and McNamara, J.R. (1980) Confidentiality: its effects on interviewee behavior. *Professional Psychology*, 11, 714–21.

Wright, P.M., Lichtenfels, P.A. and Pursell, E.D. (1989) The structured interview: additional studies and a meta-analysis. *Journal of Occupational Psychology*, 62, 191–9.

Wyer, R.S. and Gordon, S.E. (1982) The recall of information about persons and groups. *Journal of Experimental Social Psychology*, 18, 128–64.

Wyer, R.S. and Srull, T.K. (1986) Human cognition in its social context. *Psychological Review*, 93, 322–39.

Yesenosky, J.M. and Dowd, E.T. (1990) The social psychology of counselling and psychotherapy: a basis for integration. *British Journal of Guidance and Counselling*, 18, 170–85.

Young, D.M. and Beier, E.G. (1977) The role of applicant nonverbal behavior in the employment interview. *Journal of Employment Counseling*, 14, 154–65.

Name index

Ajzen, I. 74–5
Albright, L. 74–5
Anastasi, A. 173
Anderson, N. 64, 67, 69, 101, 118
Argyle, M. 21, 27, 33
Armstrong, S. 139
Arvey, R. 8, 30, 63–5, 68, 74, 148–9, 180–1
Asch, S.E. 55, 66
Authier, J. 7
Averill, J. 25

Balthazar, E.E. 79, 87, 99
Banaka, W.H. 104, 106, 108, 117, 167, 179
Barker, L. 13
Baron, R.A. 40–1, 44, 62, 64, 143, 153–5
Baron, R.M. 74
Bayne, R. 76, 144
Beattie, G. 36, 41
Bedford, T. 87
Beggs, R.M. 52, 81, 110
Beier, E.G. 64
Benbenishty, R. 152
Benjamin, A. 39, 103–7, 119, 128, 131, 164–6, 171–2, 174–9
Berger, C. 24
Berglas, S. 46
Bernstein, L. 11, 48, 51–2, 107, 148, 166, 174–6, 178–9
Bernstein, R.S. 11, 107, 148, 166, 174–6, 178–9
Beveridge, W.E. 2–3, 14
Bilodeau, E. 27
Bilodeau, I. 27
Blackham, H.J. 162, 168, 172
Bradac, J.J. 65
Bradburn, N.M. 11, 33, 183

Bradley, C. 49–50
Brannigan, C. 103, 116, 168
Breakwell, G.M. 36–7, 57, 62, 71, 81, 83, 85, 87–8, 91, 98, 101, 106, 108, 110, 118, 119, 120, 157, 174, 178
Brenner, M. 11, 39, 45, 82, 111, 113, 121, 123, 129, 132
Brown, G.A. 139
Byrne, D. 40–1, 44, 62
Byrne, P. 13, 34

Campion, J.E. 8, 30, 63–5, 68, 74, 148–9, 180–1
Cannell, C.F. 9
Cantor, N. 67, 72
Carlson, R. 10
Carlson, R.E. 74
Carroll, J. 24
Carroll, J.G. 142
Cash, T.F. 159
Cash, W.B. 1, 81, 90, 93, 96, 97, 103–6, 110, 112, 117–19, 124, 126, 129–30, 141, 146, 152, 156, 158–9, 167–8, 176–9
Cherry, N. 151
Cherry, N.M. 151
Claiborn, C.D. 52
Clark, M. 68
Cohen, A.A. 3
Cohen, L. 9
Cook, M. 74
Cormier, L.S. 51–5, 57, 82, 84–5, 88–91, 145, 163, 165–70
Cormier, W.H. 51–5, 57, 82, 84–5, 88–91, 145, 163, 165–70
Corrigan, J.D. 51–2, 55–6
Cox, B.G. 55
Cronbach, L.J. 72

Subject index